Jesus and Liberation

American University Studies

Series VII
Theology and Religion
Vol. 148

PETER LANG
New York • Washington, DC/Baltimore • San Francisco
Bern • Frankfurt am Main • Berlin • Vienna • Paris

Carlos R. Piar

Jesus and Liberation

A Critical Analysis of the Christology of Latin American Liberation Theology

PETER LANG
New York • Washington, DC/Baltimore • San Francisco
Bern • Frankfurt am Main • Berlin • Vienna • Paris

BT
198
.P52
1994

Library of Congress Cataloging-in-Publication Data

Piar, Carlos R.
 Jesus and liberation: a critical analysis of the christology of Latin
American liberation theology / Carlos R. Piar.
  p. cm. — (American university studies. Series VII, Theology and
religion; vol. 148)
 Includes bibliographical references and index.
 1. Jesus Christ—History of doctrines—20th century. 2. Liberation
theology. I. Title. II. Series.
BT198.P52   1994   232—dc20   93-6958
ISBN 0-8204-2098-0   CIP
ISSN 0740-0446

Die Deutsche Bibliothek-CIP-Einheitsaufnahme

Piar, Carlos R.:
Jesus and liberation: a critical analysis of the christology of Latin American
liberation theology / Carlos R. Piar. - New York; Berlin; Bern; Frankfurt/M.;
Paris; Wien: Lang, 1994
 (American university studies: Ser. 7, Theology and religion; Vol. 148)
 ISBN 0-8204-2098-0
NE: American university studies / 07

The author gratefully acknowledges the following for permission to reprint excerpts from:

Faith on the Edge by Leonardo Boff. Copyright © 1981 by Leonardo Boff. English translation
copyright © 1989 by HarperCollins Publishers, Inc. Reprinted by permission of HarperCollins
Publishers, Inc. *Trinity and Society* by Leonardo Boff, translated by Paul Burns. Maryknoll, NY:
Orbis Books, 1988. Reprinted by permission of Orbis Books and Burns & Oates Ltd. *Liberation
Theology and Its Critics* by Arthur F. McGovern. Maryknoll, NY: Orbis Books, 1989. *Faith and
Ideologies* by Juan Luis Segundo. Maryknoll, NY: Orbis Books, 1984. *The Historical Jesus of the
Synoptics* by Juan Luis Segundo. Maryknoll, NY: Orbis Books, 1986. *Christology at the Crossroads*
by Jon Sobrino. Maryknoll, NY: Orbis Books, 1978. *Jesus in Latin America* by Jon Sobrino.
Maryknoll, NY: Orbis Books, 1987. *What Do You Say?* by Claus Bussman. Maryknoll, NY: Orbis
Books, 1985. *Jesus and Marx: From Gospel to Ideology* by Jacques Ellul. Grand Rapids: William B.
Eerdmans Publishing, 1988.

This book is dedicated to Paty, friend and wife, who besides being a constant encouragement took care of our children so that their Daddy could finish his book.

ACKNOWLEDGMENTS

I would like to thank the following friends, colleagues and professors for their help: John P. Crossley at the University of Southern California for the constructive criticism that he offered on drafts of this work. But most of all I want to thank him for believing in me. I also want to thank Robert Eisenman at California State University, Long Beach for expediting bureucratic obstacles and reducing my teaching load so that I would have more time to write. Others that I want to thank for their encouragement and advice are: Tony Battaglia at CSULB, Sheila Briggs, Don Miller, and Dallas Willard at USC.

TABLE OF CONTENTS

CHAPTER 1

LIBERATION CHRISTOLOGY:
A NARRATIVE FOR PRAXIS

In 1968, the conference (of the Latin American Episcopal Council) at Medellín, Colombia launched a "new way of doing theology," a method which took as its point of departure the economic and politically oppressive situation in which the vast majority of Latin Americans were living (and still are today). This method produced a theology of liberation which claims to differ from traditional theology in the following ways. It has:

1. A different view of history. Unlike the traditional Thomistic view of history held by Roman Catholicism (a dualistic view), liberation theologians see history as one; there is no "separation of planes," (i.e., a spiritual and temporal, a sacred and a profane history).

2. A different view of the Church. It views the Church's action, structure, and pronouncements (dogma) as ideological and so makes the Church partially responsible (by its ignorance, indifference, or complicity) for the oppressive situation which exists.

3. A different view of the Kingdom of God. It avers that the kingdom of God can be partially fulfilled within history through human liberative action (praxis).

4. A different view of conflict. Unlike traditional theology, liberation theology views conflict, class struggle, (and in some cases even violence) as historically inevitable and something on which the Church cannot remain neutral (or attempt to escape by appeals to unity and reconciliation) (Berryman 1984, 28-29).

But like any theology that calls itself Christian, ultimately it must somehow ground itself (and the claims made above) in the person and work of Jesus Christ. And this liberation theologians have attempted to do.

One of the criticisms levied against liberation theology is that it does not have a christology. This criticism has even been noted by liberation theologians themselves. Juan Luis Segundo, for instance, acknowledges that one of the main criticisms has been that:

> . . . Latin American theology, insofar as it alleges to be an effort to understand the faith, . . . has not chosen, or perhaps dared, or perhaps been able, to structure its own coherent, systematic way of

thinking about Jesus Christ . . . [It] lacks a christology. (Segundo
1985, 14)

Spurred by criticisms such as this, liberation theologians such as Leonardo Boff, Jon
Sobrino, Segundo Galilea, Ignacio Ellacurría, and Segundo himself have, respectively, produced such christologies as *Jesus Christ Liberator*, *Christology at the
Crossroads*, *Following Jesus*, *Freedom Made Flesh*, and *Jesus of Nazareth Yesterday
and Today*, to name a few.

But in writing these christologies, these liberation theologians are not interested
in academic speculation about Jesus Christ as an object of dogmatic or systematic
theology; for them christology is not the study of Jesus Christ as an end in itself, in order
to better understand his person and his work. Rather, their interest is always that of
relating christology to the Latin American situation; their interest is in how liberative
praxis can be grounded in christology so as to make christology of service to the
oppressed. The essential question which they seek to answer is: "What is the
significance of Jesus Christ for the liberating praxis which is needed (or is occurring)
in Latin America today?" Or to put it differently: "What is the christological basis for
liberative praxis?" In short, their interest is always ethical, practical, not so much
dogmatic or theoretical.

The manner in which these liberation theologians have attempted to relate
christology and praxis gives rise to several issues that need to be explored. These issues
are connected to each step of the liberationists' christological method. This method
entails three steps; first, a "deconstruction" of traditional, orthodox christological
discourse. Here liberation theologians apply hermeneutic criteria to show how
traditional christology is inadequate to move to praxis and fulfill liberative aims. The
second step is the reconstruction of christology by bridging the horizons of the text
(i.e., the Jesus of the New Testament) and the context (i.e., the present reality in Latin
America). What serves as that bridge and mediates a new christological discourse is
ideology. More specifically, the hermeneutic key that liberation theologians utilize in
interpreting both the text and the context is a Neo-Marxist ideology that is claimed to
be distinctively Latin American.

The third step, having fulfilled the prior two steps, is the rhetorical proclamation
of christology. The story of Jesus must be told in such a way as to communicate a new
set of values and goals to the oppressed. The aim of the narrative is to encourage (or
persuade to adopt) attitudes and behaviors that result in historical liberation, in
changed social structures. Communicating the new understanding of Jesus' identity
and significance obtained through the prior two steps makes it possible for the
Christian to engage in (or continue engaging in) a liberative praxis.

Expanding on the analogy of construction, of "building," let me restate this
methodology. The christological construction, first of all, necessitates the "tearing

down" of the established orthodoxy. I call this step the "deconstruction," rather than the "destruction" of christology, because it is not a total uprooting; the foundation (the ultimate significance of Jesus for the Christian life) is maintained.[1] It is this foundation on which the builders (i.e., the theologians) erect the new christological building. This deconstruction entails the application of a variety of tools and "machines" to the edifice of orthodoxy: higher criticism, demythologization, sociology of knowledge, and critical theory.

The second step is the reconstruction of christology utilizing a blueprint, an architect's plan, that will guide the builders, a plan that will help them in their choice of building materials (what texts to use), of laborers (what theologians to marshall to their aid), a plan that will provide an analysis of the environment (What are the social conditions? What obstacles exist?) and set out the dimensions of the anticipated building (Is the form of the building adequate to its function? Is the resultant christology efficacious in promoting social change?). This is where ideology must be chosen. Ideology is seen by liberationists as the blueprint that guides them in the construction of a liberative christology.

The third step is the actual use made of the building. Having produced a structure (a form) to fulfill a specific, predetermined function, liberation theologians must then apply it to the situation. This "structure," consisting of affirmations about Jesus—i.e., titles, metaphors, and reinterpretations that communicate a framework of values for action—is to be inhabited by the hearer(s). Like an edifice, the christological narrative is meant to be "lived in," which means that the story is to be "lived out" or put into practice—no word play intended.

Each of these steps raises several questions that need to be asked of the liberationist builders, and the whole christological enterprise. Firstly, is it really necessary to tear down the building orthodoxy has been erecting for two thousand years in order to create a liberating christology? On what authority or on what basis do they set forth to demolish the "old" building? In what sense can these modern builders say they are building on the same foundation (the ultimate significance of Jesus for the Christian life)? Or has the building indeed been left without any foundation after the process of "deconstruction"?

Secondly, why is the particular blueprint (ideology) chosen? Are there no other blueprints (ideologies) that will fulfill the aim more effectively? Indeed, should theologians make conscious use of ideology in the construction of christology? Should christology be done with a particular project or interest in view? If so, what projects or interests are appropriate for the christological enterprise?

Thirdly, is the final construct adequate to its function or aim? In other words, is the resultant christology truly liberative? Is the story livable? Does the new narrative with its titles, metaphors, and reinterpretations, enable those who adhere to it to develop an identity, a meaning or value structure, that is congruent with the identity of those who have called themselves "Christian" throughout history? (This last question presupposes that there is a particular Christian identity, a Christian ethos, that all who call themselves "Christian" share.) Or does the new christological discourse ultimately make Jesus Christ superfluous in the life of the Christian?

There are many more questions that could be posed to the liberation theologians about their christology, I, however, will focus only on the process of christological construction I have described above. I recognize that liberation theology is still in the process of development, and so its christology is hardly of a piece; indeed it could be said that there are several christologies in liberation theology. Yet, these christologies do share common elements that give them their particular liberationist character and which can be said to constitute a "Latin American Liberation Christology." I will attempt to focus my analysis on these commonalities so that the issues raised in this work could be applied to all of these christologies as a whole, and will henceforth use the singular, "liberation christology," to refer to these common elements.

Since there are a variety of christologies I will focus particularly on those theologians whose christologies have reputedly had the greatest impact on the Latin American theological scene. These are Leonardo Boff, Jon Sobrino and Juan Luis Segundo, who have clearly given themselves over to the task of providing liberation theology with a christology. This is not to say that I will not allude to the christologies of other liberation theologians when it helps to show the common elements which they all share, but I will be mainly using the christologies of these three theologians for the sake of manageability.

It should be noted that the three theologians on whose christologies this study will predominantly focus are Roman Catholic. Regrettably, Protestant liberation theologians have not done very much in this important area of theology. José Miguez-Bonino has edited a book, *Faces of Jesus*, which contains several essays written by Protestants (such as Georges Casalis, Lamberto Schuurman, Juan Stam, Saúl Trinidad, and Miguez-Bonino himself), but they all seem to take their cues from the Catholic theologians (Miguez-Bonino 1985), especially the three mentioned above. Hence, since the christologies of Boff, Segundo, and Sobrino are more complete, more systematic, and are having a greater influence on Catholic and Protestant theologians alike, any serious analysis of liberation christology must begin with them.

Boff, Segundo, and Sobrino are trying to ground praxis on christology; they are trying to show that liberative praxis is the essence of following Jesus. But then it is imperative that their christology warrants it and that this christology be as coherent and consistent as possible for that is what academic or theological integrity demands in the treatment of any subject. In this work I hope to point out the key problems that I perceive from my standpoint so that a more coherent, consistent, and relevant christology can be developed. I do not intend to present such a christology here, but only to offer a critical analysis of the christology already being proclaimed.

But lest it be said that the criticisms presented herein are the result of the false consciousness of living in the First World, the product of an ideologically captive theology and experiential ignorance of oppression, let me make clear my sociological and theological standpoint. I was born and raised in poverty in Puerto Rico, a "colony" of the United States, and have seen both the blessings and the curses of economic dependence on the North.[2] Hence, if I am critical of liberation theology, it is not as an apologist for capitalism. Rather my criticisms arise out of my identification with a particular community of faith, a community of discourse which, sociologically and theologically, Latin American liberation theologians have not taken very seriously, but which they must if their theology is to have any lasting impact in Latin America. I am referring to the community of discourse known as evangelical Protestant Christianity. That Protestant Christianity, especially of the free church type (Baptists and Pentecostals, for instance) has been growing in Latin America at an astounding rate (some claim even faster than the Catholic *comunidades de base*) is an undeniable fact and presents a definite challenge to liberation theologians to make sense of the phenomenon and determine its implications for the project of liberation.[3] It is all the more important to do so since this growth of Protestantism is occurring primarily among the poorer classes, those whom liberation theologians want to consciencitize to oppression of the poor.[4] It is these people, the poor and evangelical Latin Americans, that have been my community all of my life, so that even though I live in the United States, the churches I have labored in have always been Spanish-speaking, the people who have been my friends, brethren, and parishioners have been the undocumented, the alien, those who bus tables and wash dishes at restaurants, or who pick strawberries in the local fields, or who make the beds in motels in the area. These same people, although horribly exploited by employers and "the system," would be quick to dismiss liberation theology as heresy because, in their view, it turns the Gospel of eternal salvation into a message of earthly politics. Now with evangelical Protestantism growing as fast as it is in Latin America, it would be foolhardy of liberation theologians to dismiss the phenomenon of evangelical Protestantism as simply a manifestation of false consciousness when, indeed, it could be a force for liberation.

Theologically, this critical analysis proceeds from an admittedly Protestant viewpoint that must be made explicit, for it is from this viewpoint that the christology of liberation theology will be evaluated. My view of Jesus' significance for Christian ethics is influenced by the story theology of Stanley Hauerwas, the Christian Realism of Reinhold Niebuhr, and the Christian "anarchy" of Jacques Ellul and John Howard Yoder.

First of all, from Hauerwas I derive the singular significance of Jesus for Christian ethics. I agree with Hauerwas that many contemporary theologians have gone awry in trying to ground a human, transcendental, universal ethic in Jesus Christ. Jesus Christ did not come to give humanity an ethic, but to call all to become a part of a community that would embody the virtues of the Kingdom (Hauerwas 1983, 50-64, 72-115). Secondly, I concur with Niebuhr in his assessment of the human condition (humanity is existentially alienated) and how Jesus Christ sets before the Church the "Impossible Possibility." Jesus is himself that impossibility of love made possible in history, a love that is always crucified. Jesus thus serves as a check on Christians' illusions about having realized perfect love in history, and a goad spurring us on to greater love. Niebuhr himself implies that this ethic of love can perhaps only be properly realized by the Church, not by society at large, which can at best only achieve a relative justice and must utilize coercion to achieve it. Thirdly, like Ellul and Yoder, I too follow a radical approach in the relation between Christ and culture, particularly Christ and political power. That approach is best described as Christian "anarchy,"[5] which to put it simply, sees Jesus as refusing political power, and the whole Bible as negating its validity and legitimacy (cf., Ellul 1988, 163-71). Christian anarchy sees the realm of politics as a realm of illusion, illusion sustained by cultural/historical narratives or social myths.[6] The illusion sustained by these myths is simply that politics can solve whatever problems exist in a particular society, or even the world. Politics seeks to bring under rational control the distribution of social burdens and benefits, and to mediate the interests of contending factions. By its very nature, therefore, it cannot escape the realm of necessity, of contingency; for instance, it must make use of coercion to enforce its measures or it may sacrifice the individual for the well being of the whole. But in spite of its contingency, the power of politics is often overestimated. Indeed, for some Christians, this overestimation often turns idolatrous when they begin to view secular history as the realm of God's activity, when they begin to view political programs as somehow manifesting (or being harbingers of) the Kingdom of God. The biblical image of the Kingdom given in Isaiah, where the sheep lies down with the lion, implies a transcendence of contingency or necessity. Hence, to equate the contingent realm of the political with the uncontingent Kingdom of God is to commit idolatry. But to say that the political is contingent and is not the realm of God's activity is not to say that the Christian is to abandon it. To do that would be as nonsensical as saying that the Christian should abandon his or her involvement in medicine because it has not been able to solve the problem of death!

My view of what Jesus means for us today is admittedly eclectic, but it is my conviction that the story of Jesus must be of distinctive and ultimate significance to humanity, and that the Church, the community formed by that story, must also remain distinctive in relation to the world. The story of Jesus is uniquely the Church's story.

It should also be clear from the start that I do not fault liberation theologians for trying to ameliorate the sufferings of their compatriots; I am sympathetic to the project. Indeed, I feel it would be morally reprehensible to wait until there was perfect theological clarity before doing *something* to help those in need. However, in a situation of moral ambiguity, Christian ethics should not be reduced to either-or decisionism, in which the Christian must choose either to act without theological clarity or to wait for clarity before acting. In a situation of need, it would seem that the Christian's best response (to God and neighbor) is both to act in spite of the lack of certitude and yet seek theological clarification to see if the action, in view of the Scriptures, calls for cessation and repentance, continuance, or modification. In a world of moral ambiguity, it is not always easy for the Christian to determine what should be done or what means should be used to bring about a good, if indeed anything should be done at all. And so, however laudable may be the efforts of those liberation theologians to bring about greater justice and well-being to their fellows, it is still of utmost importance to examine how christology and praxis are related to one another to see where this relation needs clarification or adjustment.

This book will present and evaluate the "what" and the "how" of Latin American liberation christology; i.e., *what* interpretation do liberation theologians give of the mystery of Jesus Christ—*What* is the identity of Jesus of Nazareth? *What* is the significance of his life (his ministry, death, and resurrection) for humanity, and particularly, the oppressed?; *How* do liberation theologians arrive at their interpretation or narrative? *How* coherent and adequate are the method they use and the narrative they proclaim?

Specifically, the argument will be set forth as follows. Chapter 2 will present an exposition of what liberation theologians Boff, Segundo, and Sobrino are saying about Jesus of Nazareth's identity and significance, i.e., an exposition of their narrative or "story" about Jesus Christ. Chapters 3 and 4 will analyze and evaluate the method by which these theologians arrive at their narrative: the hermeneutical deconstruction and the ideological reconstruction of christological discourse. Chapter 5 will assess the coherence and adequacy of the liberationist christological narrative as public discourse; i.e., does it commend itself as a valid public discourse? I will conclude by showing the implications of my analysis for liberation theology as a whole and suggesting some theses for a christology of liberation relevant to a postmodern world.

What this book will *not* do is explore the christology of liberation from the perspective of biblical studies; for example, seeking to ascertain what Jesus really did and said. Moreover, this book is not a study in dogmatics; however, we will have to look at how liberation theologians understand such dogmas as the hypostatic union and the Trinity, but in relationship to the question of praxis. The approach will be mainly ethical and methodological: How do liberation theologians relate Jesus Christ to ethics, more specifically, to liberative praxis? My approach is similar to James Gustafson's approach in *Christ and the Moral Life*, where he explores two key questions: "What claims are made for the significance of Christ for the moral life? and

"What claims can be made, and how can they be explicated from the point of view of the author?" (Gustafson 1968, 8) For my purposes, I will restate the questions more narrowly: What claims are made by liberation theologians for the significance of Jesus Christ for liberative praxis? and What claims can be made and how can they be explicated from my point of view?

It should be clear from previous allusions that, throughout this work, I will employ "narrative" as the heuristic concept with which I will query the relation of Jesus Christ to ethics in liberation theology. In recent scholarship the category of "narrative" has proven useful in illuminating many issues concerning the relation between theology and ethics. And although "narrative" is a problematic concept (being used to explain everything from the formation of Christian identity to the way to interpret Scripture), as we explore how liberation theologians connect christology to ethics, it will become clear that narrative is the most useful category in explaining this relation. Nevertheless, let me explain in what sense I will be using the word "narrative," and also give my rationale for my appeal to narrative as a way of analyzing liberation christology.

Recent scholarship has conceived of narrative in a variety of ways. Some theologians use the term to refer to some "universal inner form of human experience" (Nelson 1987, 69), and so they focus on how theological convictions are expressed in autobiography. Other scholars use "narrative" as a way of referring to all the various genres of literature present in the text of sacred scripture: epic, parable, allegory, myth, and so on. Without excluding any of the insights the previous two uses may provide, I will use the category of "narrative" to refer to a hermeneutic process, an approach to Scripture, a reading strategy, "a way of construing the Bible, as a whole or in part, which is conducive to . . . [the theologians'] display of scripture's normative role in shaping Christian self-understanding and practice" (Nelson 1987). More specifically, I want to attend to how liberation theologians construe the New Testament accounts about Jesus to display Jesus' normative role in shaping Christian self-understanding and practice. I want to examine the process by which liberation theologians arrive at their particular construal of Jesus and what is the significance of such a construal for Christian ethics.

Why do I appeal to narrative as a way of evaluating liberation christology and ethics? Firstly, because liberation christology could be seen as a Third World response to the crisis of modernity, a postmodern theology reconstructing more adequate narratives to meet the epistemological crisis occasioned by the collapse of the Enlightenment myths of progress and rationality.[7] Alasdair MacIntyre has argued in *After Virtue* that the failure of the Enlightenment project to ground objective laws of morality on reason has made necessary a paradigm shift finding its epistemological locus in "narrative" (MacIntyre 1981). The French philosopher Jean-Francois Lyotard has noted that this failure of the Enlightenment project has created an epistemological crisis of legitimation from which the only escape is a recovery of narrative knowledge (Lyotard 1988). I believe that it is the correct appraisal by liberation theologians of the failure of the liberal project of the Enlightenment, a project up to now religiously legitimated by the christologies received from Europe and the U.S. (e.g., the christologies of Rauschenbusch, Ritschl, Tillich, Bultmann, and Moltmann), which has prompted them to seek to uncover that which is subversive in the narrative of Jesus. Theology, then, for liberation theologians, becomes a language game, the aim of which is not to produce a conceptually coherent model of Jesus, the Christ, and the Trinity, but rather to re-legitimate theology, and christology in particular, by enabling it to generate new statements ("enoncés" as Lyotard calls them) or new ideas that will speak to an oppressive social reality, that will generate a liberative praxis. Narrative is what liberation theologians are utilizing to relate christology and ethics, to give a religious basis to their praxis; hence narrative is the heuristic tool that this writer will use to analyze this relation.

Secondly, narrative is a useful category for exploring the relation of christology to liberative praxis because, as various theologians, in trying to characterize Latin American theology, have shown, liberation theologians are not truly doing dogmatic theology or Christian ethics but are engaging in an altogether different genre of theological discourse. Charles R. Strain (Strain 1977) has argued that liberation theologies constitute a genre of discourse the characteristics of which are more analogous to secular ideologies than to systematic theology or Christian social ethics. Liberation theologians, he says, have eschewed the effort to understand and formulate what has been revealed through Scripture and tradition—the aim of systematic theology—as well as the effort to craft carefully the "ethical concepts necessary for making the transition from religious symbols and doctrines to political praxis" (Strain 1977, 476)—the aim of Christian social ethics.

Alfredo Fierro, in *The Militant Gospel*, notes that liberation theology, like all the other political theologies, marks a shift away from the personalism and existentialism that characterized the theologies of the 50's and '60's to a theology that is praxis-oriented, public, and critical. In this new theology, he says, "politics plays the mediating role. Thus theological language is made possible and concrete in and through the mediation of political language" (Fierro 1977, 28). Taking seriously, therefore, the exalted claims made by liberation theologians that their theologizing is a "new way of doing theology," then their christological reflection in particular must be a new sort of theological discourse, one that would best be characterized as "narrative."

South African theologian Takatso Mofokeng, contrasting Jon Sobrino's approach to the life of Jesus with the nineteenth century quest for the historical Jesus, comments:

> There is no attempt here to penetrate behind the gospel accounts
> of the story about Jesus of Nazareth with the intention of constructing
> a biography of Jesus that is verifiable by means of tools of
> historical criticism. There is no preoccupation here with the
> intellectual demands of man in the climate of the first stage of the
> Enlightenment in relation to what could be known about the
> historical data concerning Jesus. (Mofokeng, Takatso A., *The
> Crucified among the Crossbearers*, 69, cited by Witvliet, 1987, 31)

Sobrino and the other liberation theologians are not interested in entering into the
perennial discussions of christological concepts, ideas, and dogmas which have tended
to eclipse the conflictive reality in which Latin American Christians live. Instead, they
want to get back to the story of Jesus' life to see what liberating "energy" can be
released from the narrative and appropriated by the oppressed to further their own
liberation. Their genre, therefore, might be more properly considered to be narrative
theology. In short, liberation theologians are (wittingly or unwittingly) constructing
a story of Jesus and his relationship to liberative praxis.

A third reason for using "narrative" to explore the relation between liberation
christology and ethics is that liberation theology as a whole can be seen as having a
narrative structure, and its christology can be seen as one of the constitutive elements
of this structure. Anne Mullholand-Wozniak, in an incisive dissertation, points out
several constituent elements of the narrative structure of liberation theology, i.e., its
elements of "story" (Mulholland-Wozniak 1987). The first is a subversive protagonist,
namely the suffering community of Latin America. A second element is a subversive
plot, namely critical reflection on praxis. And thirdly a subversive denouement,
namely a new humanity and a new society. I would venture to add that behind this
narrative structure lies a subversive archetypal metaphor, specifically the life, death,
and resurrection of Jesus. The life, death, and resurrection of Jesus is a metaphor for
the life, death, and resurrection of the people of Latin America. Each stage of Jesus'
life corresponds to one of the other elements, although not in any chronological
sequence: the life of Jesus, a life characterized by his challenge of the oppressive
structures of his society, a challenge to all forms of false consciousness, provides the
pattern for the plot of the "story," critical reflection on praxis. The suffering and death
he endured provide the pattern for the protagonist, the suffering community (cf., Boff's
Pasión de Cristo, Pasión del Mundo). And finally, Jesus' resurrection, his victory over
death and emergence in a new mode of existence, provide the pattern for the third
element of the liberation "story," the denouement, a new humanity and a new society.
In short, liberation theologians, in the Jesus story, find a pattern for their own story.
Moreover, they also seek to establish a warrant or justification for their story and
praxis; "our 'story' is Jesus' story."

To generate in the individual an appropriate self-understanding and practice, liberation theologians and the marginalized have seen the need to retell the "story" of Jesus. Catholic theologian Johann Baptist Metz has pointed out that:

> Stories are told by very wise men . . . and by little people who are oppressed and have not yet come of age. These, however, tell not only stories which tempt them to celebrate their immature dependence or their oppressed state, but also stories which are dangerous and which seek freedom. . . . Surely there are, in our post-narrative age, story-tellers who can demonstrate what "stories" might be today . . ., narratives with a stimulating effect and aiming at social criticism, "dangerous" stories in other words. Can we perhaps retell the Jesus stories nowadays in this way? (Metz 1989, 255-56)

Liberation theologians *are* beginning to retell the story of Jesus in just this way; they're telling a subversive story of Jesus, a story that by some is perceived as dangerous because its aim is to criticize the status quo and to stimulate the oppressed to liberative praxis. While retelling the story of Jesus in this way, liberation theologians are fulfilling a pastoral need in the lives of the Latin American people; nevertheless, as Metz also points out:

> . . . in giving renewed emphasis to narrative, it is important to avoid the possible misunderstanding that "story-telling" preachers and teachers will be justified in their narration of anecdotes, when what is required are arguments and reasoning. After all, there is a time for story-telling and a time for argument. (Metz 1989, 255)

In other words, providing what the people need does not give liberation theologians an excuse for being theologically sloppy. The story of Jesus that is being told needs to be critically examined; we need to ask liberation theologians if their story is "true," not whether their account of the events is historically verifiable but whether the significance they attach to Jesus' life fulfills the criteria of narrative "truthfulness."

But what criteria are we going to use to evaluate the truthfulness of the liberation theologians' story of Jesus? Stephen Crites has pointed out in a seminal essay that experience has a narrative quality (Crites 1971), but I would further aver that narration itself is an experience-generating phenomenon.[8] There is a dialectic between experience and narration of experience. Someone's experience becomes the subject of narrative. This narrative structures a temporal world into which the reader can enter, generating a new experience which in turn becomes the subject of a new narrative. So narrative emerges out of experience, and experience arises out of narrative.

But for an experience to become a narrative or for a narrative to generate a new experience, the narrator/reader must answer the question of what the experience or narration *means*, i.e., what is its significance? Yet even before the issue of the significance of an experience or narrative is addressed, before the question "What does it mean?" is asked by the story-teller/reader,[9] there are four qualities inherent in the experience or the narrative that lead the story-teller or reader on the quest for significance, that provoke the story-teller to shape a narrative about a person or event and the reader to reflect on it. These qualities are (1) encounter, (2) uniqueness, (3) scope, and (4) pathos. Before the original story is told, there must first be an encounter between the event/person and the story-teller, an encounter that occurs within a space-time continuum and which follows a trajectory consisting of a beginning, a middle and an end. That encounter therefore could be the witnessing of an accident, a play, a movie, the reading of a novel, hearing a lecture, the sharing of a life. In other words, the story-teller must existentially confront an event/person that illumines and trans-forms his or her life "in penetrating and thoroughgoing ways" (Root 1989). For instance, I remember as a child how anxious and excited I was to tell someone about a good movie I had just seen—I had to tell the story of the encounter I had just experienced. I have yet to feel the same excitement to retell the story about a movie someone else has seen and narrated to me. We tell stories about the events and persons *we* ourselves encounter. One "comes upon" people and events that become memorable and narratable. Those events/persons which we encounter and which become memorable are those which are in some way unique, somehow affect lives and touch us on an emotional level.

Let me clarify this further. In reporting a news story, one of the questions a journalist asks is whether the story is newsworthy. Its worth is determined not only by the uniqueness of the event but also by the scope of the event (i.e., how are people affected and how many?), as well as the pathos of the event (Is the event seen as tragic, comic, ironic, or heroic?). A housewife burning a roast, therefore, is not news, but a housewife burning down a neighborhood is. If an event ceases to be unique or its scope is minimized, it loses its social significance. For example, Space Shuttle landings, drive-by shootings in L.A., heart transplants, and in-vitro fertilizations: as these events occur with greater and greater frequency, their uniqueness is lost, their scope is overshadowed by other events, their pathos trivialized. Now what does this have to do with the liberation theologians' story of Jesus? We need to see if in their retelling of Jesus' story the uniqueness, scope, and pathos of his life are somehow minimized and thus the story becomes meaningless for humanity; we need to see if the Jesus story ceases to be "News." It is in this latter sense that I ask whether the liberation theologians' story is true: is the story of Jesus that is being created and proclaimed worthy of attention? Is it still news? (At this point I'm not even asking whether it is *good* news for some and *bad* news for others.)

But a religious story is not a journalistic rendering, mere description of facts. A story is a claim to meaning; it is an argument about values. A story-teller makes this claim to meaning through the "artistic plotting of events, with a set of purposes dependent on the context" (Tilley 1985, 187). This claim to meaning is elicited by the uniqueness, pathos and magnitude of the experience on the story-teller.

When we come to the Gospels, we come to a story as told by those who had an encounter with a man they found to be unique, life-transforming, and tragically heroic. The Gospels are realistic narratives: not hard facts, but the artistic plotting of a life, in part to fulfill certain specific purposes suited to the storytellers' contexts. But besides these immediate, historically concrete purposes, the canonical story-tellers also seem to have had a common purpose: to bear witness to all generations to the universal meaningfulness of Jesus' life.

A question must be asked of all stories: Is the claim to meaning made by the story-teller through the story a valid claim? In other words, is the story "true" or valid? Whatever claim to meaning or values-argument is being made must be assessed by the listener. Such an assessment is possible by examining the coherence and fidelity to the facts as these are publicly recognized. With regard to liberation christology, then, the question is, Does the story of Jesus, proclaimed by liberation theologians, present a significant argument about values in a coherent way, faithful to the facts and to the listener as an end in him/herself (Fisher 1989, 22-23)? According to Terrence Tilley:

> A story can be assessed "true" (or "false") [i.e., valid or invalid] to
> the extent that it (1) represents the world (or part of it) revealingly;
> (2) is coherent by corresponding to the facts (insofar as we
> recognize them), by referring accurately and by attributing cor-
> rectly; (3) shows ways of overcoming self-deception; (4) shows a
> person how to be faithful (true) to others; and (5) provides a model
> for constancy in seeking to tell the truth. (Tilley 1985, 183)

In the chapters ahead, therefore, we will be looking to see if the liberationist story of Jesus: (1) re-presents the world in a revealing a way, (2) coheres with the facts, attributing qualities and actions to Jesus that are warranted by the sources, (3) opens the listener to alternative explanations so as to escape self-delusion, and (4) and (5) shows the listener how to treat others as ends in themselves.

Notes

1.   Both Juan Luis Segundo and Leonardo Boff themselves use the word "deconstruction" to refer to this first step of their christological construction. Cf. Chapter 3, Note 15 in Segundo's *The Historical Jesus of the Synoptics*, p. 194, and

Boff's *Pasión de Cristo, Pasión del Mundo*, pp. 189-90.

2. During the 1950's and 60's Puerto Rico, under the leadership of the popular governor Luis Muñoz Marín, undertook a project called "Operation Bootstrap," which sought to transform the agrarian economy into an industrial one. The results were mixed. While the standard of living of most Puerto Ricans improved as they found higher-paying jobs in American industries, the long term effects were disastrous. The sugar, coffee, plantain, and tobacco industries collapsed since no one was willing to work the fields, so today Puerto Rico has to import most agricultural commodities. As people left the rural areas in search of the higher-paying jobs in the cities where most of the manufacturing plants were located, the tremendous housing shortage resulted in shanty towns springing up almost overnight, shanty towns such as "La Perla," "El Babote," "Vietnam," and "Aguas Prietas." Many American industries, once they lost their tax-free status (15 years after an industry's arrival on the island), left the country, creating a serious problem of unemployment. Puerto Rico is now more dependent than ever as a result of such projects of "development."

3. Catholics are converting to Protestantism (especially to the Pentecostal and Baptist denominations) at the rate of 400 per hour, or three million a year according to some estimates. Guatemala, for instance, is already 25 percent Protestant and is expected to be 50 percent by the end of this century. Brazil is about 10 percent Protestant. The rate of Protestant growth has been so great as to cause alarm among the Catholic hierarchy. Cf. (Lernoux 1988; Martin 1988; Rodriguez 1989)

4. Ironically, once the poor convert to evangelical Protestantism they often adopt a rightist ideology—pro-American, anti-communist, and supportive of the status quo (whatever it might be). Although such "conversions" to the right might be easy to attribute to the simplistic equation of Christianity and Americanism made by North American missionaries and evangelists, an equation these poor Latin Americans just as simplistically accept, it might be fairer to see the rightist turn as the result of a misdirected and untutored, but fundamentally correct, intuition that the logic of Protestantism, with its emphasis on the individual, rationality, and democratic structures empowers the believer to achieve a more integral liberation. The unsophisticated Latin American often makes the following equation: Protestantism = Democracy = North America. Catholicism, rightly or not, is seen as anti-democratic, perhaps because of its historic allegiance with repressive totalitarian regimes. This is precisely what liberation theologians are trying to remedy, i.e., to change the Church's image and make it an ally of the people and not of the state. Yet ironically, the Marxist rhetoric used by many progressive priests engenders fears of *atheistic* totalitarianism in many of the people. Since religion to Latin Americans is more precious than life, it is in the

minds of many better to have a tyrant that is tolerant of religion, than to support a movement that, once it gets into power, (they fear) will programmatically do away with religion (á la the Soviet Union) as it seeks to establish economic equality. For the faithful some tyrannies are better than others.

5. The word "anarchy" as used by Ellul is *not* to be equated with the political option advocated by Bakunin. Rather he uses the term in its etymological sense, *an-arché*, the absence of authority. He means the radical, total refusal of political power.

6. Peter Berger suggests that there are two of these social myths: the myth of growth (or "progress") and the myth of revolution (the hope for a "redemptive community") (cf., Berger 1974, 18-113). Lyotard suggests that there are two archetypal narratives of legitimation in the West: the narrative of human liberation and the narrative of totality (the unity of knowledge) (Lyotard 1988, 31-36).

7. Harvey Cox has made a similar argument in *Religion in the Secular City* using American Fundamentalism and Latin American liberation theology as examples of two theological responses to the failure of liberal theology, a theology which received its inspiration from the Enlightenment myths. (Cf., Cox 1984)

8. In this view I follow the philosopher J. L. Austin, who argues that speech-acts have performative force (cf., J. L. Austin, *How to Do Things with Words*, Oxford: 1961). Here I am of course assuming that narratives are a type of "speech-act" that evoke response, and hence generate experience.

9. I will be using the words "story-teller" and "reader" to refer to the transmitter and the recipient of a narrative, respectively, but the words are used with the recognition that narratives can take many forms and can also be transmitted and received through a variety of media: film, dance, lecture, drama, mime, radio, television, and so on.

CHAPTER 2

THE SIGNIFICANCE OF CHRISTOLOGY FOR LIBERATION THEOLOGY

Liberation theologians have been reflecting christologically on the praxis that has been and is being carried out in Latin America, seeking to find in Jesus Christ a warrant for such a praxis and a stimulus for its continuance. In this process of reflection, the liberation theologians have sought to show that a liberating praxis not only is not opposed to orthodox christology, but is made necessary by it. Indeed it seems that the liberation theologians are at great pains to show that they are doctrinally orthodox, that their christologies are simply emphases of forgotten or overlooked aspects of the orthodox formulations. Their interest is not merely to demonstrate their orthodoxy to their critics, but to show how an emphasis on liberative praxis *is* consistent with (and even made necessary by) orthodoxy. So their motivations for christological reflection are ethical, apologetic, and pastoral.

Such apologetic, ethical, and pastoral concerns can best be realized by bringing together what christologies of the past have sometimes tended to split asunder: the Jesus of History and the Christ of Faith. Beginning with the early Church, through Chalcedon, even to the Protestant Reformation, the focus had been on the Christ of Faith to the disregard of the Jesus of History. In other words, the focus had been on the risen and glorified Christ. What this meant for soteriology was a focus on the salvation of the soul for an afterlife in "heaven" with this risen Christ. From the Enlightenment onward, the emphasis on the scientific and the empirical led theologians to focus on the Jesus of History, some (e.g., the rationalists and iconoclasts) disparaging the Christ of Faith and others (the "mediating" theologians) seeking to show the meaningfulness of the Gospel narratives to the modern world.[1] Such a shift in focus sparked a concern for the problems of *this* world, a "this-worldly" salvation, as made evident by such movements as the Social Gospel and the more recent "Death of God" theology. The focus on the Christ of Faith led to such an emphasis on the transcendent that christology lost all relevance to the work-a-day world; it fell short in affirming a Christian praxis. The focus on the Jesus of History, on the other hand, while advancing progress, has at times led some theologians to disparage transcendence and produce unorthodox christologies and encourage the secularization of society.

Liberation theologians Leonardo Boff, Juan Luis Segundo, and Jon Sobrino continue in the tradition of the "mediating" theologians; they have embarked on the quest of Jesus Christ Liberator, the affirmation of the Christ of Faith *through* the Jesus of History—hoping to avoid the previous excesses.

The Difficulty of Systematization

Now when we turn to the christologies of these theologians and inquire into Jesus' identity and significance, and methodically try to organize these data into a logically coherent discourse, as systematic theologians are likely to do, we find ourselves faced with several difficulties.

Firstly, as pointed out in Chapter 1, these theologians are not approaching Jesus Christ from a speculative, abstract angle as do many traditional (First World) theologians. They are concerned with how to make christology pastorally relevant, how to relate it to the lives of the people. Consequently there are lacunae on those matters that are more abstract and speculative, such as Christ's pre-existence, his kenosis, how the Logos is united to his human nature, the harrowing of hell, Christ's present role in heaven, whether it was possible for Jesus not to sin or it was not possible for Jesus to sin (*posse non peccare, non posse peccare*).

Secondly, their inductive approach militates against fitting their christological reflections into the clearly demarcated categories of Jesus' Person and Jesus' Work usually used by systematic theologians: Jesus humanity cannot be considered apart from his divinity, and vice versa; salvation cannot be considered apart from his divinity or his humanity, from his praxis, from his proclamation of the Kingdom of God, nor from his own self-consciousness.

In spite of these difficulties, in what follows I will try to synthesize what liberation theologians relate about Jesus Christ. This will involve sorting out what liberation theologians have to say about *who* is Jesus Christ, i.e., the question of Jesus of Nazareth's identity, and what is the meaning of Jesus Christ for human life. All the while, I will also aim to show how liberation theologians relate their christology to Christian social ethics.

The Identity of Jesus Christ

The Mystery of the Incarnation

The doctrine of the Incarnation is a conceptual expression of the mystery of

Jesus Christ's person. It developed in direct response to a series of conceptual challenges that arose very early on in the history of the Church. The christological affirmations found in the New Testament lacked the conceptual precision to prevent those reflecting on the mystery of Jesus Christ from offering possible explanations of that mystery. But for many in the Church, some of those alternative explanations were seen, not as explaining the mystery, but as reducing one or the other aspect of it: either Jesus' humanity was diminished or his divinity was diminished; docetism, for instance, denied his humanity, while adoptionism so emphasized his humanity that it denied his divinity. Because of the divisive potential of these explanations, the Church became very preoccupied with identifying and securing the identity of Jesus Christ as God. The climax of these conceptual controversies, which relatedly had soteriological and hence practical consequences, was the Council of Chalcedon in 451 A.D. But because the emphasis had been on conceptual clarity, on philosophical and logical coherence, Church dogma was something alien to the everyday life of the ordinary Christian. In fact, christological dogma was seen as having its own autonomy, as having to do with "faith," with religion, with the hereafter, and hence unrelated to the economic and political conditions prevailing within society. It is to this problem that Boff, Sobrino, and Segundo are addressing themselves.

The Methodological Primacy of The Historical Jesus

Boff, Sobrino, and Segundo begin with the assumption that in order to relate Jesus Christ to the current situation in Latin America it is necessary to commence any sort of discourse about him from the perspective of his concrete history. A relevant christology will be one that begins from below, that begins by looking at Jesus in his humanity so that discourse about him will be relevant to human beings. Only discourse about a human being would be relevant to human beings. Hence christology must be "from below" rather than "from above." Liberation christology does not begin with the *a priori* affirmation of Jesus' deity (which they prefer to call his divinity), but rather look to his humanity to see what in his person—namely his intentions, words, and actions—occasioned the affirmation that this man was God. That is not to say that these three theologians disavow the doctrine of Jesus being God incarnate—they do not, hence remain orthodox Catholics. Rather they disavow an exclusively ontological approach to the mystery of the Incarnation (which the Church has traditionally taken in its dogmas and polity) because such an approach eclipses the concrete historical facts, options, choices, deeds, and words of Jesus that led to (1) his eventual execution, and (2) the proclamation that this man was God.

Jon Sobrino notes the importance of beginning with the historical Jesus:

> The insistence of liberation christology on the historical Jesus
> shows the emphasis of liberation christology on the notion that in
> Jesus there appeared both God's descent to human beings and the
> manner of the human being's access to God. (Sobrino 1987, 16)

For Sobrino, then, discourse about the Incarnation (God's descent) and salvation
(human access, human ascent?) can only be intelligible and coherent only from the
point of departure of the Historical Jesus. There are also other reasons for this starting
point. By beginning with the Historical Jesus, christology can avoid becoming an
abstract discourse, on the one hand, or a tool of ideology, on the other. The Historical
Jesus can serve as a hermeneutical check on either of those two extremes. Additionally,
the totality of Christ, says Sobrino, can best be accessed, both in terms of knowledge
and of praxis, through the Historical Jesus (Sobrino 1978, 9-10).

Segundo sees this approach as paralleling the one implemented in the New
Testament and hence the normative approach for doing christology:

> The only valid approach to Jesus of Nazareth is that of the New
> Testament. It entails a process of successive readings that start out
> from the concrete, historical interest he aroused in his own time
> and place and move on to the human problems of later times and
> our own present day. Those problems are bound up with meaning-
> worlds that are radically akin to his . . . (Segundo 1985, 39)

He adds:

> . . . only one kind of christology is valid and dovetails with the way
> Jesus himself posed issues. It is a christology that starts off from
> the historical data about Jesus and *multiplies* the readings of his
> message each time *modifying* the *pre-understanding* that is brought
> to the next reading. (Segundo 1985, 39)

In other words there is a dialectical hermeneutic process in which the reader brings to
the Historical Jesus a pre-understanding, constitutive elements of which are the
present-day problems confronting the reader, which produce a new reading of Jesus
and his message (a new christology). This new reading, in turn, changes the reader's
pre-understanding, so that subsequent reading of the historical data will engender
another christology, and so on *ad infinitum*.

Segundo, therefore, clearly disavows the notion that there should be one,
definitive, universal christology. Encounter with the Historical Jesus in ever new
social contexts can and should produce a multiplicity of christologies.

Leonardo Boff also sees the need to begin with the Historical Jesus. He writes,
in *Faith on the Edge*, that ". . . liberation Christology seeks to compose and articulate

its content and style in a manner calculated to bring out the liberating dimensions of the historical Jesus' life" (Boff 1989, 121). Further on he writes:

> The reduction of Christology to a study of the Christ of faith, Jesus Christ as interpreted by the community, without any concern for the experience of the historical Jesus ... impoverishes Christianity's comprehensive vision. (Boff 1989, 150)

But Boff qualifies his approach so as to avoid any sort of historicist reductionism. In *Jesus Christ Liberator*, Boff challenges Bultmann's notion that the Historical Jesus is irrelevant for faith. Instead Boff seems to approve of the post-Bultmannian theologies that see an objective continuity and a subjectively important connection between the Jesus of History and the Christ of Faith. Although Boff is skeptical of the possibility of reconstructing a definitive biography of Jesus—since all history is necessarily interpretation—he nevertheless sees it as necessary to try to reclaim the Historical Jesus from the perspective of faith:

> History always comes to us in unison with faith and consequently any docetist watering down, be it reducing Jesus to mere Word (kerygma, preaching) or to a mere historical being that ceased to exist in death ought to be rejected a priori. (Boff 1978b, 19)

By beginning with the Historical Jesus, these liberation theologians hope to reinterpret the doctrines of the Incarnation and the Atonement in a way that might be relevant to the experience of oppression and exploitation of the Latin American people. In short, what they are trying to do is simply to give the theological attention that the life of Jesus so fully deserves but which so far has been overlooked. Their effort is best characterized by the late Ignacio Ellacuría in *Freedom Made Flesh*:

> Our new Christology must give history of the flesh-and-blood Jesus its full weight as revelation. Today it would be absolutely ridiculous to try to fashion a Christology in which the historical realization of Jesus' life did not play a decisive role. The "mysteries of Jesus' life," which once were treated peripherally as part of ascetics, must be given their full import ... (Ellacuría 1976, 26)

The Man Who Became God

Having established the methodological priority of the Historical Jesus, liberation theologians begin to discuss the mystery of the Incarnation. Since christological reflection begins "from below," since it begins with the historical, then what is clearly evident, as a rationally tenable datum, is that Jesus is a human being. The affirmation of his humanity follows logically from his historicity. Sobrino puts it best when he writes:

> Liberation christology professes the true humanity of Christ . . . *by telling Jesus' story* . . . [like] the gospels [which] present Jesus by telling his story, giving his history, by historicizing . . . his actual life. This means understanding the human nature of Christ . . . as Jesus' history. It means translating his humanity . . . into the truth of his concrete history. (Sobrino 1987, 30)

Liberation christology, then, like the Gospels, affirms Jesus' humanity narratively, that is, not through abstract speculation or philosophical argumentation about what constitutes human nature, but simply by narrating a story that identifies Jesus as intending, acting, and feeling as human beings do.

Jesus' full humanity, in conformity with the dogmas of the Church, is unequivocally affirmed by liberation theologians. But this conformity is not simply for the sake of being considered orthodox by the Church hierarchy; it is a matter of tremendous practical importance. For it is in his humanity that Jesus can be the norm for Christians, not only the goal or ideal in view, but the way to the goal, the way to realize the ideal. Jesus' humanity is eschatologically transcendent, hence normative. For instance according to Sobrino, "Christ is really a human being, indeed is *the* human being. Thereby we assert his true humanity and the eschatological character . . . of this humanity of his" (Sobrino 1987, 29).

For Boff the affirmation of Jesus' full humanity is important for liberation in two ways, one negative, the other positive. First, this humanity, revealed in Jesus' historical pilgrimage, exposes that which is non-human. His historical pilgrimage represents the realization of true humanity; he "recovers our genuine identity as human" (Boff 1989, 147). Secondly, Jesus' human nature reveals the eschatological New Human Being, the human person that God intended from eternity. This human nature comes to its full manifestation in the Resurrection. But the totality of Jesus' life, from conception to resurrection, reveals the utopian potential of humanity. The affirmation of Jesus' full humanity has enormous relevance for liberation, says Boff, for "If Jesus is truly a human being . . . then that which is asserted of him must also be affirmed in some manner of each person. Having Jesus, the most perfect of all human beings, as our starting point we can see who we are and how we are" (Boff 1978b, 204).

Segundo as well affirms Jesus' humanity but does not do so directly as a dogmatic confession. Rather Jesus' humanity is a methodological given for Segundo; he begins his "antichristology" with the assumption that Jesus *is* a human being. He seeks to approach Jesus from an angle different from that of academic christology which, he says, assumes that Jesus is humanly interesting or significant because He is recognized as God. Instead Segundo wants to argue that Jesus is recognized as God because he is humanly interesting. Jesus' divinity, therefore, follows from his humanity. He writes:

> If people came face to face with a specific, limited human being, ambiguous as everything involved in history is, and came to see him as God or a divine revelation, it was because that human being was of interest, was humanly significant. And if people today arrive at the same final vision of him today, it will only be because the latter fact is verified again: that is, because he is of interest and humanly significant to them. (Segundo 1985, 17)

So it is by examining or contemplating Jesus' humanity that his divinity can be apprehended today, and this observation applies not only to Segundo's but to Boff's and Sobrino's christologies as well. If Jesus is recognized and proclaimed as God it must be because there is something inherently present in the life of Jesus, in all its historicity, that merits it.

The full humanity of Jesus must necessarily be affirmed if he is to be of any practical relevance to human beings. If Jesus is fully human, and yet is recognized as divine—if he bore witness, in his humanity to certain values that resulted in death, resurrection, and eventual divinization—then his life, his *modus vivendi*, becomes a prototype of what is possible for all human beings. It becomes of paramount importance, therefore, to explore Jesus' life to discover what were these values to which he bore witness, what was the structure of this life, what was his praxis, if Jesus is to be of interest to human beings in the twentieth century.

As for Jesus' divinity, as has been implied above, liberation theologians are more interested in analyzing the process by which Jesus became recognized and proclaimed as divine, than in simply confessing Jesus as God. All of them are of one mind in seeing the statements "Jesus is God" or "Jesus is the Christ" as limit statements that are not open to historical or empirical verification. Rather the statements are a confession of faith, a confession that is the result of a process of reflection on the concrete history of Jesus. What is important to see, then, is what were the elements in Jesus' historical life that led the apostles, the early Christian communities, and finally and more formally, the Church Councils to proclaim as dogma the divinity of Jesus. Liberation theologians want to discover and highlight those elements in the New Testament story of Jesus, those character traits in the protagonist of the original story, that enabled the early Christian community to identify Jesus first, as human, and *consequently* as the Christ, as divine, as Lord. Access to Jesus' divinity, whether in an objective or a subjective way, must come through his humanity and not the other way around, say liberation theologians. This approach to Jesus is justifiable in that it replicates the process of "coming-to-believe" of Jesus' disciples themselves.

Jesus' divinity is apprehended indirectly, according to Sobrino, through Jesus' life. There is no other way to gain access it. Indeed Sobrino goes so far as to say that we cannot know what deity is except through Jesus' concrete life, that there cannot be any *a priori* knowledge of what God is like; we can only know God through Jesus' concrete history. It was the mistake of earlier christologies to assume what God was like and to read those conceptions into the conception of Jesus' deity and humanity. The prevailing notion of what God was like was a Greek conception that saw deity as perfection, immutability, absolute transcendence, and aseity and these characteristics were projected unto Jesus. The result was a docetic view of Jesus, a Jesus that was never truly a part of the human realm, never a part of *human* history; consequently, such divinization resulted in making Jesus irrelevant to the concrete problems faced by humanity. Liberation theologians seek to understand Jesus' divinity from the stand-point of his humanity, rather than the reverse.

According to Segundo, Jesus' divinity must be understood from a different perspective than the one that comes down to us in the Church dogmas and in the New Testament. These christologies expressed Jesus' divinization in a way that led to his de-historicization; they see Jesus as the origin and end of the universe, but only "insofar as he is above and beyond all the ephemeral conflicts of history." Segundo, like Sobrino, following Vatican II, argues that Jesus must be reintroduced into history, and his divinity must be understood from his concrete history:

> ... the concept of divinity ... must be filled with attributes arising out of the concrete history of Jesus. Which means that any "cosmic" interpretation of Jesus must begin with what we know of his history, not with what we supposedly know about what God is or may be. (Segundo 1988, 65)

Clearly, then, as with Sobrino, Jesus' divinity cannot be argued for or expressed on the basis of any *a priori* concept of divinity.

Furthermore, Segundo argues that the affirmation of Jesus' divinity is part of a language game; hence the statement "Jesus is God" is not to be taken "literally," that is, ontologically, but anthropologically. To say that "Jesus is fully God" says more about human nature than it says about ultimate reality. He writes:

> The two statements, "Jesus is (completely) human being" and "Jesus is (completely) God", are not on the same logical level. If they were, we would be led to 'mix' in Jesus properly human powers and capacities with others supposedly proper to God. The

higher level of language is a statement about the *lower*, a met-
amessage about the historical Jesus. To say that the human being,
Jesus, is God, then, is not to turn him into a demigod, an "apparent"
human being, a being "above" the conflicts and problems of
history. By the same token, the *higher* level is not a mere excla-
mation of admiration or a mere mark of my feelings. Its function
in anthropological faith is to *elevate* the concrete values perceived
in the history of Jesus to the category of absolute, and to wager that
to them the entire reality of the universe bows and submits in a
personal way. (Segundo 1988, 65-66)

To say that Jesus is God, therefore, is a way for human beings to express the ultimate
normativity of the values to which Jesus bore witness in his historical existence.

Boff, for his part, does not address the issue of Jesus' divinity directly but in
relation to the problem of trinity and unity in God, in his book *Trinity and Society*. He
works along more traditional lines of theological discourse, trying to shed light on the
Nicene-Constantinoplian affirmation of the Son's consubstantiality with the Father
and the Holy Spirit. Boff argues that rather than using the ontological conceptuality
of consubstantiality (or even the more modern existential categories proposed by Barth
and Rahner) to understand the nature of the Trinity, the model of perichoresis-
communion, the interpenetration of Persons, better manages to maintain the balance
between unity and trinity. (Boff 1988a, 137).

For Boff, Jesus is fully God. The Historical Jesus is the Son and is in a reciprocal
relationship with the other Persons of the Godhead:

[T]he three divine Persons are simultaneous in origin and co-exist
eternally in communion and interpenetration. Each is distinct
from the others in personal characteristics and in the communion
established by that Person, each revealing that Person's self to
itself and the self of the others to them. (Boff 1988a, 142)

But like Sobrino and Segundo, Boff also affirms that the knowledge of Jesus as "Son
of God," hence divine, and the knowledge of the Father, of divinity as such, cannot be
obtained *a priori*:

It is only the Son who can reveal the Father to others. . . . He alone
can provide a true guide to how the Father acts and so to what he
is. Therefore, in order to know the Father, we must see how the Son
acts. His actions and words give us access to the Father. This is
not an abstract and metaphysical approach; rather, in it the Father
is revealed through a history, by way of a revealing gesture through

> the course of his Son's life among his sons and daughters. (Boff
> 1988a, 32)

Again, access to what God is comes through reflection on the concrete life of Jesus, in all its historicity. But knowledge of Jesus as Son, i.e., as divine, can only come by a concrete commitment and praxis that replicates that of the Historical Jesus: " . .   . we cannot believe in the Son purely in terms of profession of faith, devoid of ethical content. We discover Jesus as Son through following him. . . . Ethic leads to ontology; following to believing" (Boff 1988a, 32).

Consequently, the existential "grasp" and affirmation of Jesus' divinity in liberation theology is not a cognitive assent to the witness of the New Testament; it does not even follow from a subjective, properly religious, experience as might be had in the privacy of a monastic cell after months of prayer and contemplation (i.e., as a result of a conversion experience of the type described by William James in the *Varieties of Religious Experience*). To affirm and experience Jesus' divinity is to have entered into history as Jesus entered into history; it is to make concrete, through a specific praxis, the values which Jesus, as a human being, sought to make concrete. Jesus' divinity, indeed God himself, can only be grasped or experienced, as Sobrino says, *in actu*, in the act, in a praxis of liberation.

It is "in the act" that Jesus' divinity is grasped and, subsequently, the liberative implications of other theological affirmations are illumined and grasped as well. The doctrine of the Trinity, for instance, is paradigmatic of the community or solidarity that ought to exist in society. The affirmation of God being "Three-in-One" can serve as "critic and inspiration for human society":

> The sort of society that would emerge from inspiration by the
> trinitarian model would be one of fellowship, equality of opportu-
> nity, generosity in the space available for personal and group
> expression. Only a society of sisters and brothers whose social
> fabric is woven out of participation and communion of all in
> everything can justifiably claim to be an image and likeness (albeit
> pale) of the Trinity, the foundation and final resting-place of the
> universe. (Boff 1988a, 151)

We have now seen that liberation theologians methodologically prioritize their affirmations about Jesus Christ so as to bring out the relevance of these affirmations for the oppressive situation which exists in Latin America. First is the priority of the Historical Jesus; second, and as a logical consequence of the first priority, comes Jesus' humanity; finally, and contingent on that humanity, is the affirmation of Jesus' divinity.

If by following and reflecting on the concrete path of the Historical Jesus we can discover what it means to be fully human and what it means to know and become God, what are the specific signposts of that path that guide us toward the realization of true humanity and true divinity? In other words, if Jesus is the Trailblazer, what concrete signs did he leave in order that we might be able to follow and might become, with him, truly human and truly divine?

The Significance of Jesus Christ

Jesus the Trailblazer: The Man Who Paved the Way

To speak of Jesus as a "Trailblazer" is an apt metaphor for understanding how liberation theologians conceive of his significance for humanity. Ahistorical christologies, like those of the Councils, resulted in ahistorical soteriologies, i.e., conceptions of what Jesus Christ does or means for humanity. The emphasis on the Christ of Faith resulted in views of the Atonement that de-historicized Jesus' work. But not only is the significance of Jesus' death and resurrection de-historicized, his concrete life prior to and leading to these events is overlooked as having any soteriological significance. To illustrate with an analogy the import of such an omission, such christological and soteriological construction would be similar to a literary critic trying to interpret a novel by reading only the final chapter.

By not separating christology, soteriology, and ethics and by reflecting on the totality of Jesus' life, liberation theologians hope to show that the salvation that he provides is an integral salvation, i.e., liberation from personal sin and also collective liberation from structural sin. They also hope to show that Jesus' way of saving is the best way to understand what it means to be fully human and what God is like and, hence, what it means to say that Jesus is fully God. Jesus paves the way for the realization of a full humanity, the divinization of humanity, and consequently its full salvation or liberation from every form of oppression. Along that path of realization which Jesus paved for human beings are several signposts which liberation theologians have espied and want to point out to others.

Jesus' Humanity - A Commitment to Subversiveness

The first signpost is Jesus' "person," that is, his humanity, which is laden with soteriological and ethical significance. Because liberation theologians look at Jesus from within history (rather than from "above history"), Jesus' person, his humanity, is understood in relational terms; their discourse about Jesus' person is relational, not ontological. This means that Jesus' soteriological and ethical significance is revealed in his relationship as "son" to God (what Sobrino calls "filiation") and as "brother" to the marginalized. What Boff, Sobrino, and Segundo discover about Jesus in these relationships to God and others is an uncompromising commitment to subversiveness; Jesus subverts all of the prevailing conceptions about God and how one ought to relate to Him (*sic*) as well as the prevailing conceptions about how human beings ought to relate to one another. It is this commitment that needs to be replicated today.

Jesus is a "son"

As a human being, Jesus, in all his historicity, revealed to humankind a subversive commitment to God in his filiation; that is, in his "sonship" he demonstrated to humanity what it is to be a *child* of God; he behaved as a son demonstrating all of the characteristics that are present in an intimate filial relation: faith, trust, obedience to the Father's will, loyalty, respect, devotion, love. Boff notes that "In Jesus has appeared the whole concrete reality of filiation—a child of God in all the fulness of that condition from one end of life's journey to the other" (Boff 1989, 148-49).

Boff adds that Jesus behaved as "son" (1) in his prayer life which consisted of frequent and intimate talks with the Father, (2) in his freedom, and (3) in his loyalty to the Father's cause. Concerning Jesus' freedom, Boff says:

> Because he felt himself to be the Father's Son, he took the liberty
> of eating with sinners so as to give them trust in divine mercy, to
> flout oppressive laws and to reinterpret tradition. . . . [He] sees
> himself as Son through having received the freedom of the Father,
> a freedom he passes on to men and women around him; so he frees
> them from infirmities, from the various oppressions that stigma-
> tize life, from sin and from death. . . . He forgives sins in the
> Father's name. (Boff 1988a, 180-81)

Jesus also showed that a child of God remains loyal to the Father since when "Threatened with death, he clung to his course, obedient to the Father's cause and resisting all temptations. This obedience even to death on a cross expressed his radical faithfulness as Son to the Father" (Boff 1988a, 180-81).

According to Sobrino, Jesus' filiation was demonstrated in his faith in the Father which was made explicit in a two-fold attitude, an "attitude of exclusive confidence in the Father (vertical relationship) and . . . total obedience to his mission of proclaiming and making present the kingdom (horizontal relationship)" (Sobrino 1978, 103). Jesus, like any human being, had to *learn* to trust the Father and remain faithful to his mission through his concrete history, that is, in the silence, darkness, conflict, and absurdity which is existence. This growth in faith involved a process of "conversion" on Jesus' part: of surrendering old conceptions about the Kingdom of God and taking up a new conception, of undergoing a shift in his understanding and outworking of the Father's will. Sobrino distinguishes between two stages in Jesus' life, the turning point being the Galilean crisis. It is at this point in Jesus' life that:

> Jesus comes to realize that he has failed in his mission as he had previously understood it. The crowds are abandoning him, the religious leaders of the Jewish people will not accept him, and God is not getting any closer with power to renovate reality. (Sobrino 1978, 93)

What this means for oppressed Latin Americans, as children of God, in terms of their faith made concrete in praxis, is that just as it was for Jesus, so it is for them: life is a journey of faith and the twists and turns on that journey cannot be foreknown, but whatever path they take, whatever conflicts they might encounter along the way, shattering their best-laid plans, they must nevertheless maintain their commitment to God, their total fidelity to God, since that is what it means to be a child, a son or daughter, of God.

This commitment to God to which they must remain faithful, as children of God, is not cultic in nature but subversive; it is not a privatized faith consisting of lighting candles, reciting creeds and prayers, and attending ceremonies and processions; it is a faith that expresses itself in concrete solidarity with the oppressed in their struggle for liberation; a faith that makes itself concrete by subverting everything that alienates people from God and one another.

Jesus is a "brother"

Jesus' liberative significance is also revealed in his relationship as "brother" to the marginalized. In his "brotherhood" Jesus demonstrated a subversive commitment to others, a commitment that was made historically concrete in his partisanship and in his willing impoverishment. Boff writes:

> In Jesus has likewise appeared the model of the human being as sister or brother of others. . . . Jesus draws near to all, especially to the socially and religiously marginalized and slandered, to the lowly, to the damned of the earth. And he makes of his neighbor a brother and a sister. (Boff 1989, 149)

According to Sobrino, "From a theological viewpoint, and surely from a historical viewpoint, human beings, Christ's brothers and sisters, are the poor and insignificant" (Sobrino 1987, 37).

By being a "brother" to the marginalized Jesus demonstrated three things. Theo-logically, he demonstrated that God is partisan, that God takes sides. Secondly and anthropologically, he demonstrated that to be *truly human* is to be someone who sides with the oppressed. Finally, ethically, he showed that faith is demonstrated by a subversive commitment to others; that to claim that one is a "son" of God, one must stand shoulder to shoulder with those who are also God's own, the oppressed—and therefore one's brothers—in their struggle for liberation.

The subversive commitment to others is definitive of what God is, what humanity is, and what a child of God is. But also it is through reflection on and reproduction of Jesus' partisanship that we can understand in what sense Jesus was divine as well as become able to enter that process of divinization ourselves.

Sobrino for instance writes that Jesus' partisanship, his brotherhood, reveals the nature of God, and it is in our partisanship or brotherhood that we can "know" or grasp God's nature and be able to share in that divine nature:

> The Son brings the servant to plenitude, but the Son has no
> plenitude without being servant. Precisely because the eschato-
> logical Son is also the servant, he can be the first-born, the elder
> brother, and human beings can become daughters and sons in the
> Son (cf. Rom. 8:29), can be inserted into divinization—but to be
> sure after the historical manner of servants. (Sobrino 1987, 37)

It is in being a servant that Jesus becomes the "Son" and "elder brother" and so becomes the Trailblazer making it possible for anyone to become a son or daughter of God who follows the path that he traced: servanthood, solidarity with the oppressed. One *becomes* a son or daughter by *being* a son or daughter; one *becomes* a brother or sister of Jesus Christ by *being* a brother or sister to others.

It is in reproducing this commitment, this subversive solidarity with the poor, that human beings enter the path of humanization and divinization: "[Jesus'] partisan historical filiation is the believers' path to the reproduction of the image of the Son and the path of their historical and transcendent approach to God" (Sobrino 1987, 37).

While liberation theologians appeal to Vatican II to support their view that the Incarnation is symbolic of God's solidarity with humanity, that it represents God's assumption of human history (cf. *Gaudium et Spes*, no. 22), they make this divine solidarity, as evident in Jesus' concrete history, even more specific. It is not a solidarity with humanity as a species or creature, but with a particular social class, namely the poor and oppressed; neither is it an assumption of History in the abstract, as there can be a history of the world or of the human race, but a particular history, of which there are many (the history of America, the history of the Jews, or even the history of the car, for example), but not all of them bearers of God's presence. It is the history of the poor, the history of their struggle for liberation in particular, which God assumes.

Jesus, in his historical and partisan commitment to the poor, mediates to humanity what God is like and what true human being is like. Sobrino writes:

> In accepting in faith the fundamental normativity of [Jesus']
> history we are also asserting its faith meaning. In other words, by
> associating ourselves today with the fundamental structure of the
> role of mediator and of his mediations, the God of Jesus will also
> be a reality to us as a God of life. (Sobrino 1987, 101)

We see, then, that it is in entering the history of the poor, in solidarity with them, through a voluntary impoverishment—a commitment that is selective in its object (*to* the poor) and in its project (*for* liberation)—that the Incarnation is recapitulated through and in modern-day believers.

Jesus' Ministry - A Call to Subversiveness

The second signpost that Jesus left us along the path towards humanization-divinization is that of his earthly ministry, which consisted of (1) a subversive proclamation (his words) and (2) a subversive praxis (his deeds). It is Jesus' proclamation and praxis that enables liberation theologians to understand Jesus and specify the task of Christians and the Church in Latin America. Let us look at each of these aspects of his ministry and see what they reveal about this process of humanization-divinization.

A Subversive Proclamation: The Kingdom of God

It is clear from the Gospels that "The centre and framework of Jesus' preaching and mission was the approaching Kingdom of God" (Sobrino 1987, 82, citing Walter Kasper, *Jesus the Christ*, 72). Thus to get any understanding of Jesus' "person" as Human-Divine and of the significance of his life for humanity (his work), one must delve into the meaning of his central message: the Kingdom of God. And what Jesus' words make clear is that for him the Kingdom was (1) Total, (2) Partial, (3) Historical, and (4) Radical.

1. The totality of the Kingdom refers to its extent: it involves *all* human existence and the liberation that it brings with it is an integral liberation; all forms of oppression are negated. Leonardo Boff, for instance, writes:

> The kingdom of God cannot be narrowed down to any particular
> aspect. It embraces all: the world, the human person, and society;

the totality of reality is to be transformed by God. (Boff 1978b, 55)

The kingdom of God . . . does not signify something that is purely spiritual or outside this world. It is the totality of this material world, spiritual and human, that is now introduced into God's order. (Boff 1978b, 56)

The salvation proclaimed by Christianity is an all-embracing one. It is not restricted to economic, political, social, and ideological emancipation, but neither can it be realized without them. . . . Our definitive, eschatological salvation is mediated, anticipated and rendered concrete in the partial liberations that take place at every level of historical reality. The latter are oriented toward the fulness and totality of liberation that will be attainable only in the realized kingdom of God. (Boff 1978b, 275)

What Boff is saying is that the realization of the totality of the Kingdom is, of course, eschatological in nature; it is the "Utopia of Absolute Liberation." There are, however, partial realizations of the Kingdom that are attainable in history. The vast majority of liberation theologians agree on this point. Gustavo Gutiérrez, for instance, writes in *A Theology of Liberation*: "We can say that the historical, political liberating event *is* the growth of the Kingdom and *is* a salvific event; but it is not *the* coming of the Kingdom, not *all* of salvation" (Gutiérrez 1973, 177).

Sobrino agrees that Jesus' notion of the Kingdom is one that "entails a total renovation of reality" (Sobrino 1978, 45). Sobrino, however, is somewhat critical of Boff's conception of the Kingdom in that for Boff the Kingdom "as a totality is a utopia realized in the risen Jesus but not in world history" (Sobrino 1978, 65). The Kingdom can be made partially present through functional ideologies, but *in its totality*, it remains ever eschatological. The problem with this view, says Sobrino, is that the Kingdom can remain simply an *idea*; it does not specify what form of existence the Christian is to take *now* as s/he ponders this utopia, this future Kingdom. Boff suggests a "trial-and-error" sort of existence that may or may not correspond with the "coming Kingdom": "The Christian must not be afraid to make a concrete decision and risk failure. This decision may well be a historical mediation for the coming of the Kingdom" (Sobrino 1978, 65). Sobrino, on the other hand, while not disagreeing in principle with Boff that the Christian must learn "by trial and error, which concrete mediations today bring God's kingdom near" (Sobrino 1987, 96), is more specific than Boff as to what form Christian existence is to take and is less inclined to think of the coming Kingdom as a mere idea not fully realizable in history:

Jesus' eschatology has a historico-temporal character. Jesus

> believes in a temporal fulfillment of the world which strictly
> speaking, is not the work of people insofar as it is a fulfillment. It
> is the work of the God who comes. (Sobrino 1978, 65-66)

> Jesus' eschatology . . . unveils another kind of existence that does
> correspond to the kingdom. For us that form of existence is the
> following of Jesus. (Sobrino 1978, 66)

But the "conflict" is more a matter of emphasis: In *Jesus Christ Liberator*, Boff emphasizes the expectation of the Kingdom which serves as an ideal to check our partial realizations, whereas Sobrino emphasizes the actualization of the Kingdom through a concrete following of Jesus. Or to put it differently, Boff focuses on Jesus to show *why* the Kingdom "is no longer an unattainable human utopia" (Boff 1978b, 61), while Sobrino focuses on Jesus to show *how* the Kingdom can become an attainable human utopia.

2.   Jesus' proclamation also makes clear that the Kingdom is historical; that is, it is realized in history, partially or approximately now, and fully in either an eschatological or temporal future. Although some disagree as to the ultimate realization of the Kingdom (Boff following Moltmann in seeing the ultimate realization as eschatological, i.e., beyond history; Sobrino seeing it as ultimately realized temporally, within history), all agree that the Kingdom is rendered presently in history.

Boff sees the Kingdom of God as a utopia of absolute liberation that has historical anticipations:

> The kingdom of God is not *only* future. It is not *only* utopia. It is
> present as well, and occurs in historical concretions. Hence it is to
> be thought of as a process beginning in the world and culminating
> in its eschatological end. In Jesus we find this dialectical tension
> appropriately maintained: there is the goal, total liberation (the
> kingdom of God); and yet we find mediations (deeds, activity,
> attitudes) which translate this kingdom processually into history.
> (Boff 1978a, 25)

Sobrino and Segundo as well see the Kingdom of God as being realized historically. For Sobrino, God's reign " . . . is not merely an extension of human potentialities. . . . Neither is it merely a transformation of the inner person. It is also a restructuring of the visible, tangible relationships existing between human beings" (Sobrino 1978, 44). This view of the Kingdom follows from what Sobrino sees as Jesus' conception of God, a God who reveals himself by *acting in history*: "Jesus adopts as his own the Old Testament conception of God . . . [which] is that God acts in history in a specific way, and that his action cannot be separated or isolated from his basic reality" (Sobrino 1978, 44). God makes himself known, not as he is (epiphanically), but through some situation (historically). Thus to say that God reigns is to say that God is active in history.

Segundo is even more adamant than Boff or Sobrino about the historicality of the Kingdom which Jesus proclaimed; he might go so far as to see existential interpretations of the Kingdom (such as Bultmann's) as just so much ideological subterfuge since "Jesus is doing *something more* than proclaiming a future event. He is *generating an historical conflict*" (Segundo 1985, 148). He adds:

> ... the totality of Jesus' public life ... makes clear one thing: Jesus is seeking *to place historical causality in the service of the kingdom*. And not only does he invest his all *perfectus homo* in that service; he invests his disciples' all as well.... Everything we have seen so far shows Jesus, not only announcing its coming and preparing it in history, but also associating the group of his disciples with this historical causality. (Segundo 1985, 149)

Segundo, then, sees the Kingdom as a historical project begun by Jesus and continued by his disciples, a project which consists of "consciousness-raising and of dismantling the ideological mechanisms of religio-political oppression" (Segundo 1985, 148-49).

3.   The Kingdom of God that Jesus proclaimed is not only total in its transformation, historical in its manifestation, it is also partial in its admission. The Kingdom is not for everyone; Jesus offered it to the poor and oppressed; it is they who have entrance into the Kingdom. Sobrino agrees with Joachim Jeremias that the most decisive feature about the Kingdom is that "The reign of God belongs *to the poor alone*" (Joachim Jeremias, *New Testament Theology: The Proclamation of Jesus*, New York: Scribners, 1971, 116, cited by Sobrino, 1987, 89). Sobrino continues: "When Jesus proclaims that the kingdom of God is at hand for the poor ... He is saying that this approach of the kingdom is not generic and universal. It is 'partial'" (Sobrino 1987, 90). Segundo, as well, highlights the partiality of the kingdom:

> *The kingdom of God is not announced to everyone.* It is not "proclaimed" to all. . . . *The kingdom itself cannot* be preached indiscriminately as *good news*, as *gospel*. The kingdom is destined for certain groups. It is theirs. It belongs to them. Only for them will it be a cause for joy. And, according to Jesus, the dividing line between joy and woe produced by the kingdom runs between *the poor* and *the rich*. (Segundo 1985, 90)

Although Boff is not as explicit as Sobrino or Segundo in affirming the partiality of the Kingdom, it is implied throughout his works. He agrees with the guidelines proposed by the CELAM in Medellín (1968) and Puebla (1979) that the Church should exercise a preferential option for the poor (Boff 1988b, 23-27) and that the proclamation of the gospel is not good news for everyone. In fact, "Jesus and his proclamation effect a division among human beings, a division that is the essence of the Reign. We can enter into it only by breaking with this world and changing it, not by extending its structure" (Boff 1989, 139). Entrance into the Kingdom, then, occurs by a conversion to the oppressed, by taking up their cause, through solidarity with them in their struggle for liberation.

4.   The Kingdom of God proclaimed by Jesus is also radical in its requirements: its values, its demands; indeed these values and demands serve as standards by which to judge all human attainments. According to Sobrino: ". . . the values of the kingdom will be criteria of judgment upon any type of human configuration, religious or sociopolitical, that explicitly or implicitly seeks to put itself forth as the actual kingdom of God" (Sobrino 1987, 84).

For Segundo the demands of the Kingdom which Jesus proclaims are thoroughly radical in that they subvert all of the conceptions that existed in Jesus' time, and which continue to exist today, as to how and for whom the Kingdom of God is to be established. Segundo sees Jesus as making different demands on three different groups: (1) the poor and oppressed, (2) the oppressors or the politico-religious establishment , and (3) the disciples. The demands on the poor are the most unexpected: none (Segundo 1985, 139). The demand on the oppressors is conversion, which is a willing surrender of their position of privilege and solidarity with the poor. The demand on the disciples is to "open their eyes," to become consciencitized and consciencitizers, to unmask the mechanisms of ideological oppression (Segundo 1985, 139).

Boff again is not as explicit as Segundo in expressing the radicality of the Kingdom; his tone is more conciliatory than Segundo's, and he is more ambiguous as to whom Jesus offers the Kingdom and what demands Jesus makes. He merely notes that the Kingdom requires conversion, which he defines as the "radical modification of relationships in all aspects of personal and social reality, resulting in concrete liberations and thereby anticipating the Reign of God" (Boff 1989, 138). Simply put, what the Kingdom of God demands is a change of attitude about participating in any form of oppression, which objectively would mean solidarity with the poor in the historical project of liberation. Boff, unlike Segundo, would seem to see a need for conversion on *everyone's* part, not just the non-poor.

These theologians see Jesus, in his proclamation of the Kingdom, as issuing a call to enter into a process of deploying a subversive reality, a reality that is beyond anything anyone could imagine since it is a utopia in which God rules, not human beings, but yet which can be anticipated and approximated in history. It is a message which gives reason for hope and which gives reason to act.

A Subversive Praxis: The Kingdom of God Actualized

Jesus did not simply issue a call to subversiveness, he exemplified that subversiveness through his actions: he healed the sick, exorcised demons, fed the poor, ate with publicans and prostitutes. In short, he opted for the oppressed in concrete ways, for this was the sign that the Kingdom was near. For Jesus, the Kingdom was not just a message to be proclaimed; it was also a reality to be actualized through a concrete praxis. For Sobrino:

> . . . Jesus' proclamation is not limited to God's scandalous, partisan love for the poor. It includes his quest to deliver the poor from their real misery . . . Jesus' miracles and exorcism constituted a liberative activity. . . . Jesus promoted solidarity among human beings, not in any generic and merely declaratory fashion, but by bringing his activity to bear on human beings' concrete historical situation. . . . Jesus' anathemas . . . . The denunciation of the sin of oppression is an action by Jesus in favor of the content of the kingdom now "at hand" . . . (Sobrino 1987, 91-92)

His proclamation of the Kingdom and commitment to the poor were concretized in deeds of liberation. According to Boff:

> The *acta et facta Jesu*—Jesus' praxes—are to be understood as historical embodiments of the concrete meaning of the Reign of God: a liberating change of situation. In this sense Jesus has a project like that of oppressed groups struggling for liberation. (Boff 1989, 134)

This praxis of Jesus is "eminently social and public in character [and] . . . touches upon the *structure* of society and religion in his day" (Boff 1978b, 283). His activity on behalf of the poor and marginalized had enormous religious and political repercussions, since his violations of religious law to meet human need, his emphasis on service to neighbor (orthopraxy) rather than cultic worship (orthodoxy) as a pathway to God, undermined the authority of the Pharisees and Sadducees. In *Pasión de Cristo, Pasión del Mundo*, Boff spells out some of the concrete steps (abstracted from his praxis) by which Jesus modified life and anticipated the Kingdom. Jesus, says Boff:

1. Relativized human self-sufficiency which manifested itself in religious and poli-

tical power,
2. Created a new solidarity by opting for the marginalized,
3. Respected the freedom of the other, never imposing himself by asking to be heard or served,
4. Withstood conflict unfailingly, renouncing violence but not conflict, and
5. Accepted the mortality of life by willingly dying for truth and justice (Boff 1980a, 47-62).

Sobrino sees Jesus' praxis basically as "pro-existence," as a living-for-others. It is in this way that one becomes truly human, that salvation takes place, that the process of humanization-divinization unfolds, that the Kingdom of God is anticipated:

> This pro-existence is salvation inasmuch as it includes gift to others through gift of self, saving others by delivering oneself to (apparent) destruction, loving others efficaciously out of the gratuitous love given to self. The pro-existent human being is simply the human being who loves the brothers and sisters in truth and is therefore the true actualization of what it is to be a human being. Jesus' historical pro-existence is actualized primarily in favor of the poor. (Sobrino 1987, 33)

Jesus' praxis is important, say liberation theologians, because it constitutes a strategy, consciously pursued by Jesus, to be replicated by his followers through which they can make the approaching Kingdom of God concrete. The replication by Jesus' followers, then and now, is not to be a mere imitation of Jesus' deeds, since the historicity of his life vitiates any possibility of direct imitation (the cultural and historical contexts change). Rather, the disciple is to replicate the *structure* of Jesus' life. This is expressed by Boff, Sobrino, and Segundo in different ways but they essentially mean the same thing.

Segundo argues throughout his writings that what is to be replicated is Jesus' "anthropological faith," that is, the transcendent values which Jesus espoused and tried to realize through a system of means, an "ideology," that was conditioned by his times and hence not transferable:

> We have faith in a historical figure . . . who had to try to flesh out certain human values with a system of means rooted in, and limited by, a context that was likewise limited. Hence those means are not transferable; they cannot be slavishly copied, or used directly as such to measure our reality today. (Segundo 1988, 8)

Approaches that do not recognize the historical distance between Jesus (his praxis as described in the text of Scripture) and our present context, Segundo labels pejoratively as fundamentalism.

Sobrino argues for "following Jesus as discernment," what he also calls "discipleship." Like Segundo, Sobrino disavows any sort of direct imitation since that would be anachronistic. It is, rather, the structure of Jesus' discernment "what we should in fact pursue, while the particular solutions to our discernments cannot be identical to those of Jesus" (Sobrino 1987, 134). Sobrino encapsulates the structure of Jesus' discernment in four criteria: (1) partial incarnation in history (i.e., one that opts for the poor), (2) an effective praxis of love, (3) a praxis of socio-political love (i.e., a love that becomes justice), and (4) openness to a conflictive love (Sobrino 1987, 135-36). These criteria can enable the disciple to discern the sort of concrete solutions needed to overcome oppression in his/her context.

Boff as well argues for replication of the structure of Jesus' life, his dispositions and options, his *mode of being*, but not so much his actual deeds:

> . . . the manner in which history must be taken in hand changes constantly. Jesus has prescribed, not a concrete model of an *ideal* concrete history, but a *particular* mode of becoming present in a given historical circumstance. The common, ideal element in Jesus' formula consists in his option for the wronged, his renunciation of the will to power and domination, and his solidarity with any genuine token of a more participatory society . . . It is the task of his disciples to filter this common element through the sieve of the relativity of their respective historical circumstances and thus adapt it to those circumstances in a way that will be genuine and effective. (Boff 1989, 142-43)

We see, then, that Jesus, through his praxis as much as through his proclamation, beckons his followers to pursue a strategy of subversion, to resist and overturn all structures that oppress and dehumanize.

Jesus' Death - The Consequence of Subversiveness

Liberation theologians see Jesus' death as the inevitable consequence of a praxis of liberation, the result of challenging the oppressive structures that existed in Palestine at that time. His death occurred specifically because he subverted the standard conceptions of messiahship, of God's Kingdom, and how one is to actualize it and enter into it. While Jesus could have molded and adapted his words and deeds to his society's notions of what the messiah, God, and the Kingdom were supposed to be like, he did not, resulting in his death. His death, therefore, comes to represent a life of being true to oneself and of courage and perseverance in the face of opposition. According to Raúl Vidales, a Mexican liberation theologian:

> Jesus is sentenced to death simply because he, like so many other just human beings before and after him, was not afraid to take a position outside the status quo, in words and deeds alike. (Bussmann 1985, 109)

Boff sees both a historical meaning and a transcendent meaning to Jesus' death. In *Jesus Christ Liberator* Boff notes that it was such historically concrete factors as his popularity, his interpretation of the Law, his claim to act in God's name, and the accusations of blasphemy and sedition by the authorities, that led to his execution. The historical meaning, then, is that Jesus dies as a consequence of his subversiveness. But Boff also sees Jesus' death as having a historically transcendent meaning; he sees it, to use F. Engels phrase, as a negation of negation:

> By his preaching of the kingdom of God he lived his being for others to the end, experiencing the depths of despair of the death (absence) of God on the cross. In spite of the total disaster and debacle he did not despair. He was confident and believed up to the end that God would accept him as he was. The meaningless still had for him a secret and ultimate meaning.
>
> The universal meaning of the life and death of Christ, therefore, is that he sustained the fundamental conflict of human existence to the end: he wanted to realize the absolute meaning of this world before God, in spite of hate, incomprehension, betrayal, and condemnation to death. (Boff 1978b, 118-19)

Jesus' death, therefore, has for Boff, a metaphysical meaning: the negation of the meaninglessness of existence, which is seen as essentially conflictual. Conflict, then, has meaning because in Jesus' cross God subsumes it, negates it, and infuses it with meaning. It is through Jesus' death that God reveals that meaning can be extracted from the meaningless, that it is through conflict and eventual death that history realizes its meaning.

Boff expounds several theses to show how closely interconnected are Jesus' praxis and his consequent death:

> 1. Jesus' death stands in intimate relationship with his life, his proclamation, his praxis. His call to conversion . . . and his prophetic criticism of the incumbents of political, economic, and religious power provoked a conflict that led to his death.

2. Jesus did not seek death. It was imposed on him from without.

3. The cross is the symbol of the kingdom of might and of that kingdom's power over its own duty of service.

4. This freely accepted death manifests Jesus' absolute freedom both with respect to his own person and with respect to his goals.

5. There are two motives for Jesus' murder, and both extend to the structural level. First he is condemned as blasphemer for having conceived of God in a different fashion from the status quo. . . . In the eyes of the political authority he dies as a guerilla. His preaching and his activity bring him close to the purposes of the Zealots. . . . Yet at the same time Jesus is far removed from the spirit of the Zealots. He rejects political-religious messianism based on power, for such a messianism would be incapable of actualizing a kingdom that presupposes a radical, total liberation, overcomes all breach in the human relationship of brothers and sisters, and calls for a new human being.

6. The cross manifests the conflictual nature of any liberation process that has to be carried on in conditions where injustice has the upper hand. Under such conditions, liberation is possible only in the form of martyrdom and sacrifice for others in the service of God's cause in the world. This is the path Jesus consciously chose and assumed. (Bussmann 1985, 113-14 citing *Jesucristo y Nuestro Futuro*, 31-32.)

Jesus' death then is not an accident of history, nor the result of a misunderstanding on the part of Jesus' contemporaries; neither can it be merely spiritualized away as a dying for the sins of humanity. No. Jesus' death is the direct result of a determinate praxis, the conscious challenge of politico-religious structures that oppressed and marginalized people.

In *Pasión de Cristo, Pasión del Mundo*, Boff makes explicit that Jesus' suffering and death are paradigmatic of the suffering and death which the Latin American people must endure for the sake of liberation, of trying to establish partial mediations of the Kingdom of God. Boff, however, does not want Jesus' death to be seen as a mystification of suffering, as if suffering in and of itself is what pleases God and ought, therefore, to be accepted. This is what is wrong, says Boff, with the christology of the cross of Jürgen Moltmann, in that he portrays God as subsuming the suffering of the world; it is God who suffers (on the cross, God is the crucified) and it is God who causes the suffering (of Jesus by abandoning him on the cross; God is the crucifier) (p. 226). But this view of Jesus' cross can result in (1) resignation in the face of suffering, and (2) legitimation of evil. Since this christology deifies suffering, i.e., conceives of suffering as God, "there is then no longer any possibility of overcoming suffering. It is eternal. We are irredeemably lost" (Boff 1980a, 242, my translation) and so the only alternative is resignation. But also this christology implies an acceptance of God as Jesus' assassin, that the wrath of God extends not just to his children, brethren of Jesus, but to the only-begotten Son himself. "Thus filicide assumes a sacral and theological dimension. We must deny any sort of Christian legitimation to this vision since it destroys the novelty of the Gospel and turns it into the instrument of the sacramentalization of evil in the world" (Boff 1980a, 242-43, my translation).

In the face of suffering or evil what is required is not resignation, and much less, legitimation, but struggle. Jesus death, the cross, speaks of the suffering born of a struggle against suffering. Boff notes that "Evil does not exist to be understood but to be fought" (p. 249). He continues by saying:

> The suffering worthy of man, the sort that exalts him and turns him into the image of he Suffering Servant and the Man of sorrows (Isa. 53:3), is that which results from a commitment to fight and overcome the suffering caused by men whose bad will closes itself off to the prophet, persecutes him, defames him, captures him, tortures him, and eliminates him. This suffering is not fatality, but rather is assumed within the liberating project. (Boff 1980a, 257-58, my translation)

Jesus' death, then, is to move Christians to a deeper commitment to the project of liberation, to a recognition that the proclamation and praxis of the Kingdom is costly since it will spark conflict, and arouse the death-dealing mechanisms of repression.

Sobrino argues that the "scandal of the cross" was lost by the early Christian community when it isolated Jesus' death from what went before (namely, the praxis that occasioned it) and from God himself, (specifically, His abandonment of Jesus). This "prettyfication" of the cross occurred through an emphasis on those titles that "stress (Jesus') existence as one already exalted in heaven" (Sobrino 1978, 186) as well as by the attempt to make sense of the cross in terms of an eternal plan of God for the salvation of humanity. Such explanations, says Sobrino, turned "the real-life scandal of Jesus' cross into nothing more than a noetic scandal" (Sobrino 1978, 188). Salvation became a matter of overcoming the intellectual obstacles to an understanding and acceptance of this eternal plan of God. These models for understanding Jesus' cross tended to interiorize salvation and make it ahistorical.

Sobrino not only sees Jesus' death as the consequence of a historically concrete praxis; theologically, he sees it as a mediation of God. In the cross of Jesus it is God who suffers and dies. This death of God is mediated concretely through the "death of the other human being" (Sobrino 1978, 196). In other words, not only does God die on Jesus' cross, God continues to die on every cross of history. Like Boff, Sobrino sees Jesus' death as a negation of negation, but as a negation that occurs concretely from within history, through the death of the other human being (the oppressed):

> Why does the "oppressed" person serve as the mediation of God? Is it not because in that person we find expressed what Hegel called "the monstrous power of the negative?" It is quite correct to view God as the power over the negative, as its contradiction [i.e., its negation]. But such a view remains too abstract if we do not go on to ask how and in what sense God is the power over injustice, oppression, and death. Is it from outside history or from within history? (Sobrino 1978, 196)

The answer is, of course, from within history. The cross is a historical manifestation of a metaphysical and perduring reality: that God negates the mechanisms of negation (of oppression) through the struggle and consequent deaths of the oppressed. Struggle and martyrdom, hence, have meaning in that by entering into the struggle and meeting with death one is entering into a project of liberation that is cosmic in extent, one is participating in the unfolding of Absolute Spirit within history. This is best expressed by Sobrino in one of his theses about the meaning of Jesus' death:

> On the cross of Jesus God himself is crucified. The Father suffers the death of the Son and takes upon himself all the pain and suffering of history. In this ultimate solidarity with humanity he reveals himself as the God of love, who opens up hope and a future through the most negative side of history. Thus Christian existence is nothing else but a process of participating in this same process whereby God loves the world and hence in the very life of God. (Sobrino 1978, 224)

According to Segundo, Jesus was killed because he:

> ... destroyed the foundation of that oppressive power structure [The Jewish theocracy grounded on and controlled by the religious authorities] by teaching the people to reject its theological foundations. His teaching was such a political threat that the authorities of Israel made use of Rome's authorities to eliminate this dangerous political adversary. (Segundo 1976, 111-12)

So for Segundo, as for Boff and Sobrino, Jesus dies for being a subversive, for challenging through his words and deeds the power structures that oppress and marginalize human beings.

Jesus' death, we see then, is not a tragedy, as if it had befallen him unexpectedly. It is a heroic death because it is the result of an unswerving commitment to the truth of God and the God of truth, and a determinate praxis on behalf of the oppressed. He goes to it as the price that must be paid for the actualization of God's Kingdom. He goes to it with the courage of one utterly convinced of the rightness of his efforts: unrepentant, undaunted, uncompromising. He goes to his death as the pioneer of a project of liberation, cosmic in proportions, a project for human beings and by human beings willing to pay the price for its establishment: willing impoverishment, active love, and death.

Jesus' Resurrection - The Worthwhileness of Subversiveness

Because liberation theologians do their christology "from below," from the Historical Jesus, they claim that the meaning of Jesus' resurrection cannot be grasped apart from his death and the historical causes that occasioned it. In fact, they argue that it has been the separation of Jesus' life from his death and resurrection that has resulted in christologies and soteriologies that are socially irrelevant or legitimate oppression.

Moreover, since liberationists do start "from below," their reflection on Jesus' resurrection reveals significant insights relevant to a liberative praxis. First of all, viewed christologically, Jesus' resurrection is the evidence that God approved of Jesus' praxis, for it is *Jesus* who is raised. The resurrection, therefore, should not be simplistically eschatologized as a hope of an afterlife, or a literal rising from the grave for those who believe. The resurrection is God's statement that he approved of what Jesus did, and is, therefore, a basis of hope for those who are crucified, for those who are willing to act and die for liberation.

Theologically considered, the resurrection reveals what God is like, for it is *God* who raises Jesus. So the resurrection is not only God's seal of approval on Jesus' message and praxis, it also reveals that God is just, since He would not let injustice triumph over justice:

> Jesus' resurrection is not only a symbol of God's omnipotence, then—as if God had decided arbitrarily and without any connec-tion with Jesus' life and lot to show how powerful he was. Rather, Jesus' resurrection is presented as God's response to the unjust, criminal action of human beings. Hence God's action in response is understood in conjunction with the human activity that provokes

> this response: the murder of the Just One. Pictured in this way, the
> resurrection of Jesus shows *in directo* ... that justice has triumphed
> over injustice, the victim over the executioner. (Sobrino 1987,
> 149)

Jesus' resurrection shows that it is God who has the last word since: "Surely those who have reached the top of the heap, who have a monopoly on power, possessions, or knowledge, may not define the final framework of a person's life, or the final, ultimate facts" (Boff 1988b, 134).

Not only does God reveal himself as just through the resurrection, he also reveals himself as faithful, loving, and powerful—and these qualities are inseparable from one another as the cross is inseparable from the resurrection:

> God is revealed not just by the *abandonment* of Jesus on the cross
> or by his *active work* in the resurrection, but also by his *fidelity* to
> Jesus in those two events. What reveals God is the resurrection of
> the crucified, or, the cross of the resurrected one. . . . Without the
> resurrection love would not be authentic power, without the cross
> this power would not be love. (Sobrino 1978, 261)

Not only is the resurrection a *revelation* of what God is like, it is also an *exposure* of the false "God" worshipped by the religious establishment of Jesus' time; the resurrection is the way in which God discredits the politico-religious authorities' conceptions both of God himself and his Kingdom, and how human beings can have access to either. In short, the resurrection brings into question the God who is being worshipped by the Pharisees and Sadducees, for it reveals that the God of those who put Jesus to death is an anti-God; it is an idol. The same can be said of the God worshipped today by those who oppress the poor.

For Boff the resurrection of Jesus holds a similar significance. Jesus' "resurrection would be, on the Father's part, the condemnation of the violence that assassinated Jesus, and the hope that God gives to all prophets and just ones, as these know that their death is not in vain" (González 1987, 522, my translation). Boff sees it as a protest against the so-called "justice" and "law" by which Jesus was condemned (Boff 1980a, 148).

The resurrection also has an eschatological meaning for liberation theologians. For Sobrino, for instance, the resurrection is the appearance of the final reality of history in the historical process. (Sobrino 1987, 154-56). Boff sees it as an anticipation of the Eschatological New Human Being:

> Through the resurrection Jesus steps forward as the new and final
> Adam (1 Cor. 15:45), as the human being already come to his final

term, the human being who shatters the frontiers of history and plunges into the sea of absolute fulfillment in God. [In the resurrected Jesus] The human being willed by God from everlasting is here. (Boff 1989, 151-52)

As an anticipation of the Eschatological Human Being, the resurrection is also an anticipation of Absolute Liberation:

The totality of liberation was given with the resurrection. Through it the utopic truth of the kingdom becomes topic and advent of the certainty that the process of liberation does not remain in an indefinite circularity of oppression-liberation, but that it culminates in a total and exhaustive liberation. (Boff 1980a, 147-48)

The resurrection reveals that God does not accept the death of the crucified; it is scandalous to God. It follows that it should be scandalous to anyone who calls himself Christian, a child of this God. The significance of the resurrection, therefore, cannot be conceived in terms of an individualistic hope. Says Sobrino:

Someone for whom his or her own death would be the basic scandal, and the hope of his or her own survival the basic problem, would not have a Christian hope, would not have a hope sprung from Jesus' resurrection; such a one would have a hope centered in and for himself or herself. . . . What de-centers our hope to make it genuinely Christian hope is taking as absolutely scandalous the death of the crucified today. (Sobrino 1987, 150-51)

The resurrection, therefore, has ethical significance; it opens a horizon of reflection that must include the "other"; the risen Jesus is, after all, the "*firstborn among many brethren*" (Rom. 8:29; 1 Cor. 15:20). The affirmation of Jesus' resurrection is not a doctrine merely to be intellectually assented to (simply confessing as "true" what is scandalous to reason because it contravenes the laws of nature). To affirm that the crucified Jesus rose from the dead is to profess, by words and deeds, that crucifixion (=oppression) is a scandal which will not be tolerated. The resurrection, therefore, does not only present human beings with an intellectual challenge; it is, more profoundly, a moral challenge: how can we allow the death-dealing mechanisms of oppression to continue operating, if God himself subverted them? In professing the resurrection, then, the Christian should be corresponding with God in the subversion of crucifixion and death.

This existential apprehension of the significance of the resurrection can only occur praxiologically. In simpler words, one will never truly understand what Jesus' resurrection means unless one is directly involved in the struggle for liberation. The truth of the resurrection can only be verified in liberative action, action that corresponds to that of the Historical Jesus. According to Segundo, "... the gospel narratives tell us: the pursuit of the same values that Jesus held dear is an indispensable prerequisite for being able to 'see' and recognize the risen one" (Segundo 1985, 171). And Sobrino, like Segundo, observes that:

> [T]he resurrection is comprehensible only insofar as one is conscious of building up history and trusts in the promise. . . . [T]he meaning of Jesus' resurrection cannot be grasped unless one engages in active service for the transformation of an unredeemed world. (Sobrino 1978, 380)

It is through a hermeneutic of praxis that one is able to bridge the gap between the horizon of the text, the narrated resurrection of Jesus, and the horizon of the context, the present-day struggle for liberation in Latin America. Only through praxis can the horizons be fused; only through a liberative praxis can one come to understand Jesus' resurrection today. Praxis is much more than a way of "comprehending" the resurrection, it is also the way to historicize the resurrection. The resurrection can be actualized or anticipated historically by every humanizing deed one does:

> All genuinely human growth, anything that can be really be called justice in social relationships, and whatever is conducive to the multiplication of life, represent a form of the actualization of the resurrection—the anticipation and preparation of its future plenitude. (Boff, cited by Bussmann, 1985, 126)

Jesus' resurrection, as part of the Jesus story told by liberation theologians, gives existential meaning to the liberation struggle. "The resurrection of the crucified Jesus proves that the sacrifice of one's life out of love for the downtrodden and abused is not meaningless" (Boff 1980b, ix). This part of the story is essential for liberation because it can resonate in the consciousness of the oppressed, generating or reaffirming attitudes and responses that promote liberation: indignation (because crucifixion is scandalous to God), action (because God subverts death), vision and hope (because God reveals a "promise" in the risen Jesus: that an utopic existence can be "topic").

Liberation theologians' conception of the resurrection makes faith in Jesus' resurrection a historically relevant faith; it makes "having faith," not simply and passively, intellectual assent, but also something that must be expressed through concrete feelings and action. Sobrino puts it this way:

> Because the resurrection also confirms the life of Jesus himself, we

> are now offered the possibility of living a particular way of life in
> the footsteps of Jesus. We can and should live as new, risen human
> beings here and now in history. (Sobrino 1978, 377)

It is Jesus' resurrection, therefore, that makes a life of struggling and suffering for liberation worthwhile; Jesus' resurrection demonstrates that fighting and dying for justice are not in vain, for it is God himself who vindicated Jesus and will vindicate those who replicate Jesus' praxis.

Summary and Conclusion

We have seen that liberation theologians construct a narrative about Jesus which delineates certain characteristics, attitudes, and values that he had and which Christians are to have as well. Jesus is depicted as a non-conformist, an uncompromising, aggressive activist, a social critic, a visionary, unafraid of controversy, unafraid of death, courageous, sociable, sensitive to others' needs, self-abnegating, self-confident, optimistic, hopeful, indignant over injustice, and selective in his company (the poor). He was this way because he loved.

Their christologies do not delve into such speculative matters as how the human and divine natures were united in Jesus; rather they seek to set in relief the sort of character that Jesus had; they seek to show a way of being in the world. Christology, therefore, is not faith seeking to understand the mystery of Christ (interpretation) but faith seeking to replicate the mystery of Christ today (transformation). Christology is the construction of a narrative that seeks to transform the Christian into an active agent of social transformation, an active agent of God's Kingdom.

Robert A. Krieg, in *Story-Shaped Christology: The Role of Narratives in Identifying Jesus Christ,* states that narratives are essentially recitals of events, but that we need to distinguish among three different kinds of narratives: myths (which recount 'events' outside of time), stories (fictional and non-fictional), and history (which possesses historical or empirical accuracy). Moreover, he distinguishes between myths and non-fictional stories. Myths are narratives which "can provide people of every age with a sense of the meaning of their basic involvements" (Krieg 1988, 26-27), while non-fictional stories are narratives which display historical accuracy but in which historical gaps are filled with imagined elements (Krieg 1988, 28). The Gospels, he says, fall into this latter category and further adds that in pursuing the task of Christology "we are not interested in myths" (Krieg 1988, 28) but in establishing Jesus Christ's identity (who he is). That may very well be the interest of scholars like Walter Kasper and Edward Schillebeeckx, but liberation theologians, we have seen, are not simply interested in establishing Jesus Christ's identity in the abstract, but in relation to their concrete struggles. In other words, they are indeed interested in the function of christology *as myth*: they *do* want to tell a story about Jesus that can "provide people of every age [but particularly oppressed Latin Americans] with a sense of the meaning of their basic involvements."

The story of Jesus Christ as told by Boff, Sobrino, and Segundo reveals that those who are involved (or about to get involved) in revolutionary praxis ought to see the transcendent meaning of their efforts and therefore, ought to take heart: they have embarked on a process of humanization-divinization which was pioneered by Jesus and have made themselves co-workers with him in the realization of the Kingdom of God. Their story identifies Jesus, not so much as Messiah or Logos (concepts meaningful to the first century Jew and Greek, respectively, but not to the 20th century Latin American) but as Liberator par excellence. He is identified as a subversive, as one who sought liberation in history, through his words and deeds, and was willing to pay for it with his life. Those who are followers of Jesus today follow him in this subversive course. These are the objective results of the liberation theologians' story.

Subjectively the story seeks to evoke (or to affirm if already present) certain feelings or affective responses: indignation for what has been, courage in the face of what is, and hope for what will be; indignation over past oppression, courage to confront and withstand present repression, and hope for future liberation. Jesus' life inspires us to be indignant, Jesus' death inspires us to be courageous, and Jesus' resurrection inspires us to be hopeful.

As Latin Americans involved in liberation struggles hear the story of Jesus told afresh, they find their life-experience resonating with it, and discover in the story, validation, affirmation, meaning in their present struggles.

Notes

1. Some examples of rationalist and mediating theologians are: H. E. G. Paulus (rationalist), D. F. Strauss and H. S. Reimarus (iconoclasts), Johann Neander, Johann Semler, and Friedrich Schleiermacher (mediating theologians). For a thorough discussion of this shift in focus see Hans W. Frei, *The Eclipse of Biblical Narrative: A Study in Eighteenth and Nineteenth Century Hermeneutics* (New Haven: Yale University Press, 1974).

CHAPTER 3

THE HERMENEUTICAL DECONSTRUCTION OF CHRISTOLOGY

Having surveyed what liberation theologians are saying about Jesus Christ, we can now turn our attention to the method by which they arrive at this narrative. We have seen that liberation theologians retell the "story" of Jesus in such a way as to validate the self-understanding of those already involved in a liberative praxis and to generate in the oppressed now entering the struggle the appropriate self-understanding necessary to achieve liberation. Other "stories" of Jesus, they claim, such as the stories told by the New Testament authors, by the councils of the Church, by academic theologians, and even by their compatriots through their popular religiosity are inadequate because these stories (1) carry meanings irrelevant to the pressing situation in which the vast majority of Latin Americans live, (2) do not serve to advance in the people the consciousness that they are the agents of their own liberation, and instead (3) serve as ideologies legitimating the oppressive and exploitative situation which has existed for centuries and still exists. In other words, the traditional christological discourse (Christianity's Master Story [Slater 1978] or the "Theological Code" [Glebe-Möller 1989, 3]) is being used to legitimate an oppressive narrative: that wealth and power for the few and poverty and powerlessness for the many are fates decreed by God and hence unchangeable. Christology is used to maintain an oppressive status quo.

Given the inadequacies of the prevailing christological discourse, liberation theologians have set themselves the task of dismantling or deconstructing this fruitless discourse. Segundo, for instance, sees his christological enterprise as essentially the same as Boff's:

> The task I am trying to explain and set up here [in *The Historical Jesus of the Synoptics*] is described as one of *deconstruction* by Leonardo Boff. We must deconstruct or dismantle a language that is no longer ours: [citing Boff] "My reflections here center around a labor of deconstruction. . . . To deconstruct means to see the building in terms of its construction plan and redo the construction process, pointing up the temporal nature and possible obsolescence of the representational material while, at the same time, revealing the permanent value of its import and intent." (Segundo

1985, 194-95, n. 15)

In this task of deconstruction they are guided by three methodological presumptions, each of which is linked to the perceived inadequacies. Firstly, the felt irrelevance of christology is linked to the historicist presumption with which liberation theologians approach the biblical text, conciliar christologies, and contemporary academic and popular christologies. Secondly, the need for christology to be an empowering discourse, moving Christians to be agents of social change, arises from the praxiological presumption with which they begin. Finally, the need to expose the legitimating force of christological discourse arises from the ideological presumption with which liberation theologians carry out their critique of theology in general, and christology in particular.

Let us examine how each of these presumptions makes itself evident in the deconstruction of christological discourse by the liberation theologians. By appealing to these presumptions liberation theologians hope to lay bare the weak christological edifice that has been built upon the foundation of the historical Jesus.

The Historicist Presumption

Historicity and Hermeneutics

Historicism is the theory that all sociohistorical phenomena are historically determined, hence relative. Liberation theologians, like many contemporary theologians, presuppose the validity of historicism and utilize it on various levels to deconstruct traditional christologies. They make use of it in their consideration of the biblical text, dogma, and Christian social ethics.[1] In other words, historicism significantly impacts their views on hermeneutics, theology, and ethics.

Liberation theologians begin deconstructing traditional christologies by appealing to the recognition of historical distance between past and present, the actual event and its narration. Segundo, for example, argues that it is the recognition of this distance that avoids the trap of fundamentalism (Segundo 1988, 8) and makes possible the relevance of the historical Jesus today:

> Recapturing the distance that lies between the historical figure and his interpreters opens up space and room for my dialogue with Jesus of Nazareth two thousand years later, if for no other reason than that it does away with the inhibition imposed by the false but

all too common question: *Who* then correctly interpreted Jesus?
(Segundo 1985, 19)

The recognition of historical distance relativizes all interpretations of the historical
Jesus since they are revealed as *interpretations* by human beings, constructs created
by persons living within particular socio-historical circumstances to meet specific
socio-historical needs.

Besides recognizing historical distance, liberation theologians employ historicism hermeneutically and theologically in much the same way as liberal and neo-
orthodox exegetes and theologians of the past and present, namely, applying histori-
ographic criteria to the Bible and dogma (Sobrino 1987, 74; Segundo 1985, 45-70). In
ethics, they seem to subscribe to the Hegelian historicist notion that values are
"historical facts, stages in the development of reason, which is the development of the
ideal and the real" (Popper 1966, 395). In short, values are the product of the dialectical
movement of history.

Hermeneutically, historicism has meant the application of the historical-critical
method to the text, distinguishing fact (history or *Historie*) from myth (interpretation
or *Geschichte*). The "questers" of the nineteenth century, such as D. F. Strauss and
Ernest Renan, employed the historicist presumption in constructing their biographies
of Jesus, separating the historical from the mythological, turning "to the Jesus of
history as an ally in the struggle against the tyranny of dogma" (Schweitzer 1910, 4).
In the twentieth century, Rudolph Bultmann applied the historicist presumption as
"demythologization." Unlike the "old questers," he did not seek to do away with the
mythological but to reinterpret it through existential categories, to demythologize the
kerygma, to get at a non-mythological interpretation of the kerygma. Bultmann,
influenced by his Lutheran heritage and existentialist philosophy, downplayed the
importance of the historical for faith. For Bultmann, the historical Jesus—his deeds
and words—is of no consequence for the faith of the individual. What is important is
what the Church *believes* about this Jesus.

In establishing the historicity of Jesus and its importance for faith, liberation
theologians, however, are most in accord with the post-Bultmannians, the "new
questers" (such as Ernst Käsemann and Günther Bornkamm), who recognized that the
Christ which is proclaimed by the Church is none other than the Jesus of history; that
there is continuity between the Jesus of History and the Christ of Faith. Consequently,
one cannot dismiss the historical Jesus as blithely as Bultmann did. Leonardo Boff
agrees with this conclusion of the post-Bultmannians:

> The continuity between the historical Jesus and the Christ of faith
> consists . . . in the fact that the primitive community made explicit
> what had been implicit in the words, demands, attitudes, and
> comportment of Jesus. (Boff 1978b, 13)

With the post-Bultmannians, liberation theologians point out the importance of the historical Jesus for faith. But also, with the post-Bultmannians, liberation theologians are more moderate than the "old questers" about the exegete's capacity to extract the "pure" historical Jesus from underneath the layers of historical accretion. This skeptical moderation is due, first of all, to the recognition that the only source for a reconstruction of the historical Jesus is the New Testament, i.e., the kerygma (or the Christ of faith) and as William M. Thompson points out, "If the kerygma cannot be trusted, why should a reconstructed Jesus derived from it be so trusted?" (Thompson 1985, 104). In other words, the very historicity of the evidence militates against the unearthing of the historical Jesus. Secondly, the epistemological impossibility of the interpreter bracketing his/her own worldview to "see" the past with unclouded eyes gives reason to doubt the conclusions drawn from the evidence.

Historicism, therefore, enters not only the exegetical process, but also the interpretive process. Indeed, to assume that exegesis could be separated from hermeneutics, that the acquisition of the "facts" of history could be separated from the interpretation of those "facts," is sheer self-deception. Segundo clearly points this out:

> A Jesus interpreted by no one does not exist. There is no Jesus-Jesus. Even the things that can be historically attributed to him with reasonable certainty are interpretations: because the documents available to us for that task are interpretations; because we ourselves must interpret in order to distinguish between what comes from Jesus himself and what others attribute to him . . . (Segundo 1985, 19)

Boff concurs:

> Can we reconstruct a history without at the same time already interpreting it? Historians approach their objects with the eyes of their epoch, with the interests dictated by, for example, the concept of scientific scholarship that they and their time possess. No matter how much they attempt to abstract from themselves as subjects, they can never escape the self and arrive at the object. For this reason every life of Jesus will necessarily reflect the life of its author. There will always be interpretation. It is a circle from which no one can escape. (Boff 1978b, 5; Boff 1987, 19)

Including Gospel writers, exegetes, and theologians. In the Gospels we have views of Jesus from the perspective of faith which are, therefore, not necessarily reliable as objective historical accounts. In the creeds of the Church we have interpretations of the views expressed in the Gospels, hence no more historically reliable than the

Gospels themselves. In modern-day exegesis and christology, we also have interpretations, reconstructions colored by the *Weltanschuung* of the exegete or theologian. Sobrino concurs with Segundo and Boff about the problematic of getting to the historical Jesus-in-himself:

> Latin American christology accepts the generally received observation on the literary condition of the gospels with respect to their historicity. It knows that the gospel narratives about Jesus are themselves theologized. . . . But it also observes . . . that in order to historicize Jesus, his life must be historicized in a determinate manner. . . . The historical problem, then is presented as the task of discovering the historical Jesus through the historicized Jesus. (Sobrino 1987, 73)

Evidently, the "historical Jesus" for liberation theologians, as for most liberal biblical scholars, is a misty figure lost behind myths and interpretations whom they might better refer to as the "hypothetical Jesus" since it is impossible to "get at" the actual Jesus. Nevertheless, this methodological incapacity of "getting at" the historical Jesus is not something to be lamented but celebrated in the name of liberation. It can be celebrated because the Gospels, while historically unreliable, nonetheless reliably bear witness to the *modus procedendi* of the faithful: the "hermeneutic circle," which entails approaching the historical Jesus from the standpoint of the faithfuls' current questions and problems, thus making possible the creation of ever-new gospels (Segundo 1985, 40-41; Sobrino 1987, 76; Boff 1980a, 29-32).

Among the liberation theologians, Segundo, for one, feels that christology should not begin with Jesus as he is, the "historical Jesus," (unlike Hans Küng, Walter Kasper, and Wolfhart Pannenberg) but with Jesus subordinated to the purposes, interests, and motivations of the time in which he is being interpreted. Only so will Jesus be understood and his significance grasped (Segundo 1985, 25-27). The hypothetical Jesus is sought, therefore, from the perspective of our present-day problems and desires. Segundo writes:

> I think that the only valid approach to Jesus of Nazareth [the hypothetical Jesus] is that of the New Testament. It entails a process of successive readings that start out from the concrete, historical interest he aroused in his own time and place and move on to the problems of later times and our own present day. . . . Only one kind of christology is valid and dovetails with the way Jesus himself posed issues. It is a christology that starts off from the historical data about Jesus and *multiplies* the readings of his message, each time *modifying* the *preunderstanding* that is brought

to the next reading. A complete and finished christology, consisting of one single reading of all the (biblical and/or dogmatic)
material having to do with Jesus of Nazareth, is a dead-end street.
(Segundo 1985, 39)

Boff reiterates a similar viewpoint:

The method of historical criticism tries to sift for the original
meaning of the text, insofar as this is possible, and to get beyond
later interpretations. . . . [It] obliges us to sound out the message of
another age, to critically distance ourselves from the present, and
to question ourselves from the standpoint of what is being ana-
lyzed and brought to the fore in the text itself. This does not have
to be an archaeological venture [read: a recovery of the actual Jesus
of Nazareth] but it is an opportunity to widen our very horizons,
question our evidence that appears unquestionable, and create
interior space for a possible *metanoia* (conversion). (Boff 1978b,
33; Boff 1987, 48)

The liberation theologian, then, can celebrate the "hypothetical Jesus" because his
"discovery" liberates theology from the doctrinal dogmatism that sought to preserve
a first-century mythological worldview, to the creation of "new gospels," which reflect
on this Jesus from a twentieth century, oppressed reality. It might even be through this
process of reflection, Boff speculates, that God incarnates himself [*sic*] anew in every
age (Boff 1978b, 37; Boff 1987, 52).

    To the liberation theologians, then, historicism is a boon. By demonstrating that
the christologies found in the New Testament and in the conciliar formulas are
historicized discourses on the historical Jesus—that these discourses are by-and-large
the product of particular interests, worldviews, and situations—they are able to
relativize their normativity or authority as "gospel truth," i.e., Final Truth. By
relativizing the christologies of the past there can remain the possibility of creating
new, alternative christologies for the present.

    But historicism is also a bane to liberation theology. This, however, goes largely
unacknowledged. It is a bane because if the historical Jesus, the untheologized Jesus,
is going to serve as the basis for, or be the normative model of, what a liberative praxis
consists of, then it is extremely important that this historical Jesus be recoverable. But
the prospect of successfully accomplishing such a task is dubitable. Imagine historians
in 3990 trying to reconstruct a chronology of the events at Guernica on April 26, 1937
if all they had at their disposal was Pablo Picasso's painting. They could theorize,
perhaps even approximate what really happened, but never could they achieve any
certainty or even confidence about the accuracy of the account. The same can be said

of the recovery of the unhistoricized historical Jesus: no clear portrait of Jesus-as-he-was-in-himself can possibly be drawn on the basis of the text of Scripture. This is so, as has been pointed out, because of both the text's and the historian's or exegete's own historicity.

Consequently, the majority of liberation theologians have tried to minimize the importance of a complete recovery of the historical Jesus through the historical-critical method (i.e., reconstructing a *diachronic* account), while emphasizing the importance of historicizing the historical Jesus today (i.e., reconstructing a *synchronic* account) (Glebe-Möller 1989). In other words, they have focused more on the *meaning* for today of the events in Jesus' life than on the *actuality* or historicity of the events. Sobrino states this explicitly when he writes:

> Latin American christology is not especially interested systematically in determining Jesus' "data" with exactitude, his concrete words and actions. . . . It does not make a christology based on the historical Jesus depend on the *ipsissima verba* or *ipsissima facta* of Jesus. Its interest rather consists in discovering and historically insuring the basic structure of his practice, preaching, and end through which the basic structure of his internal historicity and his person are likewise discernible. (Sobrino 1987, 73-74)

In short, the historicity of Jesus' specific words and deeds is not as important as the historicity of his overall "thrust," his intentions, attitudes, and dispositions; in short, what *is* important is the *meaning* which Jesus attached to his own life and praxis, his self-understanding.

This sounds, however, as if Sobrino is delving into the subjective causes for Jesus' words and deeds and thus building his christology upon a psychohistory of Jesus. Sobrino disavows such an effort (Sobrino 1979, 118), yet he appears to be looking for evidence in the historical Jesus for a dialectical process involving consciousness and praxis, i.e., that praxis is the expression of consciousness and this consciousness is then transformed by praxis. He writes:

> As difficult as it may be to analyze the concrete process of Jesus' life, the Gospel narratives agree that such a process, in which Jesus is transforming himself in a certain way, exists. In this transformation it is very important to note . . . the correlation between outward activity and inward attitude. The kind of inward processes, of which the Gospels give some hint, are initiated as well as made possible by his praxis. (Sobrino 1979, 118)

From a distance of about two thousand years, ascertaining this dialectical process and inner transformation in Jesus seems even more improbable than "historically insuring" his very words and deeds. As Thomas C. Oden has pointed out with regard to Jesus' self-understanding (from which proceed his "practice, preaching, and end"):

> To ask whether we can know what view Jesus took of himself is like asking whether we can know through exhaustive study what view Julius Caesar or Freud took of himself. . . . It is considerably difficult to establish such an inward self-understanding for anyone living today, much less one who lived two thousand years ago. (Oden 1990)

There are other difficulties which reliance on the historical-critical approach poses for liberation theologians. Besides appealing to questionable criteria[2] for ascertaining the historicity of an event or saying (e.g., the criterion of dissimilarity and scientistic presuppositions such as Troeltsch's principles of analogy and correlation [McKnight 1988, 46-47]), there is the hermeneutical difficulty of *why* the reconstruction of an historical account should serve to orient us in our situation today. The question is: "Why should an historical account, a life from the past, be normative for us today?" (Segundo 1985, 28)

Here we enter into the hermeneutical problem of the fusion of horizons pointed out by H. G. Gadamer: how the past (the text) and the present (the context) can mutually engage each other. Historicism problematizes this engagement. To put it simply, even if the historian could reconstruct the actual life of Jesus of Nazareth, the problem would remain of the meaningfulness or validity of this life for today. The historian could, like Pontius Pilate, say to his/her audience: "Behold the man! There you have him." To which the audience might well reply: "So what? Why should he matter *today*?" The problem, then, is finding a common horizon of understanding.

Bultmann sought this horizon of understanding in the category of "existence." The past, like the present, Bultmann assumed, was occupied with the question of meaningful existence, and in the New Testament we have the answer to this question coded in a mythological language which needs to be translated for today. Bultmann concluded that Jesus matters because he provokes an existential choice. The historicity of Jesus' life is unimportant; what is important is that Jesus—whether or not his life can be historically verified—provoked and still provokes a response and a commitment in people. This view presupposes a transcendental anthropology: that human beings in any place and time are faced with the same existential questions of personal meaning.

The liberation theologians, for their part, reject Bultmann and the Post-Bultmannians' assumption of a transcendental anthropology as ahistorical and have found the common hermeneutical horizon, not in "understanding," which they view as not being historically concrete, but in "praxis." "Praxis" is what makes possible the bridging of past and present, text and context—a horizon found within concrete history and not on some level of philosophical abstraction. It is "praxis" as an ontological and epistemological category, which can access the meaningfulness of the historical Jesus for today. In fact, it is "praxis," rather than "existence," that rescues the historical Jesus from irrelevancy for Christian faith and makes him more than "an unknown x which triggers off [the] spiritual release" of authentic existence (Bruce 1977, 55). Sobrino makes this clear:

> For us . . . the historical element in the historical Jesus is first and foremost an invitation (and a demand) to continue his practice. . . . The historical element in Jesus requires a new conception of hermeneutics. The classic undertaking of hermeneutics has consisted in a development of understanding the meaning and import of a text of the past, and of the reality appearing in it, in the presence of the difficulty of understanding occasioned by the historical and cultural distance between past and present. In view of what has been said, however, the continuity thus sought between a text's past and present cannot be primarily a horizon of understanding. It must be a common horizon of practice. (Sobrino 1987, 66)

Sobrino also shows that liberation theology's hermeneutics improves on Bultmann's:

> For the Christian, Jesus will appear as bestower of meaning for one's own personal existence when *his practice* is pursued, and not when he is made a symbol—however historical—to answer the Christian's questions without any other mediation. (Sobrino 1987, 66-67)

It would seem that with "praxis" as the common hermeneutical horizon, liberation theologians would have a considerable stake on the recovery of the praxis of the historical Jesus. But such is not the case, primarily because of the acknowledged difficulty of recovering this historical Jesus. To liberation theologians, it is not important that the specifics of Jesus' every word and deed be historically validated. What *is* important is the validation of a *minimum nucleus* of facts (i.e., certain "basics") concerning the situation surrounding Jesus and his response to it that will enable oppressed Latin Americans to find in Jesus "good news" for their situation (Sobrino 1987, 72, 75-76). Since the evidence upon which liberation praxis must therefore stand is minimal, liberation theologians could easily be charged with seeing Jesus as "little more than the [almost] unknown x that triggers off" a liberative praxis.

We have seen that through the historical-critical method liberation theologians can relativize the interpretations that have been made of the historical account—they can show that these interpretations are the products of particular cultures, circumstances, and situations no longer extant, hence by-and-large irrelevant. Consequently, the only way of bridging the horizons of the past (diachronic) and the present (synchronic) is by appealing to some transcendent horizon that puts the past in continuity with the present, that enables the past to speak meaningfully and normatively to the listening present and, conversely, enables the present to look to the past for meaning and norms.   But in assuming that this transhistorical hermeneutical horizon exists, which theologians have variously referred to as "Reason" or "Transcendental Human Nature" or "Absolute Spirit" or "Anthropological Faith," or "Praxis," they have then-and-there abandoned the historicist presumption with which they began, since they are assuming that there is some metaphysical constant that stands outside the vagaries of history. The theologians' inconsistency is evident since they relentlessly apply the presumption (through the historical-critical method) to the past but not to their own theologizing in the present.

Segundo, for instance, appeals to "faith" as a basic anthropological dimension, which he says "more or less serves as a species-memory and as the deepest bond of its unity" (Segundo 1985, 31). Anthropological faith is, for Segundo, the essential presupposition that enables us to approach Jesus of Nazareth from our meaning-world; this "faith" is the transhistorical hermeneutical horizon. But is not Segundo's concept of "anthropological faith" itself a product of the sociohistorical conditions under which Segundo himself lives? Why then should his concept have any compelling authority over anyone else living someplace else or in some future time? In his view of the historical Jesus' significance, is not Segundo projecting into Jesus his own view of human nature, a view rooted in a specific culture, class, and historical moment?

Yet that is precisely what Segundo claims for his own christology and would want for all theologians to recognize: that his christology is normative only for those living under the same sociohistorical conditions as he is (and the same could be said of the christologies of other theologians) and hence is untransferable and obsolescent (which should also be said of the christologies of other theologians) (Segundo 1985, 39). But then to appeal to "anthropological faith," to appeal to a dimension of human being that allegedly transcends history and culture and provides the horizon of understanding enabling the past to speak intelligibly to the present, is to make an exaggerated and contradictory claim, for the most that Segundo could appeal to, from a historicist presumption, for his autochthonous and obsolescent christology would be "Twentieth century Uruguayan faith."

What has been said of "anthropological faith" can also be said of "praxis" as a transcendental hermeneutical horizon. The "praxis" of which the liberation theologian today speaks cannot be anything other than a twentieth century conception[3] projected unto the past and unto the historical Jesus. Although liberation theologians have been critical of Bultmann's hermeneutics (and by association, of all the neo-orthodox and liberal theologies derived from such hermeneutics) as being too abstract and ahistorical, the liberation theologians' hermeneutic of "praxis," in order to find a point of contact with the past, must be made into an ahistorical abstraction.

Moreover, while liberation theologians criticize those using Bultmann's existential hermeneutic as approaching the text with a pre-understanding of human being as an abstraction, "a Platonic essence valid *semper et pro semper*, not real flesh and blood" (Miranda 1974), liberation theologians themselves have not been immune from that fault. They often seem to approach the text with a pre-understanding of human being as an abstraction, a Hegelian essence valid *semper et pro semper*, perpetually in historical conflict, actualizing itself as the New Human Being or true humanity, through the negation of negation, i.e., liberative praxis (Gutiérrez 1973, 145-60; Boff 1989, 147, 153-54; Tucker 1972, 41, 58-60).

In all fairness, some liberationist exegetes and theologians, such as Fernando Belo, Severino Croatto, Michel Clévenot, and Norman K. Gottwald, perhaps aware of the many difficulties with the historical-critical method, are exploring other interpretive methods, such as structuralism and socio-literary criticism.[4] The vast majority of liberation theologians, however, continue to accept the historical-critical approach to Scripture while rejecting its claim to value neutrality.

We can conclude that given the sketchy outline that, at best, can be drawn of the historical Jesus, given the heavy reliance on "Gospel *hints*," the "*basic structure* of Jesus' life," and the "*minimum nucleus* of facts," the appeal which liberation theologians make to this historical Jesus must be seen as an appeal to a symbol, a Northern Star to guide their course of christological construction. The symbol of the "historical Jesus" or the "hypothetical Jesus" serves a critical function, and its criticism is the exposure of all that is ahistorical, mythological, or mystifying in christological discourse. In short, the "historical Jesus," although providing very little in terms of positive content for liberation christology, provides the liberationist discourse with a great deal of rhetorical authority for negating or relativizing the claims of other christological discourses, i.e., for deconstructing other christologies. So, for example, by appealing to the historical Jesus, the christological claims "Jesus descended into hell and preached to the captives" or "Jesus lived a sinless life" or "Jesus will return as he ascended into heaven" can be easily exposed as ahistorical or mythological and hence as claims that are either irrelevant or in need of reinterpretation.

The alleged positive content that the historical Jesus provides for liberation christology is his praxis. I shall comment on this when I discuss the praxiological presumption, but first we need to see how the historicist presumption influences liberation theologians' view of Christian ethics.

Historicity and Christian Ethics

The historicist presumption also leads liberation theologians to see Christian ethics as emerging from the dialectic between the Scripture and the reading community, for as Clodovis Boff notes "it is only in concrete life that meaning unfolds, and 'comes to itself.' And here hermeneutics flowers into ethics" (Boff 1987, 138). Hence ethics are relative to the hermeneutic of the community which in turn is a function of socio-historical factors. Liberation theologians can thus show how particular modes of Christian conduct (especially in the socio-political realm) emerged from specific hermeneutical approaches which developed, in turn, out of specific socio-historical conditions, that is, out of particular historical circumstances and particular social loci. By presupposing historicism, not only can liberation theologians deconstruct ethical theories and their concomitant christologies, they can also justify a new ethic of liberation, one arising from its own socio-historical context (Rejón 1984, 37).

Clearly, then, there is no specific form of Christian conduct that transcends time and culture. On the basis of the historicist presumption, liberation theologians accept the relative character of all Christian social teachings and expose all claims to absolute transcendent norms as sheer delusion. In this position liberation theologians follow the generally accepted views of Ernst Troeltsch and H. Richard Niebuhr, who in their works noted that as the historical and social context in which the Church exists has changed, so has its social ethic and so have the christological discourses that give warrants to those ethics. A historicist presumption, therefore, precludes that one ethic should be seen as normative for all Christians everywhere, anytime. From this perspective, Jesus' social ethic, as well as that of the early Church, can only be fixed "stitches" in the seamless web of history; his moral values and those of the Church would have to be seen as relative to those historical circumstances and social conditions which they inhabited and hence of questionable authority today.

But liberation theologians are neither historical positivists nor ethical relativists, and be it far from them that they should be seen as such. But with historicism as a methodological presumption, it is a difficult task indeed for liberation theologians to avoid its relativizing effects and (1) demonstrate the historical Jesus' significance for Christian ethics and (2) make authoritative appeals to practise a liberation ethic, to persuade others to join the struggle.

In appealing to the historical Jesus, these liberation theologians face a special problem. This problem is best expressed by Gotthold Lessing in his dictum, "Accidental truths of history can never become the proof of necessary truths of reason." In other words, the relativities of history, such as the historical Jesus (his concrete life, work and teachings), can never become the warrant for a rational moral order. After all, if right action can be apprehended by any thinking human being, why bring Jesus into the ethical discussion at all (Schillebeeckx 1987, 583-85)? Liberation

theologians, following Vatican II,[5] themselves acknowledge that rational human beings can discern what is right and act accordingly, which is why Christians can join
with other rational human beings (which Karl Rahner has called "anonymous
Christians") in the struggle against injustice[6] and why theology must necessarily be the
second step: theology is critical reflection on praxis. The purpose of such reflection,
although called "critical," is not to evaluate the conduct as either right or wrong on the
basis of some prior biblical standards (an ethical theory), but to show how the faith can
be understood "from a point of departure in real, effective solidarity with the exploited
classes," "from a commitment to create a just society" (Gutiérrez 1983, 60). The
reflection is not a critical analysis of the praxis, for its rightness is evident to all through
reason, but a critical analysis of theology from the standpoint of praxis. The word
"praxis" itself, therefore, is not a neutral term; it connotes the "right kind of activity,"
namely efficacious activity with liberation as its aim. The oppressed engage in praxis,
not the oppressors.

The question is, then, what does Christian faith, *qua* Christian faith, uniquely
contribute to the commitment made to create a just society, a rational moral order?
How shall Jesus Christ be related to this rational moral order? Liberation theologians
have dealt with this problem by loosening both the subject of the christological
assertion, the historical Jesus, and the predicate of the christological assertion, the
Christ, from the moorings of history and turning "Jesus the Christ" into a historically
transcendent symbol that can be re-interpreted anew in any age or culture.

The predicate, "the Christ," has been disengaged from history, namely from the
historical Jesus, through the application of the historical-critical method. Through
form and redaction criticism, the appellation "Christ" has been relativized so that it can
now be replaced with the more comprehensible and currently relevant appellation
"Liberator." To call Jesus "the Christ" today is to speak anachronistically, similar to
calling Jesus "the Groovy One," and just as peculiar.

The subject of the assertion, "Jesus," has been disengaged from history as well.
The Jesus of whom the early Church bore witness is lost from view behind the mists
of historiographical methods and theoretical reconstructions. The liberation theologian, using a neo-Marxist hermeneutic key and a Hegelian philosophy of history, seeks
him—namely, the hypothetical Jesus—in the mists of speculation and "finds," in the
text, the martyred champion of the "necessary truths of reason," which truths are
simply the unfolding of Absolute Reason or Spirit, in essence, God.[7] The truths which
Jesus championed and for which he died were those of economic equality, religious
and political liberty, and fraternity among all (men, women, children, and the
despised); in short, he championed the truth of God.

As such, the significance of Jesus to the Christian's moral life is not transac-
tional (Jesus did not do something once for all, that transcends history, that each person
must appropriate and for which he/she must consequently respond in grateful obedi-

ence). Nor is Jesus' significance processive (Jesus did not initiate a process within history that enables persons to act rightly toward God and men) (Rupp 1974, 45-48). Or to use James Gustafson's typology (Gustafson 1968), Jesus functions as neither justifier nor sanctifier. Nor is Jesus "the Lord who is Creator and Redeemer." Those conceptions are seen to belong to the mythological mindset of first century Jewish Christians. Nor is Jesus the Teacher, for again the historical-critical method reveals that his teachings were tied to his eschatological expectations (expectations which have been historically falsified).

Instead, Jesus is the example, the Pattern. But his example does not lie in the particularity of his actions, as we find them in the text of scripture, for these, again are historically conditioned (Sobrino 1978, 132). His example lies, firstly, in the fundamental dispositions by which his actions are motivated, dispositions such as a preferential option for the poor, a critical and conflictive stance towards the ruling class (the politico-religious superstructure), and a willingness to suffer for the cause of liberation. Secondly, but most importantly, he is the example of the *process* by which a human being makes these dispositions historically concrete,[8] for it is not the same to prefer the poor as to become poor, nor to have a stance toward the ruling class as to fight the ruling class, nor to be willing to suffer as to suffer (Sobrino 1978, 123-26). The Incarnation, therefore, is not an ontological concept but describes the process by which these fundamental dispositions are historicized or made concrete; it reveals the path which Christians themselves must traverse in actualizing the Kingdom of God: opting, fighting, and changing to meet historical exigencies.

The historicism which liberation theologians employ in their hermeneutics lead them to discount the high (or descending) christology and personalist soteriology of the New Testament because these are viewed as irrelevant to the problems of Latin Americans today, although these may have been relevant in the past. But the same historicism which leads liberation theologians to say that the high christology of the New Testament was relevant to the needs and problems of an earlier age, also impels them to affirm the provisional character of liberation christology. Boff, Segundo, and Sobrino admit as much and this author agrees with them that christology must be continuously reconstructed in light of changing needs and changing times.

At issue, then, is not the historicality of experience—that our experience is conditioned by our historical locale—rather, the issue is how historicism is applied by liberation theologians to the witness of Scripture and the Tradition of the Church. At issue is how much of the past is recoverable and usable today because of the historicality of experience. Liberation theologians appear to have an unwarranted narrow view of the usable past. More specifically, they devalue (or do not sufficiently attend to) the personalist and cosmic interpretations of Jesus Christ that Christians of the past (and present) have proclaimed; they make the judgment that New Testament christology and conciliar christologies are no longer meaningful discourses. Such a judgment, however, is not a necessary corollary of a historicist presumption.[9] Rather, it seems to be a judgment based on the liberationist agenda of making christology politically relevant. Hence historicism is used by liberation theologians as a foil against (what in their opinion are) apolitical or politically ineffective christologies of the past. But such a total relativization of the past is not a necessary outcome of a historicist hermeneutical presumption.

The Praxiological Presumption

The Priority of Praxis

The second hermeneutical presumption which liberation theologians hold in the deconstruction of christology is "praxis." All liberation theologians, following the lead of Gustavo Gutiérrez, define theology as "critical reflection on Christian praxis in light of the Word" (Gutiérrez 1973, 13). Christology, therefore, as a constituent part of Christian theology, must have praxis as its point of departure and its goal, all the while avoiding the extremes of empiricism (drawing its content strictly from praxis) and pragmatism (orienting itself strictly to praxis) (Boff 1987, 14). It must have social change as its starting point and end-point. The absolute priority of praxis in theological reflection is made clear by J. B. Libaînio in his exposition of liberation theology when he says that liberation theology "is involved *in* praxis; it is a theology *of* praxis; it is directed *for* praxis; and it operates *from* praxis" (McGovern 1989, 33). This emphasis upon praxis marks a desire to correct the "theoretical one-sidedness of much Christian theology and its seeming social innocence and public ineffectiveness" (Lane 1984, 8). Liberation theologians hold that praxis must have priority over theory; action must precede theologizing. By assuming the priority of praxis they are able to offer a critical counter-discourse of traditional christology.

The essence of this counter-discourse is the judgment that traditional theology, and christology in particular, even though it deals with a historical personage, is by-and-large praxiologically inoperative, i.e., it does not empower people to act for their liberation. Hence liberation theologians see the need to make theology and christology practical, oriented to the here-and-now, without denying the hope of the "sweet by-and-by."[10]

Theology, therefore, must be transformed; and theology is liberated from its speculative character when reflection begins in the socially transforming activity of the people of God, proceeds to that in the Scriptures and Tradition which is most relevant to their situation, the praxis of the Historical Jesus, and concludes by articulating a discourse that animates that same historical praxis. Theology, then, to be truly liberating, must be "critical reflection on Christian praxis in the light of the Word." Praxis is the first step; theology, and hence, christology, is the second step.

Sobrino and Assmann, for instance, demonstrate that the first step to empowerment is the rejection of speculative, abstract christologies: ". . . a Christology of the historical Jesus . . . rejects any abstract, idealistic *logos* and any merely doctrinal or personalist *logos*. It seeks to affirm a truly historical *logos*" (Sobrino 1978, 83). In *Theology for a Nomad Church*, Assmann rejects any abstract Christology that describes Jesus as "the presence of the risen Christ in the world" (Assmann 1976, 103) or as "something completely ethereal" (p. 69). Sobrino makes clear that an empowering liberation christology develops through the "invisible hand" of the dialectical interplay between praxis and theology, as Christians give priority to praxis:

> Christians who had inserted themselves into a liberative practice were searching for both a way to see their historical praxis as consistent with their actual Christian faith and for the support and radicalization that faith lends that praxis. Therefore they went back to the figure of Jesus. . . . This new reflection on Christ originated in the service of historical liberation . . . (Sobrino 1987, 10)

This prioritizing of praxis, however, lacks a solid philosophical basis. Clodovis Boff, for instance, who is claimed by many scholars to present the best philosophical case for the epistemology of liberation theology, can be cited as a clear example. In discussing possible epistemological approaches to employ in articulating the relationship between theology and the social sciences, Clodovis Boff sets aside or excludes those approaches which do not take praxis as their point of departure. Only so, he implies, can the status of the question (of the relationship of theology to sociology) be expressed correctly (Boff 1987, 3-6). This, however, seems to beg the question (Why can theology and sociology be correctly related only from a point of departure in praxis?) since he is presupposing the truth of a praxiological epistemology for the articulation of the relationship of theology to social science. In other words, he has already decided *a priori* how theology and the social sciences are to be related: theology is a second word in the interest of praxis. Moreover, by presupposing the priority of praxis, the "social sciences" of which he speaks which can be related to theology, can only be those which see in praxis a valid approach to social reality. This would exclude, *a priori*, all functionalist sociologies.

Praxis: The Basis of Critique

We mentioned earlier that praxis functions as the hermeneutical key or bridge that enables the Latin American Christian to fuse the horizons of the past (text) with the present (context). But praxis functions as more than a hermeneutic key; it also functions as a basis of critique, as a basis for a counter-discourse. In spite of the ambiguous referent liberation theologians attach to the word "praxis," christological discourses that do not meet certain criteria implicit in the praxiological presumption held by liberation theologians are set aside as defective discourses. In other words, "praxis" is a concept which has its own theoretical criteria which serve to distinguish it from human activity (or practice) in general. What are these criteria?

Firstly, "praxis" is concerned with *social* transformation. It is not activity orientated toward the transformation of individuals and their particular circumstances (for instance by converting them or giving alms to selected needy ones), but orientated toward the transformation of generic humankind, the transformation of social structures, particularly political and economic institutions. The focus of praxis, then, is the structural, the institutional, the systemic, the collective, the macro-social.

Secondly, praxis is concerned with *efficacious* transformation. The sort of action sought is not some helter-skelter activity that seeks to ameliorate the circumstances of the oppressed by working with or within the "system," neither is it a repetition of methods and approaches (for instance, developmentalism) that have either failed or succeeded only partially or temporarily. Praxis, then, is activity which efficaciously obtains the liberation of the oppressed. This obviously demands an attentiveness to means. And so unless the proper means are being used one cannot be said to be engaging in "praxis." The means must be in keeping with the task at hand: so for instance, to transform political institutions, political means are necessary; to effectively resist and overcome repressive violence, violence must be one of the options available to the Christian. There cannot be an *a priori* theoretical rejection of any historically concrete means. I make the qualification of historical concreteness because for an action to be viewed as "praxis," the means employed must be as historically concrete as the task at hand. Hence prayer and fasting, for instance, are not historically concrete means for opposing the forces of repression or challenging capitalist exploitation. These might be seen as concrete forms of spirituality (that nourish and inspire liberation praxis), but they could not properly be viewed as types of liberative praxis in themselves.

Thirdly, praxis is concerned with *total* transformation. In other words, liberative praxis is not the sort of activity that seeks to effect change in a piece-meal fashion, altering bits and pieces of the "system" while leaving other parts of it intact. One is not talking about "reformist" activity when calling for liberative praxis. Rather liberative praxis implies the subversion of the entire system, for every institution within that system is in ideological collusion for the continued exploitation of the oppressed.

Fourthly, because praxis is social, efficacious, and total, it is inherently *conflictual*. The "system," which holds power, does not cooperate in the process of transformation. It resists change; it resists surrendering its power to the powerless. As a result, praxis necessarily implies conflict.

The Ambiguous Use of "Praxis"

Although the word "praxis" has a clear meaning, a specific kind of activity having characteristics that enable one to distinguish it from "practice" or "activity" in general, liberation theologians are not clear or consistent in their use of the term. For instance, "praxis" is often used to refer to the "commitment" made to the oppressed, the "*option* for the poor*." What that means concretely remains as vague as the word "praxis." Does that option entail giving away every material possession one has and joining the poor in their plight? Does it entail joining a guerrilla group to fight for the overthrow of the oppressors? Does writing and lecturing against oppression as a university professor count as "praxis," as "opting for the poor?" For Leonardo Boff, it counts. In an essay in which he attempts to thematize the christological discourses present in Brazilian liberal Christianity, he states:

> Our reflections here will be based largely on the *praxis* of theology
> as we discover it in our theological activities, in talks, courses,
> meetings, and contacts with the living thought of theologians,
> priests, and bishops in this immense country of ours. (Miguez-
> Bonino 1985, 11)

Theologizing, then, is itself a form of "praxis." Gustavo Gutiérrez, in his more recent works, uses the word "praxis" "to include all that the poor 'experience' in their lives— their sufferings, their joys, and their experiences of God in the daily struggle to survive" (McGovern 1989, 34). Theology then is reflection on "the 'action' of the poor in confronting their lives" (McGovern 1989, 34).

Such plurality of meanings accorded by liberation theologians, however, is not indicative of the profundity of the word "praxis" nor of the complexity of their thought but rather is indicative of their vagueness and of their use of "praxis" as little more than a rhetorical device for calling people to align themselves against the status quo.

Arthur F. McGovern argues at length how critics have unfairly grouped together the mainstream theologians (i.e., those who advocate historical praxis like Boff, Sobrino, and Segundo) and far more radical proponents like Christians for Socialism.

It would certainly be unfair to paint all liberation theologians with the same brush. But if critics have done that, I would put some of the blame on the liberation theologians themselves for their vagueness about praxis. McGovern notes that these theologians are all clearly against capitalism, but they should not be grouped with Christians for Socialism, for like Gutiérrez they certainly do not want to baptize any one political option as Christian (McGovern 1989, 44, 46, 49). But if they are neither for capitalism nor for socialism, then what sort of economic alternative do these liberationists have in mind as the goal of praxis? Peronism? Sandinismo? Some sort of economic "anarchy?" A "mixed" economy? Is to engage in liberative praxis simply to be against capitalism? Or against developmentalism? Or both? Is the goal of praxis the transformation of the entire international economic order or just the national socio-economic order? Should a Christian seek change through the electoral process or is violent revolution the only hope? Or does "engaging in praxis" mean that, as a Christian, one must simply act on behalf of the poor without asking which political/ economic programme will enable the poor to get a hold of their own historical destinies? The question is, however, if these liberation theologians do not want to "baptize" any one political option as "the Christian option," how is their stance any different from that of the Vatican and the progressive stance of CELAM?

Again, the ambiguity with which liberation theologians use the term "praxis" leaves one in the dark as to the concrete means and aims of such action; it becomes a "catch-all" word for any action whose aim is an equally vague "liberation." Liberation theologians' ambiguity on what they mean by "praxis" has been the reason for many of the criticisms raised against the movement.

McGovern himself, a very sympathetic critic, says that Gutiérrez uses the word in *A Theology of Liberation* to describe:

> a wide array of movements and groups that fall under the general heads of "the process of liberation in Latin America" and "the church in the process of liberation." These processes involved ranges of events from the formation of guerrilla groups to bishops speaking out against injustices. As a basis for generating some new theological concepts, such as liberation, such a broadly based praxis might suffice. But in determining concretely the direction that liberating praxis should take, this broad base seems hardly adequate.... One finds few concrete examples of critical reflection on specific problems and strategies in liberation theology itself. A move in that direction, along with the development of some explicit ethical criteria for judging the best actions to take, would greatly advance the work of liberation theology, in my judgment. (McGovern 1989, 33-34)

I am in agreement with McGovern on this point, but he seems to forget that the development of such ethical criteria (moral *a prioris*) for judging the best actions would imply a return to the "old" epistemology which gives priority to theory rather than praxis. To do as McGovern suggests would be to subvert what is "new" about the liberation theology method, the priority of praxis.

In fact, the ambiguity attached to the word "praxis" is evident not only in the variety of referents attached to it but also, and consequently, in the variety of theological currents found in Latin American liberation theology. In other words, it is not altogether clear to the liberation theologians themselves what would be a proper point of departure for theologizing since they are in disagreement as to what actually constitutes liberative praxis. Juan Carlos Scannone, for example, distinguishes between four currents of praxis found in the liberation theology movement which are associated with concomitant currents of theologizing.

One current of praxis is that which can be described as ecclesial denunciation; in other words, the theologizing begins with the praxis of the institutional church. It makes no use of social analysis. This approach is the one most favored by the Vatican and CELAM, but an approach often criticized by theological luminaries like Gustavo Gutiérrez, Leonardo Boff, and Juan Luis Segundo as ineffectual.

A second current of praxis can be described as revolutionary militancy. The theologizing begins with the praxis of revolutionary groups. This approach makes much use of Marxist analysis and feels theology should be in the service of revolutionary ideology. Scannone puts Hugo Assmann and Christians for Socialism in this current. I would venture to say that Boff, Sobrino, and Segundo would be somewhat critical of this approach for disdaining the liberating resources available in the theological traditions of the Church (the Scriptures and the *magisterium*).

A third current of praxis can be described as historical praxis. The theologizing begins with the praxis of the poor themselves, particularly that of the ecclesial base communities as they reflect on different aspects of the faith in light of their oppression. This theologizing, therefore, is formal, somewhat systematic reflection on informal, popular reflection and action. This theological approach makes use of Marxist analysis but also seeks to show how the Church's traditions and doctrines can contribute positively to the struggle for liberation. Boff, Sobrino, and Segundo would fall into this camp.[11]

A fourth current of praxis is that favored by Scannone himself, which might be described as a praxis of historical-cultural identity. The theologizing begins with the praxis of "the people," a more generic category than the "poor." This approach is averse to only using Marxist analysis because such analysis places the people in economic categories and overlooks other forms of oppression afflicting Latin America. Arthur McGovern is of the opinion that this last approach "seems representative of only a small group in Argentina" (McGovern 1989, xvii). That leaves us with the three approaches mentioned above as truly representative forms of liberation praxis.

Historical Praxis and Defective Discourses

Of the three representative forms of praxis, however, it is historical praxis that serves as the norm for those theologians we are considering in this work and is their norm for evaluating traditional christological discourse and for constructing their own liberating discourse. Their conclusion, briefly put, is that traditional christological discourse has failed to meet the norm of historical praxis and so must be deconstructed.

For instance, the christological discourse that gives the warrant for the first form of "praxis," i.e., denunciation without socio-analytic mediation, is viewed as defective for two reasons, (1) for not giving praxis the primacy in the dialectic of theory (theology) and praxis (in other words, praxis is seen to follow from correct theory, orthopraxis follows from orthodoxy), and (2) for not meeting the criteria of efficacy and totality. This christological discourse is what Jens Glebe-Möller calls "the Theological Code," (Glebe-Möller 1989) which portrays Jesus Christ as descending from heaven to fulfill a spiritual mission, that of dying on a cross to atone for the sins of humankind. Implicit in this "code" is that Jesus' approach to social reality was an apolitical and non-partisan one and that his "praxis" consisted of issuing a call for individual conversion, which would result in changed attitudes toward "neighbors," putting an end to the oppression of human being by human being. The theological code assumes that Jesus called the Church to pursue the same approach to social reality as he did.

This account of Jesus Christ's work and "praxis," i.e., this christological discourse, is defective on the grounds already mentioned. It gives priority, not to praxis but to theory or theology. To "act out" this code it is necessary, first, to *understand* a variety of theological certitudes (doctrines), such as Jesus' pre-existence, his relationship to the other members of the Godhead, the doctrine of the Fall of humankind, the doctrine of Atonement, and the doctrine of future Judgment. It is only in the context of such "theoretical knowledge" that denunciation makes sense as a "praxis," as a necessary ingredient of a call to conversion. This theological code takes the concrete experience of oppression and spiritualizes it or theologizes it, eliminating the possibility of the oppressed taking historically concrete action to effect an immediate and lasting change in the situation. This code also individualizes the act of oppression so that it is not sinful structures (causing the oppression) what needs to be changed but rather the sinful individuals which compose these structures. In light of this code or discourse, this orthodoxy, the only proper course of action in the face of oppression is denunciation and evangelization, understood as issuing calls to conversion.

Leonardo Boff is critical of this approach. In *Jesus Christ Liberator,* Boff argues that the denunciatory sort of praxis emerges from a "Sacramental articulation of liberation christology" which arises out of an *intuition* of an unjust situation but is an inadequate way of expressing efficacious agape. According to Boff:

> On the basis of their faith many Christians have come to realize that this situation contradicts the historical plan of God. Poverty is a social sin that God does not will, and so there is an urgent obligation to change things. . . .
>
> This perception generally finds expression in the language of prophetic denunciation and hortatory proclamation. Ethical indignation is transformed into an appeal for changes. This summons is fleshed out in a praxis of committed love. Since this lifestyle does not entail an analysis of the mechanisms and structures that have generated the existing situation, the efficacy of its commitment is short-range and unpredictable. (Boff 1978b, 269-70).

Although Boff finds some value to this praxis and its concomitant christology, he finds it limiting "Since it does not broach any social analysis, [and so] has little political force or impact" (Boff 1978b, 271). He clearly prefers a "Socio-Analytic Articulation of Liberation Christology," i.e., a christology and a praxis based on a careful analysis of the mechanisms that produce social iniquity. It is only such a Christology (and such a praxis) what Boff considers "liberative in the real and strict sense" (Boff 1978b, 272).

Segundo, like Boff, sees the denunciatory approach as ingenuous: "One might very well come across a very ingenuous kind of liberation theology which assumed that it could deduce its content for any given situation from the gospel message itself" (Segundo 1976, 83). It is ingenuous, he says, because it "assume[s] that the straightforward words of the gospel message [the New Testament, the Theological Code] by themselves are enough to convince the Christian that the maintenance of the existing social structures is incompatible with his or her faith" (Segundo 1976, 83). He further argues that this "praxis" deduced from a "correct" theological discourse (orthodoxy, the Theological Code) is inadequate because it was not the approach employed by Jesus himself. He writes:

> No truly liberative theology can seriously entertain the question as to whether it should or should not descend from its own proper certitudes to the shaky terrain of concrete history, sociology, and politics. Why? Because that is precisely the kind of approach that is ruled out by Jesus. (Segundo 1976, 80)

Segundo is posing the question as to whether theology should begin with orthopraxis or orthodoxy and the answer to him is clear: a truly liberative theology begins with praxis (employing the analytic mediations that history, sociology, and political science provide) not with the theoretical, abstract speculations of academic theology. Implicitly, then, christological discourses that take Scripture and Tradition as their point of departure and which seek to establish some Christian ethic (a theory) deduced from them are dismissed as defective because such an approach does not conform to the theological method employed by Jesus himself and results in an ethic or practice that cannot adjust to meet historical exigencies. In short, it is ineffectual (Segundo 1976, 77).

Hence the warrant for the priority of praxis over theory (theology) is found in the approach of Jesus himself. Any sort of approach to Christian action that inverts the praxis-theory dialectic, i.e., which gives priority to theory over praxis, theological speculation over concrete action, is seen as a defective approach christologically (in that it does not conform to Jesus' own method) and politically (in that it fosters an essentially conservative politics).

Inasmuch as this Theological Code embodies the christologies found in much of the New Testament and in the traditions of the Church throughout its history (for instance, in the christologies elaborated by Anselm, Peter Lombard, Aquinas, Duns Scotus, Luther, and Calvin or in the canonical doctrines established by the Councils of Nicea [325], Carthage [418], Ephesus [431], Chalcedon [451], Constantinople [381, 553], and Lateran [649]), liberation theologians view most of the traditional "descending" christologies as defective discourses since they do not empower the oppressed to use historically concrete means to obtain liberation and bring the Kingdom of God closer to its realization.

But liberation theologians are equally critical of many contemporary theological discourses with their ascending christologies, such as those of Political Theology in Europe and Process Theology in the United States. The reasons for their rejection of these christological discourses are essentially the same as for their rejection of descending christological discourses, namely that they do not take the concrete historical praxis of the people as their point of departure but remain highly theoretical, even when discussing the necessity of praxis, as in Political Theology. As a result the sort of "praxis" suggested by political theologians tends to be a conservative one that does not sufficiently challenge the status quo.

This criticism was raised early on in the liberation theology movement. Rubem Alves, for example, called for a humanistic messianism rather than the political theologians' messianic humanism. In other words, whereas the political theologians call for humanity to wait for the future, the Eschaton, to take hold of it, Alves and other liberation theologians call for humanity to realize its future, to become captain of its destiny, take hold of the reins of history and overthrow capitalism. Gutiérrez, in *A*

Theology of Liberation, is critical of political theology's lack of social analysis (Gutiérrez 1973, 224) and Hugo Assmann is very critical of the timidity of political theology which has "not dared to continue [its] analysis of the historical mediations of the role of power"; it has not dared to ask *where*—with whom and against whom—Christ's power is acting in human history. (Assmann 1984, 132-33).

Political theologians and liberation theologians have much in common in regard to their views on traditional and many contemporary christologies. For instance Johannes B. Metz, a political theologian, "faults modern christologies for not bringing out the practical structure of christology, for adopting a non-dialectical relationship between theory and praxis, and therefore for remaining too idealistic" (Lane 1984, 14). Liberation theologians would certainly agree with Metz's assessment, but the Latin American liberationists are nevertheless critical of the European political theologians for not being radical enough in their praxis, for taking a reformist approach to society and not making sufficient use of socio-analytic tools to inform their praxis.

Other contemporary theological discourses are equally excluded, such as the transcendental theology of Karl Rahner and the theology of history of Wolfhart Pannenberg, for being abstract and speculative. Sobrino gives an extensive "list" of the sort of christological discourses Latin American liberation theology is *not* interested in, primarily because of their praxiological inefficacy (Sobrino 1987, 64-65).

A second sort of liberation theology is criticized by those who advocate historical praxis as not being theological enough or "popular" enough (too elitist) and for turning the Gospel into an instrument of Marxist ideology. Hugo Assmann, for instance, is put into this category by Juan Carlos Scannone. Assmann sees social reality as the only text to be interpreted and the only valid source for theologizing. He avers that we must:

> ... look at the given situation as our primary and basic reference point . . . The Bible, tradition, the *magisterium* or teaching authority of the Church, history of dogma, and so on . . . do not constitute a primary source of "truth in itself" unconnected with the historical now of "truth in action." (Assmann 1976, 104)

Unlike Assmann, Sobrino and Boff give considerable attention as to how the New Testament and Chalcedonian formulations can be "translated" so as to engender a liberating consciousness in the oppressed and become a motive force of historical praxis. It is not clear whether Segundo would fall into this current. He has been marginalized by "mainstream" liberation theologians on several occasions, such as not being invited to the twentieth anniversary celebrations at Maryknoll in July 1988 or to participate in international meetings of liberation theologians (Sigmund 1990, 64). He was not included in the recently published Festshrift honoring Gustavo Gutiérrez

(Ellis and Maduro 1989) in spite of being one of the major intellectual contributors to the movement. What reasons there might be for marginalizing Segundo from the mainstream liberation theology movement are not altogether clear, but his claim to have invented liberation theology before Gutiérrez or his notion that a minority must lead the oppressed majority into liberation, which makes him sound elitist, may have something to do with it.

Jesus Christ: Warrant for Historical Praxis

Having given praxis the priority in the dialectic of theory-praxis, the theologian takes the route to theology and back through three mediations: (1) a socio-analytic mediation, that interprets the context, social reality, (2) a hermeneutical mediation, that interprets the text, the Bible, and (3) the practical mediation that synthesizes the prior two mediations through concrete political activity orientated toward transformation. In all of these mediations it is praxis what serves as the heuristic value enabling the theologian to choose from among the plurality of sociologies, biblical interpretive methods, and political ideologies, programmes, or means. In other words, whatever approach is chosen—socio-analytic, hermeneutical, or practical—it must conform to the epistemological priority which has been given praxis in the theory-praxis dialectic. The choice of approach is contingent on the value the approach places on praxis. In other words, does the approach being considered, have praxis, transformative action, as first in its interpretive agenda? If it does not, then the liberation theologian excludes it as faulty.

Granting the validity of this praxiological presumption, we would expect that the christology which should be hermeneutically mediated would be one that would give a great deal of attention to the Historical Jesus' activity and which would seek in that activity a basis and an impetus for continued praxis. But after scrutinizing the liberation theologians' christologies, we find that this inference is only half true. In the previous section I pointed out that because of their commitment to a historicist presumption, liberation theologians end up dismissing the specifics of Jesus' activity as practicable in the Latin American situation while trying to find in these specifics some historically transcendent thrust or disposition that might be applicable today—a good idea but methodologically contradictory. Ironically, liberation theologians get far more rhetorical mileage from the doctrine of the Incarnation, than from biblical exegesis, or to put it differently, not so much from the Historical Jesus as from the Christ of Faith. Their arguments for praxis are far more persuasive when they appeal to the doctrine of the Incarnation than when they appeal to the praxis of the Historical Jesus.

By appealing to the Incarnation, some liberation theologians present Jesus

Christ as the basis, the mystical origin and fulfillment, and the apotheosis of liberating praxis.

First, because God is Incarnate in Jesus, he can be seen as the basis or ground of praxis. Juan Carlos Scannone, arguing how theology as reflection on praxis is still theology, says:

> Thus theology does not cease being theology. In fact, it is all the more theology for being appropriately historical and practical. For the *Theós* whose *lógos* it expresses (and this makes it theology) is the God of history, and the Word that articulates that history. He is the Word of God become flesh, who gave his life to liberate brothers and sisters. (Bussmann 1985, 20)

Hence the theological basis for the orientation to praxis is a theology of the incarnation: God is a God active in history, and through God's incarnation, Jesus is the articulation of God's liberative action in history.

Secondly, Jesus, as the Christ, is seen as the mystical origin and fulfillment of liberative praxis. Gustavo Gutiérrez writes:

> In Christ the all-comprehensiveness of the liberating process reaches its fullest sense. His work encompasses the three levels of meaning mentioned above [political liberation, the liberation of man throughout history, liberation from sin and admission to communion with God]. (Gutiérrez 1973, 176)

He goes on to quote a Latin American text on missions:

> All the dynamism of the cosmos and of human history, the movement towards the creation of a more just and fraternal world, the overcoming of social inequalities among men, the efforts . . . to liberate man from all that depersonalizes him . . . , all these originate, are transformed, and reach their perfection in the saving work of Christ. In him and through him salvation is present at the heart of man's history, and there is no human act which, in the last instance, is not defined in terms of it. (Gutiérrez 1973, 178)

Thirdly, Jesus is seen as the apotheosis of liberative praxis. Claus Bussmann, for example, commenting on Segundo Galilea's christological enterprise says that he:

> places the accent on a recovery of a Christology of the incarnation. His purpose . . . is to afford Christians involved in the Latin American liberation process, who lack a political Christology, the

opportunity to orientate their involvement on the model of Jesus' political involvement. (Bussmann 1985, 50)

Jesus, God Incarnate, is the example of liberative praxis. However, what that historical praxis of Jesus consists of, liberation theologians obtain from biblical exegesis, through the historico-critical method (as pointed out in the previous section), and has the following four-fold characteristics (Bussmann 1985, 51-65):
1. His activity is not on the basis of theological criteria, but on humanistic criteria (what is good for people).
2. His activity is prophetic (profane), not priestly (sacred).
3. His activity is aimed at structural change, not just individual conversion.
4. His activity is revolutionary and constitutes a challenge to revolution.

Regrettably, each of these characteristics is exegetically debatable, but can only be cursorily discussed here. For instance, that he acts on humanistic as opposed to theological criteria is contradicted by the Lazarus narrative, where Jesus "lets" him die, delaying three days before going to raise him—hardly a humanistic thing to do. That his activity is profane rather than sacred is contradicted by the many instances related by the Gospels in which Jesus went away to pray, observed the Jewish holy days, and was found in the Temple ("about his Father's business"). As to structural change, the Gospels *do* present Jesus as challenging the religio-political hegemony of the Pharisees and Sadducees, but he says and does almost nothing about the imperialistic Romans. That his activity was revolutionary and challenged to revolution is true, but it was not the sort of revolution the Jewish people were expecting nor what liberation theologians may want to advocate. It was a revolution of the heart, not a conflict of power against power but of love against power.

In their appeals to liberative praxis and how Jesus exemplifies it, liberation theologians commit a hermeneutic fallacy which Jacques Ellul has pointed out in *Jesus and Marx*; they read a modern concept *into* an ancient text:

In no way can one refer to Jesus' praxis, since, . . . (1) no proletariat was involved; (2) the interpretation of Jesus as having had a revolutionary practice in the modern sense depends on word plays and forcing the text; (3) no one could begin claiming Jesus had a revolutionary praxis until the time when the ideology of Marxist revolution became part of our thinking. In other words, *this* Jesus is discovered not on the basis of what He is, but in the basis of a presupposition acquired from one's social milieu. (Ellul 1988, 130-31)

In other words, in order to make Jesus the all-in-all of liberative praxis (understood in the Marxist sense of revolutionary activity to change the existing material relations), the liberation theologian must read into the text an ideology, a worldview that was not part of the First century Semitic worldview held by Jesus himself or those bearing witness to Jesus through that text. Therefore, Jesus can serve as the warrant for liberative praxis only if the text and Jesus himself are hermeneutically tortured to fit a contemporary ideology.

Moreover, in spite of the criticism and rejection of traditional christologies for not engendering praxis because of their abstract and speculative characters, liberation christology itself is not anymore practical or unspeculative. Again, Ellul in his vitriolic criticism of Marxist Christians (which, in his view, includes the majority of liberation theologians) says of the "practical" aspect:

> What then is the praxis of Marxist Christians? As far as I can tell, their practice consists of giving lectures, writing articles, travelling to congresses and colloquia, attending demonstrations, signing petitions and manifestos, and organizing seminars. . . . Such actions do not amount to praxis . . . , praxis cannot be separated from the exercise of an economically situated profession. To the degree that Marxist Christians' verbally revolutionary activities have nothing in common with their profession, to the degree that they continue to be bourgeois professors, lawyers, pastors, or Dominicans, we cannot consider their actions praxis. (Ellul 1988, 128)

As for the abstract, rather than practical, character of liberation christology, one need only look at Fernando Belo's *A Materialist Reading of the Gospel of Mark* or Juan Luis Segundo's *An Evolutionary Approach to Jesus of Nazareth* to discover that these works were not written with the campesino in mind. A couple of examples will suffice. Belo, for instance, often writes in code: "In the FS characterized by the MPE, the STR Z cannot respond to the STR AA," or "the STR of Jesus is vanquished by the STR AA" (Ellul 1988, 90, 114). Segundo is just as theoretical:

> . . . we can say that the "enslavement of corruption" noted by Paul enters the circuit of an organism or project precisely through the cracks or openings left by poorly integrated subcircuits, by those subcircuits that have been integrated at a very low price in terms of the overall energy calculus. (Segundo 1988, 87)

Are these liberation christologies any less theoretical than such traditional ones as the Chalcedonian Formula or the Second Helvetic Confession?

Strengths and Weaknesses of a Praxiological Presumption

Liberation theology's emphasis on praxis does serve to correct several weaknesses of previous christological discourses. First, it recognizes the need to relate "Christ" to "culture," i.e., that whatever one has to say about Jesus Christ's person and work it should somehow be related, not only to the transformation of individuals, but also social structures. This is well and proper, for a faith that is purely private is a clear denial of the communal, indeed universal, intention of God for humankind as presented in the Scriptures.

Moreover, the emphasis on Jesus' praxis corrects christological discourse by recovering the totality of Jesus. By focusing so much on the death and resurrection of Jesus Christ, traditional christological discourses had completely overlooked the soteriological significance of Jesus' life, i.e., his pre-paschal experience. His life, as narrated in the Gospels, was merely seen as a preparatory stage for the death he would endure for the sake of humankind; the death and resurrection were the climax of a divine plan and so the actions/words of Jesus, leading up to that death, simply set the stage for that climax. Consequently, these actions and words (confrontations with the Pharisees, for example) were of secondary importance in God's plan and, therefore, soteriologically irrelevant. In other instances, the pre-paschal narratives served a sort of apologetic function in Christian discourse, namely to demonstrate that indeed Jesus was God: that he healed, raised the dead, forgave sins, and so on. The emphasis by liberation theologians on the Historical Jesus and his praxis, establishes the soteriological significance of Jesus' life; that it is not only his death and resurrection that is saving but also his concrete life. The aim of liberationists is to articulate in what sense this concrete life is a saving life.

Regrettably, that is where they fall short. Although their emphasis on Jesus' praxis recovers the significance of Jesus' total life, from birth to resurrection, the saving efficacy which is accorded to this life by liberation theologians for the individual is a subjective rather than an objective efficacy. Throughout history, Christian orthodoxy has maintained the objective efficacy of Jesus' work: that by faith in Jesus Christ, by acknowledging his sacrifice for one's sins, one's status before God is changed, that one becomes a member of a New Community, the Body of Christ, the Church, that one becomes a member of the New Israel, a citizen and an heir of the Kingdom of God. Liberation theologians, however, see the significance of Jesus' life as effecting in the Christian a mere change in consciousness; Jesus becomes a model for the sort of disposition one ought to have toward oppression, a model for the attitude one ought to have in the midst of class struggle. He is made into a source of inspiration, but hardly the consummator of our integral salvation. The salvation that such a Jesus offers is purely subjective and temporary. Once the historical struggle is over, once liberation from exploitation is obtained and capitalism overthrown, Jesus is dispensable, perhaps held unto as a nostalgic memory. Following Jesus, as Sobrino enjoins, is what is saving, but once we get to our "destination" (a liberated Latin America), what do we do with him? What is his significance then?

Juan Carlos Scannone makes a similar criticism when he writes that some liberation theologians:

> ... place what is proper to the faith and the order of the religious symbols which express it, celebrate it and institutionalize it as the believing community, only—and here is the problem—in the consciousness of salvation and in the conscious reference to Jesus Christ, a reference which on the level of practice offers "only new motivations." In that way the same history of revelation is made into a "merely sectorial phenomenon, although charged with metonymic (*pars pro toto*) and symbolic (*sacramentum salutis*) value." [It] is thus overlooked that the *sacramentum salutis* is not only *sign*, but efficacious *sign*—efficacious not only on the order of the consciousness of salvation as in the theologal reality of the same—, besides being the *analogatum princeps* with respect to the salvation of all mankind and its ontological reference to Jesus Christ. Thus the real efficacy of the Christian religious symbols is undervalued in relation with the ethical commitment that they not only demand and express, but that they also promote in the order of the psychological motivations and, above all, in that of the theologal realities. (Scannone 1987, 58-59, my translation)

What Scannone is saying here is simply that liberation theologians emphasize so much the motivational efficacy that christological discourse has for liberation praxis, that they end up forgetting about the transcendent efficacy of Jesus' work and how that work is represented symbolically/analogically in the Church. Or to put it differently, liberationists so emphasize the efficacy of Jesus' life and work on the horizontal dimension (which ends up being merely motivational), that they fail to emphasize the efficacy of Jesus' life and work on the vertical dimension. Consequently, in their christological discourse they fail to insufficiently explore or call attention to the liberative significance of the conceptual verbal and non-verbal symbols of Jesus Christ (doctrines, narratives, and rituals such as the Eucharist, Baptism, and the other Sacraments) which the Church mediates to the people in its liturgy. The logical consequence of this horizontal overemphasis by liberation theologians might very well be that the liturgical, institutional expressions and mediations of this saving (liberating) work of Christ become dispensable and their psychological efficacy in motivating ethical behavior in other areas of life (such as in sexuality, medicine, commerce, and interpersonal relations) is lost.

Sobrino and the other liberation theologians have relied so much on functional categories (such as praxis, or Sobrino's term "discipleship") for their christological discourse, that the ontological categories, which serve to define Jesus Christ's uniqueness and transcendent significance, are lost from view. While the approach of liberation theologians has provided a corrective to the excessive abstractionism and speculation of much Christian theology with its ontological approaches, liberation theologians have now gone to the other extreme with their functional approaches. What is needed is a balanced discourse, one that will give ontological grounding to the functional christologies of the liberationists, or put differently, a discourse which will be both practical and yet faithful to the tradition of Jesus' uniqueness. Lamberto Schuurman in discussing Jesus' divine "Sonship" gives expression to this problem:

> We need a vocabulary that will not only express divine sonship as a projection with which Jesus identifies and which in no way can be expressed in static ontic form, but which will also be a terminology in which divine sonship attains to a certain "institutionalization"—a terminology through which it manages to be converted into substance. (Miguez-Bonino 1985, p. 167)

The development of such an ontological vocabulary, such a discourse, is one of the crucial tasks that liberation theology needs to and has yet to fulfill.

The Ideological Presumption

Ideology as Distortion

The third presumption which liberation theologians hold in their deconstruction of christology is the influence of ideology. Accepting the validity of the sociology of knowledge, liberation theologians have applied the concept of ideology to the construction of theology. They understand the concept in a two-fold sense: pejoratively as "false consciousness," and positively, as "a way of translating ideas into action" (Geuss 1981, 11). For the deconstruction of christology, liberation theologians appeal to the negative sense of the concept. In the next chapter we will be looking at how it is used in its positive sense.

It is clear from their writings that liberation theologians have been genuinely challenged by the ideological critique of religion posed by Marx; that religion, and especially theology, functions as an ideology of legitimation, that it serves to give religious sanction to exploitative socio-economic systems or to dull the critical faculties so that one remains indifferent to exploitation. Accepting this view of religious discourse, liberation theologians expose christological discourses to an ideology critique, i.e., to uncover how christologies function as discourses or narratives of legitimation.

Indeed, one of the reasons for their "rejection" of the "Theological Code" is that it has functioned as a legitimating discourse for centuries. It legitimated the conquest of the New World, the enslavement and decimation of the Amerindians, the *encomienda* system of the 18th and 19th centuries, and the "liberal" developmentalism of the 20th. Except for a few exceptions, such as Bartolomé de las Casas (in the sixteenth century) and Fr. Miguel Hidalgo y Costilla and Fr. José María Morelos (in the nineteenth century), the Church hierarchy in Latin America remained either closely allied to the ruling elites or sought their favor (Dussel 1981).

Liberation theologians derive their conception of ideology from the sociology of knowledge, which originated with Marx and was then theoretically developed by Karl Mannheim, Louis Althusser, and the Frankfurt School. From Marx is derived the thesis that consciousness is the product of the material relations which prevail in the society. Mannheim agreed with Marx that "there is a correlation between the economic structure of a society and its legal and political organization, and that even the world of our thought is affected by these relationships" (Zeitlin 1968, 281). Mannheim argued that human beings "act with and against one another in diversely organized groups, and while doing so they think with and against one another" (Zeitlin 1968, 302). Thus he makes clear that thinking or theory follows action or praxis; theology, therefore, reflects the position those theologizing hold in the socio-economic structure.

Althusser, for his part, argued that ideology is not a thought that one assumes, but rather is something within which one thinks. "There are concepts *through which* we think and *with which* we think" (Ricoeur 1986, 120). Ideology, therefore, is an anonymous and unconscious field of concepts which serves as the backdrop, the scenario, for an individual's thoughts. Theology, therefore, as the conscious reflection of the theologian is very much conditioned by this unconscious, anonymous field.[12]

The Frankfurt school, in its critique of modernity, pointed out that the claims to rationality, the ideal of progress through technological and managerial advance, upheld by the "liberal" societies of the West, were only an ideology. "Modernity has appropriated the language, arguments, and findings of modern administration, science, and technology to promote and continue the illusion of rationality, while masking otherwise morally unacceptable arrangements and exercise of power throughout society" (Pottenger 1989, 37). First, Latin American sociologists and economists (such as Henrique Fernando Cardoso and André Gunder Frank), and then the liberation theologians, applied this critique to the concrete efforts of the Alliance for Progress to achieve Latin American development. Such efforts (developmentalism), and their theological legitimation, were only a mask for the continued exploitation of Latin America.

The upshot of all this is that liberation theologians view theology as a form of ideology, either legitimating oppression (if produced by the privileged) or furthering liberation (if produced by the oppressed). When theology develops in a society where the socio-economic system is a capitalist one, or where those doing theology enjoy positions of economic and social privilege, then the resultant theology is suspect, since in all likelihood, it is a non-critical discourse, one that legitimates or protects the material interests of those who are theologizing. Theology, therefore, can be either a form of false consciousness or a form of liberating consciousness, depending on its source.

This view of ideology makes clear why liberation theologians feel that theology must have its origin in the praxis of the people, that it must begin from the "underside of history," that it must be the creation of the communities of the oppressed struggling for liberation, for the oppressed enjoy an "epistemological privilege": they see reality in a different way (Miguez-Bonino 1983, 43). Only by beginning from their standpoint can theology avoid its ideological (legitimating) character. This also explains why liberation theologians reject theologies that have their loci in "Academia" or in the "First World."

Ideology and Defective Discourses

The appeal to ideology provides a basis for counter-discourse, for challenging a variety of theological or religious discourses. It functions as a criterion guiding the evaluation of various christologies by posing the following questions:

1. Who is the source of the discourse? What is his/her social locus? To what cause is s/he committed? This means asking about the socio-economic position of the source, his/her practical involvements, and even the geo-political realm of which s/he is a part, for all of these factors surrounding the theologian are crucial in determining the liberating viability of his/her theology in Latin America.

2. What tools of social analysis does the theologian employ to mediate the discourse to the situation? Is the social analysis Marxist or functionalist? Does it see Latin America as a society of class struggle or as a maladjusted organism?

3. What concrete actions does the discourse engender with respect to structural injustice? Does the discourse produce effective praxis, reformist attempts, or no

action at all?

Using these questions liberation theologians have evaluated various theological discourses, and have "classified" as suspicious two types of christological discourses: (1) those of Academic theology and (2) those of popular religiosity.

Hugo Assmann, for example, rejects North American and European theologies for their "insensibility to the political dimension of the problems" of Latin America, for their inability "to generate hypotheses which might transform the status quo" and for their "vague sociological content" (Assmann 1976, 57). In short, he rejects these theologies with their respective christologies (such as Moltmann's and Pannenberg's) for their lack of historical realism, their idealization of reality.

Juan Luis Segundo, in *The Liberation of Theology*, criticizes Schillebeeckx for holding "the naive belief that the word of God is applied inside some antiseptic laboratory that is totally immune to the ideological tendencies and struggles of the present day." The liberation theologian, however, suspects that "anything and everything involving ideas, including theology, is intimately bound up with the existing social situation in at least an unconscious way" (Segundo 1976, 7-8). Theology, therefore, must be liberated from its ideological captivity and this can only be accomplished by putting oneself, as one theologizes, through the "hermeneutic circle."

But in order for the hermeneutic circle to function, the theologian must accept two preconditions: (1) conceptions of reality must be questioned or suspected, and (2) interpretations of the Scriptures must be seen as changeable with each new historical situation. Having met these preconditions, the theologian must go through four stages to complete the hermeneutic circle. First, the interpreter must experience reality in a way which evokes ideological suspicion. Secondly, the theologian applies this ideological suspicion to all of reality in general and to theology in particular. Thirdly, as the theologian experiences a new theological reality, exegetical suspicion develops, i.e., "the suspicion that the prevailing interpretation of the Bible has not taken important pieces of data into account" (Segundo 1976, 9). Fourthly, and finally, the theologian arrives at a new hermeneutic, at a new way of interpreting the Scriptures (Segundo 1976, 9).

Only by going through this hermeneutic circle can a theologian avoid falling into the ideological traps that are laid all along the way of the theological enterprise.

Most theologies, regrettably, fail to complete the circle or even to meet the preconditions, and so Segundo dismisses them as ideological. For instance, he analyzes Harvey Cox's secular theology, the "political theology" of the Chilean bishops in their document "*Evangelio, política, y socialismos*," "The Gospel Message, Politics, and Brands of Socialism" (p. 130-31), Reformation theology (Luther, R. Niebuhr) (p. 142-43), German Political theology (Moltmann) (p. 144), and even other

Protestant "liberation" theologies such as Rubem Alves' and Richard Shaull's (p. 147-49), and finds that they all fall short of completing the circle.

Segundo discounts traditional and academic discourses because, by-and-large, they assume that absolute certitudes can be deduced from revelation (Scripture and Tradition). He finds two problems with this approach: (1) the problem of applicability and (2) the problem of objectivity. Regarding the former problem, which we discussed previously in the section on "praxis," Segundo argues that by establishing theological absolutes from which a Christian practice is to be deduced, the Christian is faced with being unable to deal with historical contingencies. The latter problem is that the entire theological methodology assumes the objectivity of the theologian. In other words, the process is not critical; it fails to recognize the hidden interests which are at work in such a deductive process. It is, therefore, ideological (Segundo 1976, 77-78; Segundo 1988, 7).

Leonardo Boff, unlike Segundo, does not impugn any specific theologian, but he does note that certain sorts of discourses are "pathological" for propounding a logic of bureaucratic maintenance or a radical experiential dilettantism both of which, Boff says, usually lead to isolationism (Boff 1989, 46-47). Could Boff be alluding to the Vatican (which silenced him) and Catholic charismatic movements (which ignore him)?

It is clear enough, however, that Boff attributes these divergent discourses about the meaning of the Gospel and the mission of the Church to ideology. He argues at length that theology, like all ideas, reflects the material interests of those propounding it. He writes:

> Any idea, theory, worldview, however universalistic and objective it claims to be, is bound up with the material conditions, theoretical and practical, of its location . . . all discourse refers to a social locus. . . . Every social locus permits or prevents particular discourses. . . . The social locus produces the epistemic locus. That is, the social locus guides the development of ideas and worldviews. . . . Underlying the theoretical differences [between theological positions] are different social loci. Divergent, indeed conflicting and antagonistic, interests are at stake. . . . Distinct interests help determine the choice of themes addressed. (Boff 1989, 48-50)

Boff, therefore, following Mannheim's notion that "forms of consciousness [such as is theological reflection] are ideological because they are 'expressions' of the class position of those who hold them" (Geuss 1981, 19), finds several theological currents or discourses as functionally defective in that they conceal or overlook the contradictions in Latin American society and provide a world-view that legitimate domination or hegemony.

He rejects the discourse of the ultra-conservative reactionary Catholic theologians who support, through their reflection, the movements of Archbishop Lefebvre, Dom Sigaud, and Dom Castro Maier. Their discourse reflects the interests of elitist groups who, distrustful of the people, anachronistically seek a return to the "old" order in which they controlled all power. Christologically, Boff says, they are uncomfortable with the historical Jesus and "prefer a made-to-order Jesus, arrayed in all the magnificence of Byzantine culture" (Boff 1989, 52).

Boff then criticizes the conservative discourse of the Vatican for its "emphasis on the transhistorical nature of the Church and thus on the apparent (not real) neutrality of political and social questions" (p. 53). He adds that because of its authoritarian structure it implicitly legitimates authoritarian regimes. This discourse, he says, "Based on authority, . . . erects the kind of Church that dovetails nicely with authoritarian political regimes. One never lodges a basic criticism against this kind of Church" and implicitly, against this kind of regime. To the Church, Boff adds sarcastically, "A dictator can be good and also devout. But the inherent violence of the fact of dictatorship is left out of account" in its reflection. "Theological reflection is linked to the mentality of an authoritarian state" (p. 53). In other words, such reflection is ideological, hence it must be regarded as defective.

A third type of defective discourse, Boff calls progressive in that it seeks to bridge the gap between modernity and Christian faith. It takes science and technology seriously and wants the Church to modernize itself. Boff seems to be referring to the reflection of those Catholic theologians who, like the Protestant neo-orthodox, seek to make the faith relevant to the modern person, the person whose scientific, secular mind-set keeps him/her from believing. But such a discourse, says Boff, "expresses the social locus of the upwardly mobile—university graduates who will be joining a progressive, bourgeois society" (p. 54). This discourse, although more critical, avoids the basic question facing Latin America, not unbelief, but injustice. The discourse is, therefore, functionally ideological.

Sobrino is not as explicit as Boff or Segundo in discounting traditional discourses because of their ideological character, but he is influenced by the presumption that one's social locus has a determining effect on one's consciousness and theologizing. For instance, he agrees with the diagnosis of Boff and Segundo that other christological discourses (for instance, those concerned with demythologizing christology) are meaningless in Latin America. What is needed rather is a de-ideologization of christological discourses; they must be liberated from their ideological captivity. He writes:

> Christ's demythologization is important . . . but more urgent in

> Latin America is his rescue from manipulation and connivance
> with idols. Demythologization is important because without it
> Christ remains dangerously abstract and ideal; but it is insufficient
> unless it leads to Christ's rescue from manipulation . . . More
> urgent than Christ's demythologization, therefore, will be his
> 'depacification . . .' Christ must not be forced to leave reality in
> peace. . . . The most profound crisis to which Latin American
> christology must respond, then, lies not along the lines of pure
> demythologization, but along those of the rescue of Christ from
> appropriation as the alibi for indifference in the face of the misery
> of reality and especially as an excuse for the the religious justifi-
> cation of this misery. (Sobrino 1987, 58-59).

I quote Sobrino at length to show that although he never uses the word
"ideology," he clearly accepts as valid the analysis of the sociologists of knowledge
that consciousness is ideologically conditioned. One need only reflect on some of his
statements above to see that, in his view, ideology in christological discourse is a major
hindrance to effective liberation. He argues that christological discourse is captive to
"manipulation" and must be "rescued," that some of these discourses are "in conniv-
ance with idols," i.e., collaborating with false gods (perhaps destructive values and
institutions) that "shape reality" (p. 59) and consume victims. These discourses have
"pacified" Christ so that those who follow Him "leave reality in peace." Furthermore,
these discourses have provided an "alibi" or "excuse" for not changing that oppressive
reality; they provide the Church with an alibi for allowing the continued "worship" of
"idols" which consume millions of victims. Sobrino uses many metaphors, and does
not specify discourses by name or source, but his meaning is clear: these discourses
legitimate oppressive realities and so they must be deconstructed to recover their
liberative significance.

So far I have been referring largely to the discourses coming from academia, but
some liberation theologians also point out that christological discourse coming from
the people must also be deconstructed because of their lack of a critical perspective on
society. These popular christologies, with their verbal and nonverbal discursive
elements, are equally ideological, in that they reinforce the status quo in various ways.
The Protestant João Dias de Araújo identifies five images of Christ that verbally or
nonverbally communicate attitudes of indifference or resignation in the face of
injustice: (1) a dead Christ, (2) a distant Christ, (3) a powerless Christ, (4) a Christ who
inspires no respect, and (5) a disincarnate Christ (Dias de Araújo 1984). The dead
Christ can be seen in the crucifixes present everywhere in Brazil (and in all Latin
America), the message of which, says de Araújo, "has been a great generator of the

fatalism and conformism that are so deeply rooted among the people." The distant Christ is symbolized by the Christ of the Andes situated on a mountain peak. This image both reveals and communicates the irrelevance of Christ to the lives of the people; he is absent from their spirituality, his place having been "taken over" by saints and spirits. That Christ is seen as powerless is evident from the pamphlets the people read and from their actual practice. Saints and charismatic figures are seen by the people as having power and are petitioned in their prayers. Jesus, however, is weak and needs the help of others. The Christ who inspires no respect is communicated through the prevalent profanation of Christ's name and image; crucifixes and pictures of Christ are found in bars, houses of prostitution, gambling establishments, and even on syphillis cures. Finally, the disincarnate Christ is revealed in the Catholic devotion to the saints and in the Protestant emphasis on Christ's divinity. Latin American Catholics seem to view the saints as more human than Jesus who is seen as "out of touch" with human life. Latin American Protestants, for their part, so stress Christ's deity to the neglect of his humanity that unwarranted Platonic dichotomies are created which see only the spiritual and heavenly as good and all that is material and earthly as evil. The earthly, therefore, is to be forsaken.

All of these images communicate essentially one message: Christ cannot change anything in this earthly realm. Clearly, then, these discourses, these images, are serving to sustain oppression by engendering in the people a consciousness of resignation and indifference. Liberation theologians, therefore, see the need of deconstructing these discourses that are being communicated through popular piety.

One of the most convincing arguments for the deconstruction of popular christological discourses because of their ideological character is made by Georges Casalis, in the essay, *"Ni Vencido, ni monarca celestial,"* "Neither defeated, nor celestial monarch" (Miguez-Bonino 1985, 72-76). In this essay, Casalis criticizes the popular christology that, on the one hand, depicts Jesus as beaten, tortured, and hanging on the cross and, on the other hand, depicts him as the Santo Niño dressed in royal robes, bearing a crown and a royal scepter. These images of Jesus serve to perpetuate and legitimate two complementary ways of thinking: first that suffering and death are part and parcel of the life of Latin Americans (after all not even Jesus, the Son of God, was able to escape suffering and a tragic death), and secondly, that authoritarianism, the totalitarian state, wealth and power are legitimated by God since God himself, in the figure of the Santo Niño, enjoys the wealth and power, the pomp and circumstance which he so *deserves*. In the defeated Jesus, says Casalis, "All discover a reason for resigning themselves to their lot, for accepting their destiny as a defeated and beaten people. The essence of such a religion is passivity in the face of misfortune and evil—acceptance of life as it is" (Miguez-Bonino 1985, 73). In the monarchical Jesus, the ruling class has a symbolic "minister of propaganda" legitimating the "governments that govern by authoritarianism and torture." The christology that

Casalis calls for is "a christology of a suffering servant who suffers because he fights" (Miguez-Bonino 1985, 76).

So christology, in order to be liberating must itself be liberated from ideologies. This is what Segundo argues in his work *The Liberation of Theology* and what Casalis echoes above with respect to christology. But taking the assumption (revealed by sociology of knowledge) that a non-ideological stance is impossible, liberation theologians argue that it is not enough to de-ideologize christology, it must also be re-ideologized; it must be made clear to the people that Jesus "suffers *because he fights*" (italics mine), because of his political praxis, because of his subversiveness. The ideologies of resignation and authoritarianism must be replaced with an ideology of revolutionary subversiveness. A christological discourse is needed, therefore, that will bear the stamp of this subversive ideology. That is the subject of our next chapter.

Notes

1. Historicism makes itself evident in various ways in the works of those formally trained in theology. In the base communities, where liberation theology is also produced, the people view and approach the Scriptures, the Church's dogma, and Christian ethics less critically and more freely than the professional theologians (Mesters 1980).

2. For discussion on the limits and weaknesses of the historical-critical method and the need to move beyond it see (Oden 1990, 109-38), (Maier 1977), (Glebe-Möller 1989, 5-20), (McKnight 1988, 22, 67-109).

3. "Praxis" as it is understood today by liberation theologians is certainly not what Karl Marx meant by it. Latin American theologians use it as a generic term for any activity, including their own theological activity, the aim of which is the liberation of the oppressed. "Praxis" is used almost as a synonym for "experience." Marx used the term in a narrow economic and materialist sense to refer specifically to the activity of the proletariat. Activity (and even *opinion* (Min 1989, 72)) *on behalf of* the oppressed is called "praxis" by liberation theologians, but Marx limited the term only to the activity *of* or *by* the oppressed themselves (Ellul 1988, 101-03, 131-33).

4. Structuralism, unlike the historical-critical method, presupposes a transcendental horizon that bridges the past and the present; what Claude Lévi-Strauss calls "*bricolage*," the capacity of human beings to mediate binary oppositions through sign-systems such as myths. Structuralism avoids the relativist pitfalls of the historical-critical method because, as Terry Eagleton points out, "Structuralism . . . was hair-

raisingly unhistorical: the laws of the mind it claimed to isolate—parallelisms, oppositions, inversions and the rest—moved at a level of generality quite remote from the concrete differences of human history." These laws were "universal, embedded in a collective mind which transcended any particular culture" (Eagleton 1983, 109). Gottwald, who in his sociological exegetical method revises the historical-critical method by using new reference points (social as opposed to political and religious), hints at adopting structuralism's presupposition: "if structural criticism of texts presupposes a constantly structured and structuring human mind . . . sociological data will at least appear as instances of this unitary mind at work, parallel in a sense with literary instances of that mind. This outlook could provide a harmonizing of the two kinds of structures." (McKnight 1988, 112, n. 32) It could also provide the common horizon necessary to bridge the past and the present.

5. Cf. *Gaudium et Spes*, n. 22, n. 38, n. 42.

6. Leonardo Boff writes in *Faith on the Edge*, "Church groups must seek connections with other social groups whose aim, like ours, is structural change and the liberation of the oppressed" (Boff 1989, 64).

7. As we said in the previous chapter, liberation theologians do not view Jesus as ontologically divine, i.e., as *being* divine, but rather as realizing or unfolding his divinity through praxis, a view which dovetails nicely with Hegel's concept of human being as "finite, self-conscious spirit" and of Jesus as one "who could not deny [his] feeling of selfhood" nor objectify "his own absolute self as an external deity" (Tucker 1972, 39-40). In other words, Jesus was the one human being who self-consciously realized the absolute, the divine, within himself.

8. Sobrino writes: "Jesus does not constitute the moral standard for his disciples because he incarnates vague or generic moral values, however lofty they might be. Jesus serves as the moral standard through the concrete history whereby he turns those values into reality" (Sobrino 1978, 123).

9. To liberation theologians New Testament christologies and conciliar chris-tologies (creeds) are useful in providing limits of what may be said about the historical Jesus. Creeds are only "limit statements" (Sobrino 1978, 316-37). But such a view is not made necessary by a historicist assumption applied to these christologies in the first place. For instance, just because the early Church equated the historical Jesus with God as a result of the influence of its own socio-historical circumstances, does not mean that today—living under different socio-historical circumstances—these dis-courses from the past are no longer meaningful to human experience and can only

function as limits in theologizing. More importantly, such limit statements bear witness to the attempt by Christians throughout history to define the boundaries of the experience—the existential encounter—that each one had with Jesus of Nazareth. Such statements, then, are more than limit statements. They are confessional statements; they not only define what *can* be said about Jesus of Nazareth, they define what *must* be said of Jesus of Nazareth by any one who claims alleigance to him.

10. Clodovis Boff distinguishes between two types of theology, both of which are necessary forms of reflection: first theology, the focus of which are those transcendent realities which are commonly viewed as the proper content of theology (God, Christ, Salvation, Sin), and second theology, which is concerned with theologizing about the concrete aspects of existence such as a theology of marriage or of work or of politics or of economics or of play. Liberation theology should be considered a "second theology," a theology of the political. (Boff 1987)

11. Sobrino, for instance, writes: "Another source for Christology today is the life and praxis of the specific church community" (Sobrino 1978, xx). Boff, as well, sees the necessity of of utilizing the traditions and doctrines of the Church. He writes: "The only proper and correct theology . . . will be one developed first in view of a good and relevant cause, and then, through all the methodological rigor, following the rules of theological discourse and in respect for reality, the Bible, sacred tradition, the magisterium, theological reason, the *sensus fidelium* . . . , and so on" (Boff 1989, 51).

12. Segundo appears to have been influenced by Althusser's views and tries to relate Gregory Bateson's *Steps to an Ecology of Mind* (especially his concepts of entropy and negentropy) to the lack of reflexivity in human thinking and valuing, and consequently, the conservatism evident in Catholic theology.

CHAPTER 4

THE IDEOLOGICAL RECONSTRUCTION OF CHRISTOLOGY

In the previous chapter we discussed how liberation theologians, in order to create a liberating christological discourse, must first deconstruct traditional discourses or narratives about Jesus Christ. This required the presumption of three hermeneutical criteria: historicism, the priority of praxis, and ideological suspicion. In the ideological presumption, we said, liberation theologians assume the pejorative sense of the word in order to point out the forms of false consciousness engendered by other christological discourses. But liberation theologians also hold a positive view of ideology; the concept is also utilized in its positive sense to develop a relevant christology.

Raymond Geuss defines ideology in the positive sense as the invention, construction, creation of that "set of attitudes and beliefs which would best enable" the members of a group "to satisfy their wants and needs and further their interests" (Geuss 1981, 22-23). Geuss's definition of ideology in its positive sense is very broad and could very well refer to a world-view or outlook.

Jorge Larrain gives a more detailed description of this notion of ideology. He says it refers to a system of opinions, values, and knowledge which are connected with certain class interests and whose cognitive values may vary. In this view distortion is not of the essence of the concept of ideology. Ideology can be scientific or non-scientific. The determinative factor is "the specificity of class interests which condition knowledge." In other words, if the ideology is proletarian and revolutionary it can be considered "scientific," whereas if it is bourgeois it is considered non-scientific (Larrain 1979, 172).

Taking both of these definitions together we can analyze what liberation theologians claim. They grant epistemological privilege to the oppressed, meaning that the oppressed can see reality for what it is, that their knowledge is not distorted. That is why the liberation theologians take as their starting point for theologizing (creating a christological discourse) the locus of the oppressed and their praxis, for it provides an undistorted epistemological locus for reflection.

Furthermore, this reflection on the Scriptures must be mediated through another discourse, what the Boffs call a "socio-analytic mediation." Theological reflection on praxis is mediated through Marxist social analysis (sociological discourse), grounding this theological reflection on a "scientific" view of Latin American reality. Christological discourse, in other words, must not only be liberated from those ideologies which legitimate oppression, it must be re-ideologized so as to make it into a discourse that facilitates effective social liberation. Christological discourse must engender those attitudes and beliefs which would best enable the oppressed "to satisfy their wants and needs and further their interests" (Geuss 1981, 22). Ideology (in the positive sense), then, serves as the tool that makes possible the creation of a liberating christology.

We will first examine how Boff, Segundo, and Sobrino conceive of ideology in this positive sense and then offer a critique of this process of re-ideologization.

Positive Concepts of Ideology

Leonardo Boff's Positive Concept of Ideology

In *Church, Charism, and Power*, Boff, citing and agreeing with Heinrich Schlier, writes:

> The Church lives in the measure that it continually decides to accept the divine decision in confronting the decisive challenges of history. It is in this way that Christian faith is constantly incarnated in the world, in ideas, ideologies, and customs. (Boff 1985, 73)

Here Boff is not using the word "ideologies" in the negative sense of false consciousness for he is prescribing what the Church ought to be. Faith is incarnated; it becomes real in ideologies, when the Church gets historically involved. The question, of course, is which ideology best incarnates the faith as the Church becomes historically engaged. Boff uses the plural, "ideologies," but does he have any particular ideology in mind? Does he consider any one ideology best at incarnating the faith?

We find the answers to these questions as we examine his view of which christological discourse is truly liberating.

> Confronted with this situation [of underdevelopment], some groups of Christians have become more consciously aware and have reacted to it ... Two basic reactions can be noted ... and they have generated two corresponding Christologies centered around the

image of Jesus Christ Liberator. One effort attempts to work through the sensible realm of lived experience in christological terms; the other effort attempts to deal with the realm of thought and analysis in christological terms. (Boff 1978b, 269)

The first effort Boff calls a "Socio-analytical Articulation of Liberation Christology" and the second, a "'Sacramental' Articulation of Liberation Christology." Although he sees both articulations as valid in "rescuing the practice of the faith . . . from its traditional historical cynicism" (p. 269), he clearly prefers the "socio-analytical articulation." The "Sacramental Articulation" in his view, "does not propose a line of strategy or a set of tactics. It does not offer any concrete definitions of goals because it is not guided by an analysis of the situation or a consideration of viable pathways to liberation. Its praxis is basically pragmatic." He adds that this type of christological discourse is of limited value because "it does not broach any social analysis, [and so] it has little political force or impact" (p. 271). The Sacramental christological discourse, therefore, as we pointed out in the previous chapter, is faulty on the grounds of praxiological efficacy.

Boff prefers a christology mediated through a socio-analytic discourse because such analysis enables the theologian to detect:

the mechanisms that generate . . . [the] scandalous poverty [of Latin America] and to elaborate a praxis that is liberative and effective. . . . If we are to arrive at a praxis that will achieve its goals, there must first be as careful an analysis as possible of the mechanisms that produce social iniquity. . . . This second brand of Christology undertakes such an analysis, and hence I consider it liberative in the real and strict sense. (Boff 1978b, 272)

The theologian must make a determinate choice of a socio-analytic theory to detect these mechanisms of oppression, and, presuming the conditioning which class interests play on consciousness, it is necessary that such a choice proceed from a locus of commitment and involvement with the oppressed classes. The ideological presumption we discussed previously operates as the criterion of discrimination in the choice of a socio-analytic theory, a positive ideology. According to Boff:

Every intervention of theology in the social arena . . . presupposes some underlying sociological theory. It may be a theory held unthinkingly or spontaneously; or it may be a truly critical theory. . . . A spontaneous or intuitive reading . . . tends to reinforce the status quo and to prevent one from articulating a theology or a Christology of liberation. So we are forced to ask ourselves which

> social theory is to be used to articulate a liberation Christology. .
> . . The choice of an explanatory theory of society usually entails
> criteria that are not exclusively concerned with objectivity and
> rationality; they also have to do with the underlying option of the
> analysts and their social place or setting. All reflection on human
> reality is guided by a basic underlying "project," i.e., a "utopia"
> that some group fashions and then uses to project its own future.
> Such a project or utopia is not merely ideological; it is also based
> on social and material conditions. . . . We can identify two such
> kinds of projects and associate them with two different sets of
> advocates. One project is that of the dominant classes of society;
> the other is that of the dominated. (Boff 1978b, 273)

In choosing a positive ideology with which to mediate his christological discourse,
therefore, it is imperative that the theologian be committed to the project or "utopia"
of the dominated classes.

Boff distinguishes between two types of social analyses or sociologies: the
functionalist, which is preferred by the dominant classes because it stresses balance
and equilibrium, and the dialectical, which is preferred by the dominated classes
because it stresses struggle or conflict and sees society as full of contradictions. He
adds that the discernment of the Christian faith:

> goes further to determine which type of analysis ties in better with
> the demands of a faith that is to be fleshed out in practice. Faith will
> guide our choice toward the socio-analytical framework that is
> best at discovering the mechanisms that generate injustice, that
> offers us suitable means for overcoming them, and that does most
> to foster the notions of brotherhood and participation. Thus
> liberation Christology presupposes an option for the dialectical
> approach to social analysis and for the revolutionary "project" of
> the dominated. (Boff 1978b, 274)

Boff assumes the validity of the primary insight of the sociology of knowledge, that
all thinking, consciousness, or knowledge is socially constructed and, depending on
whose social construction it is, such knowledge can serve to legitimate or subvert the
material relations which prevail. Boff, therefore, assumes that christology, being a
noetic construct, is also conditioned by the social circumstances and can, therefore,
legitimate or subvert the socio-economic relations:

> Every Christology is relevant to its particular social and historical
> circumstances. In other words, [every] Christology is socially

engaged and committed. . . . The real question, then, is not *whether*
a particular kind of Christology is partisan or engaged, but *to whom
and to what* this particular kind of Christology is committed and
engaged. (Boff 1989, 120)

Since all christologies are partisan or ideological, it is necessary to have the
"right" ideology; one must be committed to the "right" (as in "righteous") side, one
must identify in action and reflection with the oppressed class, so that christology
will not function to justify oppression but to justify liberation, so that christology
will not function to protect the oppressors but to conscientize or radicalize the
oppressed.

At this point the distinction between socio-analytic theory and ideology
becomes blurred, for if "ideology" is conscious or unconscious partisanship, then *that*
socio-analytic theory is but the "scientific" ratio and justification of those partisan
options. The choice of socio-analytic theory is the choice of the model or paradigm
into which the "facts" of experience can best be fitted or correlated, and which can best
give the experience some coherent meaning. In other words, the ideology or the socio-
analytic theory makes possible a narrative about the Latin American social reality by
which Latin Americans can comprehend and give meaning to their social existence.
That socio-analytic theory, for Boff, is Marxism (Boff 1989, 77-78).

Boff makes very clear that it is as a method of social analysis, rather than as a
philosophy or political program, that he aims to use Marxism to mediate his christological discourse. Its virtue lies in its scientific capacity to reveal the "truth of things,"
and must be regarded as an instrument provided by the God of Truth (Boff 1989, 75).
What exactly is *scientific* about Marxism? Boff answers that it is the theory of
historical materialism which is most helpful in mediating a liberative christological
discourse. He contends that Marxist historical materialism "is a valid scientific theory
and can help Christians acquire a better knowledge . . . of social reality, especially the
conflicts of that reality, together with its mechanisms of popular marginalization"
(Boff, 1989, 76-77). By "scientific" Boff certainly does not mean empirically
verifiable but uses the word in the Marxist sense of "fundamental theory" or
fundamental knowledge (Ricoeur 1986, 103).

Boff appears to disregard the reductionist assumptions of historical materialism
(Coste 1985) and the possible incompatibility of those assumptions with Christian
faith and the contradiction this entails for his own affirmations. What do I mean?
Historical materialism asserts that the movement of history can be explained in terms
of the changes in the material relations. Clearly Boff holds a different notion of
historical materialism than what orthodox Marxism has maintained throughout its
theoretical history, otherwise he would have to deny the involvement of God (or the
transcendent) or the influence of any other non-material factor (such as ideas or values)
in history.

Boff espouses a revisionist Marxist conception of historical materialism since he gives some autonomy to the superstructural elements of social reality (Boff 1989, 76). Boff nowhere explicitly tells his audience which thinker is the source for his views on historical materialism (in fact, Boff may be combining the thought of such neo-Marxist philosophers as Ernst Bloch, Louis Althusser, and Jürgen Habermas) but it is clear that he sees "historical materialism" as "science" and so as *the* theory which provides the fundamental knowledge of Latin American reality. All other explanatory theories are ideological in that they fail to penetrate to the real basis of Latin America's problems, which is "the interplay of productive forces and productive relations" (Ricoeur 1986, 104). Historical materialism is for Boff the *only* theory that provides *real* understanding of the Latin American infrastructure. Christological discourse, therefore, in order to be relevant to the problems of Latin America and to harmonize with scientific truth, must be mediated through the analytical categories of historical materialism.

Boff's claim, however, that historical materialism provides a truly *scientific* analysis of the historical phenomena of Latin America and, therefore, that it can serve as a proper socio-analytic mediation for christological discourse is debatable. For instance, Paul Ricoeur makes a criticism of Louis Althusser's views that is equally applicable to Boff: that the "scientific analysis" provided by historical materialism is mechanistic since the real basis of history or social phenomena is not lifeless material/ economic factors but "real individuals in determinate or definite conditions," and that historical and social "phenomena are better understood in the framework of motivation than of causation" (Ricoeur 1986, 106).

There are other incoherences in the appeal to *historical materialism* as *the* scientific tool for social analysis of which Boff and other liberationists do not take account. Jacques Ellul presents several criticisms of Fernando Belo's materialist hermeneutic of texts which can certainly be applied to Boff's materialist hermeneutic of history and society. First, historical materialism denies a "God" intervening in history; "Scientifically, one cannot relate a given action or event to God" (Ellul 1988, 97). The presumption of such methodological atheism, however, is not unique to Marxism nor is such materialism the exclusive domain of dialectical sociologies; functionalist sociologies are materialist analyses in this sense as well. Second, Boff opts for historical materialism (Marxism) because it explains historical processes on the basis of economics. Ellul contends, however, that "Explaining history on the basis of economics has become a commonplace" (Ellul 1988, 97). In other words, taking account of economic factors in explaining historical and social processes has become common practice for all historians and sociologists, whether Marxist or bourgeois. Third, Boff opts for historical materialism (Marxism) because it sees society as characterized by class relationships and class struggle and so corresponds to the Latin American reality more adequately than other theories. But such a view of society is neither necessarily materialist nor Marxist. Ellul points out that "Before Marx affirmed this, A. Turgot (1727-81) used the idea and these terms to explain societal change . . . " (Ellul 1988, 97).

This socio-analytic discourse by Boff, therefore, is not coherent. It claims to be materialist, when in fact there is nothing in it that could be called materialist analysis. Boff proclaims it to be a *scientific* discourse, but is better characterized as a *mechanistic* discourse since it does not take into account human agency, motivations, traditions, and values and proceeds from non-material effects to search only for material causes. Such a discourse is hardly capable of grasping the complexity of the problem of economic disparity in Latin America.

J. L. Segundo's Positive Concept of Ideology

Segundo views ideology as an anthropological dimension; it is the mediation of "faith," the means by which that faith is concretized. He avers that ideologies are "all systems of means, be they natural or artificial, that are used to attain some end or goal . . ." (Segundo 1984, 27). Human beings, then, choose ideologies in an allegedly value-free and objective way, as "how-to" plans or projects for the realization of values. For Segundo:

> Every technique, every methodology, every science, everything that proposes to be effective and to master facts, is part of an objective experience of a system by which we believe we have grasped the real, however precarious our knowledge may be. Thus ideology connotes . . . a vision of things that claims to be objective: i.e., nonvaluational. (Segundo 1984, 16)

He defines ideology very narrowly as "all human knowledge about efficacy (or effectiveness)" and adds that "this type of knowledge always arises in subordination to values, or to satisfactions. So understood, an ideology never provides . . . a meaning-structure (or, a scale of values, a life-meaning)" (Segundo 1984, 27).

By making ideology an anthropological dimension of life Segundo hopes to show that a leftist ideology, socialism in particular, is best for the working out of the Kingdom because the humanistic values the ideology seeks to establish most closely correspond to the values of Christianity.

Segundo's conception of ideology is especially problematic for christology, for if Jesus Christ fully shared in our humanity, i.e., if he was fully human, then he must have had "faith" (something which theologians like Boff and Sobrino, for instance, readily affirm). If he had "faith" then that faith had to be mediated through ideology.

If Jesus then had an ideology for the concretization of his faith, what was it? And if we could discover what Jesus' ideology was, then why is it not normative for Christians? In what sense can Jesus be a norm for Christians, if they are not supposed to follow Jesus in all things, both in his faith and in his means [ideology]? Are not liberation theologians making a disjunction between Jesus' faith and means, and saying that the faith is what ought to be followed while not the means because of Jesus' historicity? And if they aver that Jesus had no ideology (in Segundo's sense), then is not Jesus being made less than human? [the Docetic heresy]

Segundo argues that Jesus cannot be the sole source of "faith," that appeal to Jesus as God's revelation (God's Word) will not suffice to find answers to our modern problems.

> As reality and its unforeseeable twists and turns increasingly relativize every attempt to give ready-made, conclusive solutions to the problems of one's values, one sees the growing importance of having faith in people who have learned how to learn as they lived their lives and moved from one problem to the next. . . .

> [When we have matured] it will normally no longer be possible for one single person to serve as the basis or trustee of our own "faith." We know that even the most perfect human being is limited, even if only by virtue of the circumstances in which he or she has to live. However rightly and creatively that person may have lived, he or she was forced to set aside problems that were alien to his or her own culture, age, and personal abilities.

> Jesus was no exception to this rule. . . . he did not confront the problems and tasks facing a Christian today. Hence Jesus did not present himself as the *one solitary* revelation of God, his Father.

> In reality Jesus identified himself with a "tradition," a specific history. It entailed a long series of referential witnesses to certain values , a process involving defeats, victories and retreats. Jesus made clear his continuity with a group of human beings who were deeply united in their anthropological "faith" and who found support in each other for the task of *learning how to learn*. (Segundo 1984, 75-76)

Elsewhere Segundo points out that "Jesus adheres to a history of human beings who learned how to learn by looking to the experience of others for support. . . . Neither in the tradition nor in Jesus himself does the 'divine' show up as some 'pure,' extrinsic element. Instead it shows up as the very quality of the values in each witness and in the tradition as a whole" (Segundo 1984, 82). Christologically, this means that Jesus does not reveal some *unique* set of values or meaning-structure for human life, unknown up to that point in history.

This has serious christological and soteriological implications, particularly in defining the uniqueness of what Jesus reveals, and relatedly his *singular* significance for human beings. Jesus is no more "divine" than Isaiah or Jeremiah. What is "divine" are the values to which Jesus, like Isaiah and Jeremiah before him, bore witness. Jesus is simply one among a succession of witnesses that pointed human beings to transcendent ("divine") values through their very lives. "Divinity," therefore, is an intrinsic part of the lives of all these witnesses and not a quality unique to Jesus.

Ethically, the quote above means that "ideologies," the means of actualizing that "tradition" or "meaning structure" or "values" or "faith" to which Jesus bore witness, are negotiable. What is required of the moral agent, therefore, is the identification of those transcendent values and thereafter he or she can choose whatever ideology best enables (with the greatest economy of energy) the realization of those values. The ideologies are negotiable because Segundo sees them as historically conditioned; they are the products of particular historical circumstances and conditions, and consequently, they are untransferable to other circumstances and conditions. The ideology which Jesus implemented in realizing his values is a product of his time and hence cannot simply be transferred into some other time and culture. We see here how the historicist presumption is intimately linked to praxis and ideology in Segundo's thought. He states:

> Jesus had a concrete, historical, human destiny. He worked with human hands (65:22) in the construction of the kingdom [i.e., he used an ideology to realize his values] . . . The means which Jesus used to reveal the Father to us . . . bear the stamp of history and its irreversibility. In short they bear the stamp of any and every "ideology." (Segundo 1985, 165)

Ideologies, therefore, are of transitory and relative value.

It is not enough to recognize the relativity of these ideologies, however, for according to Segundo, there is the danger that the Church will remain passive—not doing anything in expectation of the eschatological "absolute," the Kingdom of God. These relative ideologies must be absolutized, for: "Far from *relativizing* any given present, the eschatological aspect of any Christian theology *links that present to the absolute*. Absolutization is necessary for all effective human mobilization" (Segundo 1979, 256).

Does Segundo have any specific ideology in mind as to what should be absolutized *today* in Latin America? He is critical of Marxism on various counts, but nevertheless argues that the Church cannot claim neutrality but must opt for the political left. Ideologies of the left share with the Church a "not-yet," utopic sensitivity to history that makes openness to the future and experimentation with systemic arrangements possible (Segundo 1979, 257).

It should be clear by now that, unlike Boff, Segundo does not write about mediating christological discourse through a particular social analysis or ideology. Ideology is not a means of revealing the truth of social reality, but a means for concretizing values. Also unlike Boff, Segundo notes the problematic aspects of appealing to historical materialism as a tool of social analysis. He argues that historical materialism cannot simply be viewed as a "science" but is also a "faith," since there are transcendent values that are implicitly connected with the method of analysis. "Historical materialism" must be conceived and implemented as the revisionist Marxists understand the term, for otherwise it is philosophically and practically inconsistent. "Historical materialism" must leave room for "spiritual" aspects of production (such as intentionality); it must give some degree of autonomy to the superstructure, otherwise efforts at consciousness-raising would be futile. It is only by granting a relative autonomy to the superstructure, by positing some transcendent values, that Marx could avoid the paradoxical annihilation of his vision for society (his utopia) by his own method.

All of the above can also be said of Boff's use of historical materialism as "science." If the ideology (the system of means) is going to mediate successfully christological discourse, then such "science" must smuggle in a set of transcendent values that correspond with the transcendent values held by the Historical Jesus. Segundo argues that the set of transcendent values (the "faith") which Marx and Jesus sought to realize through their respective ideologies was a humanism. These humanistic values must be "smuggled in" because the dialectic of history, historical materialism, does not provide evaluative criteria for directing praxis toward the most liberating outcome (Segundo 1984, 218). These scientific methods do not provide values to guide praxis or judge what constitutes liberation. The evaluative criteria have to come from elsewhere, i.e., from anthropological faith.

Segundo finds the basis for this *modus operandi*, i.e., for the absolutization of relative means/systems/ideologies, in the *modus operandi* of Jesus himself. He sets the pattern: he opts and acts without giving guarantees of long-term outcomes, and it is in that opting and acting that the Kingdom of God makes itself present. Jesus, argues Segundo, absolutizes relative anticipations of the Kingdom (deeds like healing and raising the dead) calling them "salvation," knowing full well that those healed would get sick again and those raised would one day die (Segundo 1979, 255-56).

Thus socialism, a relative ideology, may very well be the project to be absolutized and realized by Christians in Latin America, but there is no point in asking that guarantees be given as to the sort of shape this socialism will take. Like Jesus, Christians are to see and make the Kingdom present *now* in and through praxis in the here-and-now, regardless of what changes may occur in the future because of the vicissitudes of history. To conceive of the Kingdom as an "eschatological reserve" that relativizes all human accomplishments (as do the Political theologians Metz and Moltmann, for instance) can only lead the oppressed into an acceptance of the status quo or, at best, half-hearted efforts at social transformation. Only when one sees one's action as actually realizing or *causing* the realization of the Kingdom does one's action seem truly worthwhile, i.e., as having transcendent worth. Otherwise one remains in a state of existential *angst*, seeing every human effort as nothing but "spitting into the wind."

The question is, however, why does Segundo appeal to Jesus as the warrant for this *modus procedendi* if Jesus is just one referential witness among many to a set of transcendent (humanistic) values? Wherein lies his uniqueness, which is the presupposition for his normativity? Why does Segundo make Jesus' approach (his *modus procedendi*) normative, if he is but a referential witness in the tradition of the prophets?

In Segundo's antichristology, Christian and non-Christian alike find the Historical Jesus interesting or appealing because he holds the same humanistic values, the same anthropological faith, as they. In fact, it is the commonality of values, the humanism which these values embody, that makes it possible for Christian and Marxists to work together for the transformation of society. Marxism and Christianity are but two ideologies, two systems of means, seeking to concretize a similar set of humanistic values. Humanism is the anthropological faith.

The problem is, however, that this humanistic faith and the values which it embodies have been variously defined throughout history. Some philosophers (J.S. Mill, and John Rawls, for instance), have valued equality over liberty as what is required for the actualization of true Human Being; others (Immanuel Kant and Robert Nozick) have valued liberty over equality. In short, this "faith" is historically conditioned and subject to ideological distortion. This "faith"—what it means to be truly human—has been defined in a variety of ways throughout history, usually to serve the interests of the defining parties. This means that there are a variety of humanisms, a variety of anthropological faiths.

To claim, therefore, that Christianity is compatible only with Marxism or ideologies of the left is sheer nonsense, for ideologies of the middle or of the right seek to concretize humanistic values as much as ideologies of the left. "Developmentalism," for instance, is an ideology (a system of means) for concretizing a humanism. "Humanism" is not the exclusive province of the left. The crucial questions are, then, why should a leftist ideology be preferred over a middle or a rightist ideology? In the plurality of ideologies, why is one ideology preferable over another? Secondly, what criteria are going to be used in the selection of the ideology? Clearly, seeking a correspondence in humanistic values will not be an adequate criterion since all "faiths" are in one sense or another "humanistic."

We see, then, that despite all of his tortuous meanderings in *Faith and Ideologies*, Segundo leaves Christians no better off in terms of understanding their ideological options in the face of injustice. They are left asking, "Which system of means should we employ in concretizing the faith (the humanism which we have inherited from the tradition)?" Non-Christians, however, can find in Segundo's antichristology the assurance that their options are not so far removed from Christianity and its values, although I am befuddled as to why it should matter to them in the first place.

Given the common anthropological faith which Christianity, Marxism, liberalism, and even libertarianism share [because of their humanistic values], Segundo's claim that the Church *must* opt for leftist ideologies (systems of means) (Segundo 1979) must be seen as an ideological claim (in the negative sense) that must be regarded with suspicion. Although in more recent affirmations, Segundo does demonstrate a greater degree of realism and flexibility, his basic ideological stance has not changed: he still continues to present Latin American social reality as the conflict between two ideological options: the reactionary national security state ideology (of the oppressors) legitimated by "cultural traditional Christianity" and the socialist revolutionary ideology (of the oppressed) supported by critically-minded, "philosophical" Christianity (Segundo 1984, 326-38). His realism and flexibility have not made him any more sympathetic toward middle-of-the-road reformist and conservative ideologies, and in his more recent works he simply issues caveats against those of the left who are naively hopeful, "who nurture simplistic dreams" (p. 301) of seeing all the problems of Latin America solved through a socialist revolution. Nevertheless, he believes that the Church today has but one option: a critical Christian-Marxism.

Jon Sobrino's Positive Concept of Ideology

Although Sobrino is more circumspect in appealing to a specific ideology for the mediation of the christological discourse and the actualization of the faith, he does give clear indications that Christian faith can only be actualized today through some ideology. For instance, he argues that Christians cannot simply emulate Jesus' concrete historical behavior but must actualize certain absolute values of Jesus through relative means. These values are, briefly, the Kingdom of God and its corollaries: universal reconciliation and re-creative justice (Sobrino 1978, 118-23). Those absolute values have a radical character reflected in Jesus' own praxis: a radical choice between this world or the Kingdom of God, a radical perseverance, and a radical discernment (Sobrino 1978, 127-30).

In order to choose the best means for the actualization of those values the Christian must exercise "discernment"; to follow Jesus is to live a life of discernment. What this means in terms of conduct is that there can be no *a priori* right or wrong, good or bad; right choices or good acts are discovered "along the way," in praxis, through the attempts to historicize concretely these absolute values. The means for historicizing these values are different in each historical situation; the means cannot be absolute since these must be adjustable to meet historical exigencies.

Sobrino writes that Christology, as a theoretical discipline, is subject to historical conditions; in other words, that social, political, and economic realities have a formative impact on christological reflection. Consequently, christology must take an explicit stand regarding the historical conflicts which surround it. It cannot remain neutral or claim that the Christ the discourse presents is above and beyond "the alternative of oppressors and oppressed" (Sobrino 1979, 111). The claim to neutrality is but ideological self-delusion; such a discourse is ideological (in the pejorative sense) for it clearly favors the oppressors. In order to avoid becoming pejoratively ideological, therefore, "Christology must integrate into its own discourse the real historical conditions and, accordingly, make an option for the type of christological discourse which can better unface the sin of the objective situation and better lead to its defeat according to the Kingdom of God" (Sobrino 1979, 112).

Which method of analysis will reveal and explain the objective conditions, and how this analysis is going to be integrated into christological discourse, Sobrino is very vague about. His vagueness is understandable given the life-threatening situation in which he lives in El Salvador. Any explicit reference to Marxism might very well mean a death sentence. Juan Alfaro states in the preface to Sobrino's *Jesus in Latin America* that: "In his reflection on the situation of the Latin American people, Sobrino never resorts to the Marxist analysis of society, nor does he ever draw his inspiration from any ideology alien to Christianity" (Sobrino 1987, xii). This may mean two things: either (1) social analysis is unnecessary to mediate a liberating Christological discourse, since the Gospel provides its own criteria of analysis and discernment, or (2) Sobrino does not want to give the rightist extremists any basis for accusation.

Sobrino implies that christological discourse should be mediated through some socio-analytic discourse that will enable the theologian to locate "the truth of Latin America" and place himself/herself within it in his/her theologizing, for:

> The theologian reflects not only within the church but also within
> Latin America. This may appear evident, but it is not, for what is
> at stake is a placement within the truth of Latin America. . . . The
> truth of Latin America . . . is a totality of multiple elements, which
> calls for determination of which element or elements contain a
> greater concentration of the total truth and afford a better access to

the total truth. (Sobrino 1987, 62)

It is in determining which element(s) contain a greater concentration of the total truth of Latin America (whether the religious, the political, the economic, or the cultural) where a method of analysis is needed. So it would seem that social analysis is indeed necessary. However, Sobrino is indefinite as to the method which he believes should presently be used and which would best afford access to the total truth. Whether he is vague about the method of analysis because he fears for his life or because he wants (himself and the Church) to remain open to all the possible methodologies, either reason is laudable and understandable. But whatever method of analysis is chosen and used, Sobrino is clear that it must enable the transformation of society, concretely and efficaciously, through the praxis (or discipleship) of the church. Sobrino contends that "As [the Church] allows itself to be swept along the channel of discipleship, [it] will gradually learn from within, by trial and error, which concrete mediations today bring God's kingdom near; what social, economic, and political systems render the kingdom-at-hand more illuminating" (Sobrino 1987, 96).

In comparing Sobrino with Boff and Segundo, we can conclude that he is the least ideological (in the positive sense) of the three since he does not specify a method of social analysis for the mediation of christological discourse nor prescribe a particular socio-economic arrangement to be sought. However, his own christological discourse reflects the use of certain conceptual categories that have enabled him to arrive at some discernment of the "truth of Latin America." These categories are: (1) the structural nature of injustice, (2) the priority of praxis over contemplation and the necessity of praxis for social transformation, (3) the ideological conditioning of thought, and (4) the reality of class struggle. Sobrino strives to ground these conceptual categories on christology[1] but they certainly resonate with Marxist thought.

Dangers of Ideologization

Liberation theologians, then, in order to mediate christological discourse employ ideology in the positive sense of a set of beliefs and attitudes which make possible the realization of liberation. Although some are more explicit than others, they all feel that a leftist ideology, a revisionist Marxism, is what best provides the analytical tools, i.e., the images and narratives necessary to enable the coherent understanding of the Latin American social experience for its subsequent transformation. Christology is re-ideologized; christological discourse finds itself complemented by a particular sociological discourse, a preferred sociology: Marxism. There are, however, a variety of problems and dangers in such re-ideologization.

The first problem is that there is nothing in the ideology itself that of necessity makes *it* complementary to christological discourse. If any complementarity exists, it lies in the humanistic values which both Christianity and Marxism espouse. But, as was pointed out previously, Marxism or any other leftist ideology cannot lay exclusive claim to humanistic values; every ideology, whether of the right or the left, seeks to actualize some sort of humanism as that humanism has been defined by the ideologizers. So for instance, the advocates of liberal ideology seek to establish and protect the natural (positive) rights of all individuals to life, liberty, and the pursuit of happiness—humanistic values. The advocates of libertarian ideology seek to establish and protect the natural right to non-coercion, i.e., individual liberty, as that which best enables the realization of humanity. The advocates of Marxist ideology seek to protect the basic right of the proletariat to the product of its labor. Equality, liberty, and solidarity, therefore, are humanistic values that Christianity certainly shares with all of the above mentioned ideologies. Consequently, to say that *only* Marxism is ideologically compatible with Christianity because of its humanistic values is a presumptuous and frivolous claim.

The point is that liberation theologians choose leftist ideology to mediate christological discourse, not because it *alone* allegedly enables the realization of the humanistic values it shares in common with Christianity, but rather because that is the ideology preferred by these theologians as best enabling them to realize their humanistic vision. Given their incoherent arguments for the mediation of christological discourse through a specific ideology, we can see how the resultant discourses are rhetorical narratives, but narratives that fail to meet the criteria of fidelity and coherence. Consequently, the rhetoric fails to be persuasive.

There is another problem with the liberationists' mediations of christological discourse through positive ideology and that is that this ideologization easily changes into a negative form of ideology. Raymond Geuss notes that the distinction between positive and pejorative ideology becomes blurred rather easily because "of the fact that historically satisfaction of one's interests and oppression, pursuit of a sense of identity and false consciousness have been inextricably linked. Thus the major way in which ideologies (in the pejorative sense) have traditionally maintained themselves is by harnessing what are in themselves perfectly legitimate human aspirations [humanistic values?] . . . so as to create a situation in which the agents can satisfy legitimate existential needs only on condition of accepting the repression the ideological world-view imposes" (Geuss 1981, 24-25). Thus the ideology which supposedly is only a tool for social analysis or a system of means for concretizing values can easily become a dangerous means of legitimation and repression. Segundo himself points out how liberal ideologies (like democracy) can become legitimating and repressive ideologies (Segundo 1984, 289-300). This same caveat, however, must be made concerning leftist ideologies, which Segundo does make[2] (but not very forcefully) (Segundo 1984,

300-01) but which the majority of liberation theologians do not.

Ideology in the pejorative sense is most easily communicated through narratives,[3] and thus there is the very real danger that christological discourse may unwittingly become a means for mediating a false consciousness, i.e., a distorted and distorting interpretation of reality. While liberation theologians are quick to point out this problem with regard to the traditional christologies (i.e., that they are ideological and hence must be de-ideologized), they are not as quick to point out the problem with regard to their own christological discourses. Yet the communication of pejorative ideologies through narratives appears to be a not uncommon phenomenon noted by sociologists of knowledge and sociologists of religion alike.

We can cite as an example of this phenomenon Freud's development of his psychoanalytic theory as the "scientific" explanation for conscious behavior. Gregory Baum, in his book *Religion and Alienation*, notes that Freud chose the Oedipal myth (story or narrative) as "the one single model story, one Story with a capital S, that applies to all individuals wherever they may live; and if people learn to tell their own story in dialogue with the normative story . . . they will acquire a realistic understanding of their own past and eventually experience a marvelous deliverance from the symptoms that made them suffer. . . . The Oedipal story is the salvation myth in Freudian therapy" (Baum 1975, 120-21). He goes on to note that

> Freud based the universality of the Oedipal complex not on metaphysics . . . but upon the biology of the family: He thought that being born of a woman and being nourished and protected by this woman and the man to whom she belonged would inevitably introduce the male child into the oedipal constellation. What Freud overlooked was how much the structure of the family and hence the experience of infancy and childhood depended on cultural factors and the social order. . . . Freud did not realize that by making Oedipus Rex the normative myth of human life, he excluded women from his essential imagination; the typical human being was male. (Baum 1975, 120-21)

So Freud makes the Oedipus Rex story *the* Story that explains the nature of every human being's psychic problems. He ignores those relativities in the original story and in the cultural context which would vitiate his Story, for instance the fact that the child in the myth was male, or that not all family structures are patriarchal. The crucial conclusion to which Baum arrives is that "By investing this story with universal validity, orthodox Freudian psychoanalysis becomes an ideology that subjects people to a pre-conceived image and possibly imprisons them in a false imagination" (Baum 1975, 122).

Thus here we have one example of a story, a narrative or myth, which serves to carry an ideology. Alleging to be scientific, the theorist chooses (or creates) a story that supposedly describes or explains all reality and which, therefore, has universal, absolute validity. In giving metaphysical or absolute validity to a story which has its starting point in historical, cultural relativities, the "story-teller" turns the story into a pejorative ideology. As such, the story is no longer a means of deliverance, of obtaining an accurate appraisal of oneself and of reality, but rather one that obscures self-understanding and the understanding of reality.

With the exception of Segundo, most liberation theologians, in their exclusive use of a dialectical method to interpret Latin American social reality, come danger-ously close to absolutizing their narrative or explanation of reality, and thus there is the danger of imprisoning people in a false imagination. (Not only are they in danger of turning their secular narrative into an ideology [false consciousness] by claiming scientific status for it, they are also in danger of turning their religious narrative [christological discourse] into an ideology as well. Ideology as false consciousness can occur with secular as well as with religious narratives.)

This ideological problem within religious discourse is best seen within the genre of rhetorical narrative known as the "American Jeremiad" (Bercovitch 1978). Ber-covitch defines the genre as "a ritual designed to join social criticism to spiritual renewal, public to private identity, the shifting 'signs of the times' to certain traditional metaphors, themes, and symbols" (Bercovitch 1978, 11). This seems very much what liberation theologians are doing in mediating christological discourse through a socio-analytic discourse (or are they mediating a socio-analytic discourse through christol-ogical discourse?) They seem to be engaging in a Latin American Jeremiad.

These Jeremiads, however, slip easily into forms of false consciousness as the story-tellers ignore those aspects within the original story that would call their modern "application" or re-telling into question. One such example of the American Jeremiad is the Puritans' narrative of their "Pilgrimage." The Puritans viewed themselves as being in an "Exodus" fleeing from "Pharaoh" (the king of England), being led by God into the "Promised Land," the new Jerusalem, the New World, where they would build the Kingdom of God (McCann and Strain 1985, 21-22) and where they had to show themselves faithful to the Covenant or else suffer God's judgment. The original story had its starting point in the historical and cultural relativities of the conflict between the Hebrews and the Egyptians thousands of years before. This original story is appropriated by a people in an analogous situation (but with altogether new historical and cultural relativities) who make it *their* Story. But by giving the story metaphysical status the actual relativities (both in the original story and in their own situation) are obscured and hence the Story becomes a metaphorical "carrier" for ideology. In other words, whatever would bring their Story into question (what would de-absolutize the Story) is denied, and whatever, in the original story, conflicts with their view of reality is unconsciously or consciously ignored or accommodated to fit their views. Instead the original story (now retold as their Story) becomes a warrant for the pursuit or imposition of their own self-interests, whatever these might be.

Liberation theologians do something similar with the Exodus and Jesus narratives. For liberationists, the Exodus narrative is paradigmatic of the liberation which God desires for the oppressed (Croatto 1981). Since the focus of this work, however, is the Jesus narrative or christological discourse, we will not explore how liberation theologians turn the Exodus into a rhetorical narrative in order to communicate an ideology. As for the Jesus narrative, in a previous chapter we saw that liberation theologians argue that Jesus Christ is the Trailblazer who sets before the oppressed the path to be followed (i.e., the values and virtues to be sought) in their quest for liberation. This narrative must be mediated through a socio-analytic discourse, a social science, in order for it to be efficacious in the transformation of Latin America. Hence liberation theologians are engaged in a two-fold story-telling process.[4] While the liberation theologians are not as prone to absolutize their christological narrative (because of the presuppositions used in approaching Scripture), the same cannot be said (of the majority of them) concerning their socio-analytic discourse. In spite of the claims to be using historical materialism as a tool of analysis, it is seen as the *only* tool of analysis that can rightly be called "scientific" and which can enable one to access the "truth" of Latin America. If it is claimed that there is only *one* truth about Latin America and only *one* way of getting at that truth, and that only the oppressed[5] with their epistemological privilege, and the theologians as their intellectual representatives, are able to articulate that truth or *analysis*, then that socio-analytic discourse becomes an ideology, false consciousness, since it excludes alternative analyses and closes itself off to criticism.[6]

We said in the previous chapter that liberation theologians, such as George Casalis, argue that it is not enough to de-ideologize christology, but that it must also be re-ideologized; it must be made clear to the people that Jesus "suffers because he fights" (Miguez-Bonino 1985, 76); he suffers as a consequence of his political praxis, his subversiveness. Jesus thus provides the pattern to be followed by the oppressed in their suffering. Such a christological discourse, however, illustrates the process mentioned above, i.e., that of ignoring those details in the original story which would call the implementation (the re-telling) into question. Clearly, Casalis uses loaded language—"Jesus *fights*"—but such language can be effective only if the audience is not very attentive to or very knowledgeable of the text of Scripture. When we look at the relevant details, we find that the original story and the liberationists' version of the story have little in common.

We do not want to get bogged down in the murky waters of exegetical scholarship concerning the Historical Jesus, but suffice it to say that there is a great deal of consensus among New Testament scholars that Jesus was not interested in fighting the Romans, the "party" most directly bent upon, and benefitting from, the *economic* exploitation of Palestine (Bammel 1984). Jesus does not "fight" even the direct collaborators with the Romans in this economic exploitation, the tax-collectors. In Latin America, the oppressed fight against the national security states (military juntas and wealthy elites that, with the support of First World ["center"] nations, seek to protect their common capitalist interests). In comparing the two scenarios, therefore, Jesus' "fight" is hardly analogous with the "fight" of the oppressed in Latin America, where their struggle *is* properly economic (and only secondarily religious). Those whom Jesus *does* "fight" are the Pharisees and Sadducees, but this struggle is one having to do more with religious oppression—Jesus attempting to humanize or reform Judaism—than with economic oppression. The means which Jesus employs in this fight, moreover, were certainly not the sort of means which many are calling the oppressed to employ in Latin America: Jesus hardly sought to overthrow the Pharisees from power nor did he encourage people to join the Zealots in their struggle for liberation.

All of these incongruities are of little consequence to the liberation theologians in their retelling of the story of Jesus and their intended purposes for telling it. In their view, one can simply blame those incongruities on historical relativity and set them aside. What *is* important is the symbolic depth of Jesus' unjust suffering, and that is sufficient for Jesus' story to be functionally effective. It is enough to provide a warrant for an ideology of subversiveness.

But on what basis do the liberation theologians choose this ideology of subversiveness? Do they stand on privileged intellectual high ground so that they and only they can look over the landscape of ideas and determine which ideology will be truly liberating and which will not? Instead of Jesus the Liberator, why not Jesus the Libertarian? Would not Robert Nozick's libertarian ideology with its minimal state and freedom from coercion be more liberating?[7] Would not John Rawls' liberal ideology, with its maxi-min principle of the greatest benefit for the least advantaged, be as liberating as a neo-Marxist ideology? Would not the revisionist socialism of the Christian Democrats be an option? Regrettably most liberation theologians argue that in Latin America, a liberating discourse, a liberating christology, can only be cast in terms of one "correct" ideology: neo-Marxism. This we must judge as intellectually presumptuous.

Many of the christologies of liberation, then, are as ideological, in the pejorative sense of the word, as the christologies liberation theologians criticize, for these discourses falsely lead people into pursuing a course of action, into taking a stance towards self and society, that is for the most part, the capricious choice of a few intellectuals.

Notes

1. See for instance his ten theses in "The Epiphany of the God of Life in Jesus of Nazareth" (Sobrino 1983).

2. Segundo calls for historical flexibility, employing ideologies to realize humanistic values but always attentive to any imbalance which might be brought upon the social ecology through their implementation (Segundo 1984, 308-09).

3. According to John B. Thompson, "ideology is expressed in discourse, [which] is to say . . . that it is realized in *extended linguistic constructions which display an articulated structure. . . .* Linguistic constructions may be studied, for example, as *narratives* which display a certain logic. . ." (Thompson 1984, 198).

4. Actually three narratives are being related by liberation theologians: a secular narrative (social analysis), a meta-theological narrative (theology must be changed, a new method is needed) grounded on quasi-theological assumptions (theology should be functional), and a theological narrative (liberation christology: Jesus Christ is Liberator).

5. Not all of the oppressed are articulating this "truth" or analysis since many of the poor are joining the ranks of the Pentecostals and other Protestant Fundamentalist groups, who eschew political conflict; so here the "oppressed" represented by the theologians are those which belong to the CEB's, the Ecclesial Base Communities.

6. Lest I be accused of being one-sided, it should be clear that I have no particular axe to grind against liberation theologians; the same can be said of "analyses" propounded by social scientists and religious adherents of any stripe; what I seek to encourage is an attitude of openness to the other, that truth and love are furthered not by absolutizing or propounding as unquestionable fact what is only a glimpse of the total truth, but rather that truth and love are furthered when one proceeds with humility, acknowledging that one's views are only partial and hypothetical, functional enough to be of help, but flexible enough to stand correction. Such an approach may not be as rhetorically effective—it will not mobilize people very quickly and efficiently; it will not work very well as propaganda—but it will be far more intellectually honest. Such an approach will be truer to the depth and complexity of all social phenomena and truer to the spirit of empathy and reconciliation which the Gospel enjoins.

7. One could very well defend a libertarian christology in Scripture as much as a subversive liberation christology! For instance, on entitlements, see Luke 20:24, 25 "Give to Caesar what is Caesar's and to God what is God's;" on the right to be free from coercion, John 19:9-11, "You have no power over me that was not given to you from above;" on the libertarian principle of distributive justice, "From each as they choose, to each as they are chosen," see the miracle of the woman with the issue of blood (Lk. 8:43-48), the miracle at Cana (Jn. 2:1-11), the parable of the talents (Lk. 19:11-27), and the workers who were employed late in the day (Mt. 20:1-16). The doctrines of divine sovereignty and divine election (Jn. 15:16; 17:6; Eph. 1:11) as elaborated by Calvin, for example, could serve as warrants for a libertarian ideology and the theory of entitlements: God does not grant the gift of salvation to everyone, but gives it to whom he will, out of the goodness of His grace, and cannot be called unjust for so choosing.

CHAPTER 5

THE RHETORICAL PROCLAMATION OF CHRISTOLOGY

In the previous chapter we saw how liberation theologians reconstruct christology by mediating the biblical discourse through ideology. The discourse that is reconstructed through ideology is then proclaimed to fulfill its apologetic and pastoral intents, i.e., it is proclaimed as a defense of Christian involvement in the liberation struggle and as a warrant for a Christian ethic of liberation. The liberationists' christology is therefore a rhetorical discourse: it aims to persuade (1) those who would be critical of Christian involvement in political conflict, (2) those, not yet involved, who would be undecided or debating the issue of Christian involvement, (3) those already involved who have doubts about the Christian merit of their involvement in the struggle for liberation. This rhetoric, however, must be assessed.

So far we have been assessing the *method* by which liberation theologians arrive at this rhetorical discourse; now we must examine the discourse itself. We argued at the beginning of this work that liberation theologians, in their christological discourse, are not engaged in the same sort of genre as traditional theologians are when *they* construct christologies, but rather that liberationist christologies are a form of narrative discourse. The sort of rationality employed in building traditional forms of christology is the classical form of rationality, specifically, inductive and deductive logic. In assessing the rhetoric of the liberationist christological discourse, however, we cannot use the classical rhetoric principles which themselves presuppose classical rationality. We must employ criteria appropriate to the genre, principles of narrative rationality, a narrative rhetoric. In this assessment, the work of Walter Fisher, *Human Communication as Narration: Toward a Philosophy of Reason, Value, and Action*, has provided much of the conceptual basis that I here apply to liberation christology, and thus I will be referring frequently to this work throughout the chapter.

According to Fisher the criteria for evaluating the logic of rhetorical narratives are coherence and fidelity:

> The essential components of this logic [narrative rationality] are the following. Human communication is tested against the principles of probability (coherence) and fidelity (truthfulness and

reliability). Probability, whether a story "hangs together," is
assessed in three ways: by its *argumentative* or *structural coherence*; by its *material coherence*. . . and by *characterological
coherence*. . . .

Fidelity, the truthfulness of a story, is assessed by applying
what I call "the logic of good reasons." The logic of good reasons
is a logic formed by combining the means of analyzing and
evaluating arguments offered by such writers as Toulmin, Perel-
man, and Ehninger and Brockriede with critical questions that can
locate and weigh values. These are questions about *fact, relevance, consequence, consistency,* and *transcendental issues.*
(Fisher 1989, 47-48)

We will, therefore, test the rhetoric of liberation christology against these two
principles of narrative rationality: coherence and fidelity.

The Narrative Coherence of Liberation Christology

In assessing the coherence of a rhetorical narrative one must examine its
structural coherence, its material coherence, and its characterological coherence.
Structural coherence has to do with the inner unity of the argument posed; one must
ask whether there are any internal contradictions: is the story, and the argument it
poses, self-contradictory? Does the argument "hang together?" In this regard, the
liberation theologians' christological discourse can be assessed on two separate levels:
on a methodological level and on a theological level.

Structural Coherence

Methodologically, the question is: Do the claims made about how christological
discourse should be constructed "hang together?" Do the methodological claims made
by liberation theologians such as Segundo, Boff, and Sobrino avoid self-contradic-
tion? In the previous two chapters of this work I have sought to demonstrate that the
christological discourses elaborated by most liberation theologians are methodologically incoherent in that either (1) they appeal to presumptions in deconstructing other
christologies that are not in turn applied to their own christologies or (2) in reconstruct-

ing christology, they opt for a particular ideological mediation on unconvincing warrants.

Theologically, the question is: Do the claims made about Jesus Christ hang together? On this level, we can say that liberationist discourse is internally coherent. We showed in Chapter 2 that liberation theologians relate a coherent narrative, namely that the man Jesus, through his subversive praxis, becomes divine and thus sets the pattern for Christians to follow. Thus the liberationist discourse processually interrelates praxis and divinity, challenging the internally incoherent traditional christologies that, through their ontological approach, divorce Jesus' concrete praxis from his divinity and also from his death and resurrection.

Material Coherence

In assessing the narrative's material coherence, we must ask how the liberation theologians' christological argument fares in comparison with other arguments made through other narratives. It is on this point where the weaknesses of liberation christology become evident. Liberation christology presents a Socinian-like[1] argument about the person of Jesus Christ and an Abelardian[2] argument about his significance for human beings: reflecting on the memory of his life, death, and resurrection exerts a moral influence upon one's consciousness. The liberationist christological discourse presents Jesus Christ as exerting a consciencitizing influence on the individual; Jesus shows us that oppression is to be challenged and that such a challenge will have ultimate costs (crucifixion, death) but that God is well-pleased with such gumption (as confirmed by Jesus' resurrection). The discourse proclaims and aims to effect only a subjective change in the listener.

Traditional Christianity has affirmed the christological discourse elaborated at Chalcedon and soteriologically, the narrative elaborated by Anselm which relies upon the ontological categories of the Chalcedonian formula. This traditional discourse (the Theological Code) proclaims an objective (forensic, statutory) change in the relationship between God and humanity (or in Protestant theology, the one who believes). The metaphors employed in the New Testament, for instance, to describe this work of Christ focus not so much upon the psychological changes within the believer as upon the objective changes in the relationship between humanity and God. Words such as salvation (σωτηρια), reconciliation (καταλλαγη), propitiation (ιλαστηριον), and redemption (λυτροσισ) speak metaphorically of this "before-and-after" transformation of the status of humanity before God effected through the life, death, and resurrection of Jesus Christ. In the New Testament, almost every change of attitude and every ethical injunction is enjoined on the basis of this objective change. If Jesus' pre-paschal life is normative in any sense it is by virtue of the objective efficacy of the totality of his life.

Liberation theologians, on the other hand, present the life of Jesus as if it were normative in-and-of itself, but in losing sight of Jesus' role in the celestial drama, there is little reason why his pre-paschal life should be normative at all. In the liberationist discourse, Jesus ends up being little more than a martyr, his life possessing a "structure" that is found throughout history, both before and after his particular existence: a life of witness, in word and deed, to the truth of humanistic values and a willingness to suffer and die for such a witness. If Jesus Christ reveals anything about God to humanity, it is that God approves of the faithful witness to such humanistic values.

Beginning "from below," with an ascending christology, liberation theologians have problems making soteriological affirmations as compared to those who begin with descending christologies. The reason for this is that in ascending christologies, Jesus of Nazareth is bereft of any uniqueness or ultimate significance, and so his contribution to humanity's salvation cannot be clearly discerned. Ascending christologies, like all inductive theologies, methodologically seek to exclude transcendent realities (or universals) as much as possible; there is, therefore, a tendency toward nominalism. Such was the case with Abelard, for instance, whose nominalism finally led him to an agnosticism concerning how the atonement affected God (Wells 1984, 117). Liberation theologians, by their silence on the matter, seem to evince the same sort of agnosticism concerning how God is affected by the atonement[3] and how humanity is affected in relation to the Transcendent. Whenever they do refer to salvation (or reconciliation, or redemption) as revealed through the Historical Jesus, it is existential and historical, horizontal (intra-worldly, i.e., in relation to one's fellows), and mostly self-wrought.[4] To make such claims is legitimate, for the totality of salvation includes an anthropological dimension, but it is not the totality of salvation. Salvation is bipolar, having an anthropological dimension and a theo-logical dimension, a historical dimension and an eschatological dimension. The liberationists' over-emphasis on only the anthropological/historical dimension leads to a lopsided christological and soteriological discourse.[5] Moreover, since from this perspective (i.e., beginning from below with the "Historical Jesus"), Jesus cannot be claimed to hold any particular soteriological uniqueness, there is no ultimate reason for becoming a Christian, remaining a Christian, or proclaiming Jesus as the Christ.[6]

Paradoxically, Jesus Christ is ultimately made irrelevant to liberation ethics even as the theologians seek to put him at the center of their ethical reflection. This occurs for two reasons. First, and as just noted, they implicitly deny any particular uniqueness to Jesus' life and work. By beginning their christological discourse from below and adopting a historical and existential viewpoint that sees history as one, liberationists obviate any sort of historical transcendence; the implication is that Jesus and his praxis are localized to a particular moment in history. Jesus and his praxis can only be rescued—in and for the present—as a historical memory, but not a unique memory. For liberation theologians, the remembrance of his deeds has the same efficacy as the remembrance of the deeds of various other "saints" such as Bartolomé de las Casas, Camilo Torres, Néstor Paz, and more recently Rutilio Grande, Oscar Romero, and Ignacio Ellacuría. Such remembrance provokes a greater depth of commitment to the struggle for liberation—it makes one count the cost—and it engenders a hope: that death for the sake of justice is not pointless and will find its historical vindication. This is not an insignificant result in itself, but it significantly diminishes the unique role and status accorded to Jesus by traditional christologies.

The second reason for the paradoxical irrelevancy of Jesus for ethics is that liberation theologians try to find common ground between Christian ethics and humanistic ethics. In his book *The Peaceable Kingdom*, Stanley Hauerwas points out that much of contemporary theology has had difficulty making Jesus relevant to social ethics because of the abstractionism "characteristic of both Catholic and Protestant ethics," an abstractionism which reifies such concepts as "nature" and "grace" in particular (Hauerwas 1983, 57). But moreover, these concepts are not only reified but actually "grace" is collapsed into "nature," such that the content of morality is derived from "nature." Ethics ultimately rests on an anthropological foundation. Hauerwas cites Catholic theologian Timothy O'Connell as an example of such ethics:

> ... the fundamental ethical command imposed on the Christian
> is precisely to be what he or she is. "Be human" ... Christian ethics
> is human ethics, no more and no less. .... Christians are uncondi-
> tionally humanists; that is our pride and our privileged vocation.
> (Hauerwas 1983, 56)

In such an ethics Jesus Christ is seen as the fulfillment of the human vocation, what it means to be truly human. And so he simply functions as a warrant for a natural law ethic; by his incarnation in Jesus, God declared "nature," and more specifically the "human," "good" and so a proper locus for ethical reflection. But, says Hauerwas, such a view of ethics loses "the particularity of Jesus, his historicity as God's decisive eschatological actor" (Hauerwas 1983, 56).

The issue may be restated as a point I made in an earlier chapter: if the content of morality is derived from nature through reason, then why bring Jesus into the discussion at all? Or:

> [If] Jesus is regarded as normative because He is believed to have
> experienced what it is to be human in the fullest way and at the
> deepest level. [then] Christian ethics does not and cannot add to a
> human ethical self-understanding as such any material content that
> is, in principle, strange or foreign to man as he exists and experi-

ences himself. (Hauerwas 1981, 39)

In other words, if Christ only provides a warrant for humanistic ethics, "an ethics acceptable to non-Christians, then at least in matters of content Jesus is irrelevant" (Hauerwas 1981, 39).

Liberation christology suffers from this weakness (the irrelevance of Jesus to ethics) precisely for the reasons just stated. Gustavo Gutiérrez, for instance, like O'Connell, argues in his seminal work, *A Theology of Liberation*, that in doing theology a distinction of planes (sacred-profane, nature-grace) can no longer be maintained. History, he says, is one.[7] Instead Gutiérrez argues for "a recovery of the historical and existential viewpoint" which affirms "there is but one vocation: communion with God through grace. [That] In reality there is no pure nature and there never has been; there is . . . no one who is not affected by grace" (Gutiérrez 1973, 70). The Christian's vocation, he says, is to "worldliness," which is "a necessary condition for an authentic relationship between man and nature, of men among themselves, and finally between man and God" (Gutiérrez 1973, 67). This viewpoint, therefore, makes nature into an abstraction into which "grace" is absorbed. What this means, in terms of Jesus Christ's significance for ethics, is that he is brought in *a posteriori* as the warrant for a humanistic ethic, as is evident in Gutiérrez's discussion about encountering God (grace) in history (nature):

> God is revealed in history, and it is likewise in history that men encounter his Word made flesh. Christ is not a private individual; the bond which links him to all men gives him a unique historical role. God's temple is human history. . . . We find the Lord in our encounters with men, especially the poor. . . . An act of love towards them is an act of love towards God. (Gutiérrez, 1973, 201)

Jesus Christ, then, does not provide the content for a Christian social ethic, but only the warrant. At best, in this viewpoint, Jesus functions as motivation for right conduct, but by looking to Jesus himself (as he is found in the text of Scripture) there is no way of knowing *a priori* what that right conduct might be. That action, that orthopraxis, is revealed by history itself, by the "signs of the times."

Another example is Juan Luis Segundo's christology. In his book *The Humanist Christology of Paul*, he argues at length that "faith" is an anthropological dimension, that "Faith, as understood by Paul, is compatible with the situation of any and every human being both before and after Christ" (Segundo 1986, 152). He proves this by appealing to Paul's reference to Abraham in Romans 4. The concrete content of Abraham's faith was a transcendent datum, namely that "*loving is worthwhile* , whatever it may cost in self-giving and even death" (Segundo 1986, 152). Now the content of the expression "Faith in Jesus Christ" is "the very same *transcendent datum*, accessible to all humans from the very start but this time spelled out in terms of the message, life, death, and resurrection of Jesus of Nazareth" (Segundo 1986, 152-53). Jesus Christ, therefore, does not reveal any new content to Christian ethics but is simply the best model, the warrant for, and the clearest expression of what every human being can discern from nature through reason and has been able to discern throughout all history—that loving is worthwhile.

We see, then, that the liberation story of Jesus makes him irrelevant to Christian social ethics because his story is not unique. By positing a monistic, Hegelian view of history, the possibility of Jesus being "God's decisive eschatological actor" is closed off. By employing a narrowly conceived historicism for the construction of their discourse, liberation theologians could just as well use the life of anyone else who dies for the sake of social justice as a paradigm for liberative praxis. In contrast, throughout history, Christians have claimed Jesus' life and praxis to be efficacious beyond his historical locale through their witness to an experience that is both personal and cosmic in extent; they have affirmed their belief in a *Heilsgeschichte*, a salvation history, generated from their existential encounter with Jesus Christ. But while many of these Christians have been ingenuous about the historical conditioning of their alleged common experience of personal and cosmic "salvation"—to the neglect of the social and historical implications of Jesus' life and praxis—liberation theologians, for their part, have obscured the personalist and cosmic implications of Jesus' life, death, and resurrection by taking a too narrow "historical and existential viewpoint." To the degree that Jesus is circumscribed to the historical moment in which he lived, he becomes no more than an activist and political martyr. As such his story is no different from the story of Ernesto "Che" Guevara or Mahatma Gandhi or Martin Luther King, Jr. And if the story of Jesus Christ *is* the story of "El Che" then the story of "El Che" is sufficient to generate a proper self-understanding and a liberative ethic. But while these heroic figures have generated a following, unlike Jesus of Nazareth, they have never generated a salvation history.

This liberationist christological discourse overlooks the fact that the christology of reflection that we have in the New Testament and which was subsequently dogmatized at Chalcedon (Platonic philosophy notwithstanding), was formulated on the basis of a christology of witness, a *lex orandi*, an oral body of affirmations about Jesus, that soon after his death, ascribed personal and cosmic significance to his life and work. In other words, the Christian Story was—even prior to the christology of reflection we find in the Gospels and Epistles, for instance—a story of cosmic implications, not historically localized (Hawkin 1985, 40-51). From very early on, the followers of Jesus came to the conclusion that their story was one of *cosmic* implications, launching them, and any willing to join them, on a world-wide mission to tell the "good news" to all, irrespective of nationality, gender, or social class. Because the Story was of *cosmic* significance, a community of memory (and a self-understanding) was able to form that could call into question any claim by the relative to absoluteness.

Hence the liberation story of Jesus is materially incoherent because it does not sufficiently emphasize those elements that would make this story a *Christian* Story of Jesus; i.e., it does not sufficiently maintain continuity with the christology of witness; it does not keep in tension the bipolarity of Jesus Christ's person (human-divine natures) and work (personal-social, historical-cosmic salvation).[8] In other words, liberation theology has too narrow a concept of Jesus' person and work. Throughout history, those who have told the Christian Story of Jesus have consistently claimed that its meaningfulness transcends time and place; that its efficacy is both subjective and objective, that the scope of this efficacy is not only historical, but also personal and cosmic, and that the mode of conduct to which the Story calls the hearer is closely related to the identity of Jesus of Nazareth as God's eschatological actor (i.e., the initiator and consummator of the New Covenant).

Characterological Coherence

The third element of narrative coherence that must be assessed is characterological coherence. In assessing characterological coherence we are asking whether the characters (narrators, actors) are reliable. To assess character one must look at "interpretations of the person's decisions and actions that reflect values," i.e., actional tendencies. "If these tendencies contradict one another, change significantly, or alter in 'strange' ways, the result is a questioning of character" (Fisher 1989, 47). That is, there is characterological incoherence.

The first character that must be evaluated is the "narrated Jesus," the subject of the narrative. The question that must be posed to the liberationist's story is "Does Jesus the Liberator behave characteristically?" Given the fact that in their proclamation liberation theologians presuppose that their audience will identify Jesus the Liberator with the Jesus of the Gospels—that their story is not a different story, but the same story told differently—the answer would have to be "No," for the Liberator Jesus does not cohere with the Jesus of the Gospels, particularly in the account of the Passion.

Jesus the Liberator, who identified with the poor and oppressed and challenged the systems of oppression, whose concrete historical praxis led to his being put to death as a subversive, who challenged injustice at every turn, is well-known to have remained silent before his accusers (Mt. 27:14; Lk. 23:9). Would not the Liberator seek his own liberation? How is justice served by remaining silent? How are the oppressed served by Jesus' remaining silent? Would not the Liberator encourage his followers to fight for his and their freedom? (Cf., Jn. 18:36; Lk. 22:49-53) If as Casalis states, "Jesus suffers because he fights," why does Jesus stop "fighting" from the moment of his arrest? If Jesus is the model of those who would take hold of the reins of their destinies, why do the Gospels present him as one who has surrendered himself to fate, who has made himself subject to the whims of the political and religious authorities?

The christological narrative of liberation theology does not deal convincingly with these final enigmatic actions of Jesus. Leonardo Boff, for instance, simply says that Jesus was willing to accept death rather than renounce truth, justice, and the ideal of universal brotherhood (Boff 1980, 60). That would still not explain why Jesus accepted his condemnation and death *in silence*. After all, death for truth and justice's sake can be accepted in suicide (as the Jews at Masada) or in struggle (as Che Guevara in Bolivia and Camilo Torres in Colombia).

Unless the liberation theologians are hoping, through some pedagogical magic, to demolish the implicit authority which the publicly-known Gospel story has for most Latin Americans and then write new gospels to suit their christological discourse, in order to effectively proclaim Jesus Liberator, liberation theologians will have to make their narrative cohere with that of the Gospels. The problem for the liberation theologians in appealing to the Gospels, however, is that from their perspective, these Gospels present a Jesus (1) who fails in his liberative project (Boff 1980, 30) and (2) whose actions are not consistent with the liberationists' characterization. (In fact, if Jesus' actions during his passion were indicative of his character, he should be called Jesus the Willing Victim rather than Jesus the Liberator). Liberation theologians must explain these discrepancies. Boff acknowledges the problem but argues that the differences are explicable and justified by the respective rhetorical intents of the Evangelists and the liberation theologians:

> Their [the Evangelists'] interest [in writing] consisted in persuading, proclaiming, defending, polemicizing and witnessing to Jesus as Christ and Savior of humankind. That is why in the Gospels we find, in a unity difficult to separate, history and theology, story and confession of faith, narrative and dogmatic thesis. . . .
>
> . . . The [Gospel] narratives seek to strengthen the faith of converts and express the self-understanding of the primitive community. But furthermore, the Gospels seek to provide a bridge that will facilitate the acceptance of the thesis: the Messiah suffers because he is the Suffering Servant [lit.: Just One]. . . . They [the Evangelists] needed to justify the new figure of the Messiah as suffering and crucified that they presented and preached.
>
> . . . .If the Evangelists had had a politically liberating interest, surely they would have written the Gospels in a very different way,

underlining other aspects of the passion of Christ. (Boff 1980, 25, 27-28, 30)

Segundo, as well, acknowledges that when Jesus' life and message are inter-preted politically, i.e., using a political key, the narrative "shows great coherence and significance. . . . But . . . there comes a point . . . when the political key seems to give out, when some other type of interpretation seems needed to account for the facts" (Segundo 1985, 178-79). However, rather than changing his interpretive key so as to harmonize Jesus' actions with his character, Segundo prefers to escape the dilemma by appealing to "the mystery of a person" and attributing the discrepancies between character and action (particularly Jesus' enigmatic non-actions) to the natural miscal-culations to which any human being is subject:

> Because he was perfectly human, we cannot assume he had something improper for human nature: knowledge of the future that would do away with the risk of any and every option.

> Perhaps he thought he had much more time ahead of him to carry on his long-term policy of consciousness-raising on behalf of the poor and the kingdom. Perhaps he was counting on some powerful intervention of the kingdom itself. . . . It is even more likely that he was surprised by the crucial moment that brought him his death and by the silence of God. We just don't know for sure. But that does not invalidate the overall key to his ministry, forcing us to replace it with another. (Segundo 1985, 182)

In other words, for Segundo, it is of little consequence that his characterization of Jesus does not cohere with Jesus' actions as presented by the Gospels; it appears that since interpreting Jesus politically makes sense of *most* of his life and is praxiologically useful, christological characterological coherence is not necessary.

The separation by liberation theologians of the historical Jesus from the noumenal Christ, results in an incoherent Jesus. His character is incoherent; his actions, in crucial moments of his life, make little sense. The narrative of the Evangelists, however, seeks to put Jesus' enigmatic behavior not only within a historical framework but also within an eschatological and noumenal one. Their story seeks to maintain the bipolarity of reality as Jesus and the disciples experienced it, with all the tensions present in such a bipolarity. The Gospels implicitly "argue" that only within this noumenal framework could one begin to make sense, as the disciples gradually "made sense," of Jesus' words and actions, and the attendant circumstances. Jesus is "identified" by the disciples not only by what he said and chose to do, but also by what happened to him; his identity (as any person's identity), was constituted not only by what he was able to control but also by those events and circumstances over which he had no control.[9]

In their portrayal of Jesus' character, liberation theologians have provided a corrective to the traditional depiction of Jesus as gentle, meek, and mild. He has been given a strength of character that had been lost from view; he is presented as one having determination, perseverance, and faithfulness to a set of values. Yet they also seem to go too far in characterizing Jesus as some sort of political activist with a utopian vision, a man whose intentions were laudable (namely to liberate the oppressed and especially the economically poor) but whose choice of means was questionable, lacking in pragmatic wisdom (Segundo 1985, 165, 182; Boff 1978, 286). Liberation theologians' story of Jesus, therefore, is cartoonish; their identity description of Jesus is reductionistic;[10] they have Jesus "all figured out." Whereas the Gospels present Jesus as the tragic hero, liberation theologians end up presenting Jesus as the comic fool: Jesus, well-meaning but ignorant, ends in failure (getting himself killed in the process), but God vindicates him by raising him from the dead, demonstrating that it was all worthwhile, that loving is worthwhile, and that in the end, injustice will not win.

The Gospels, on the other hand, present Jesus as an enigmatic figure. He is often depicted as blunt and confrontational, direct in his challenge of the Pharisees, and even angry in the cleansing of the Temple, but in just as many instances he is shown as patient (something emphasized by the New Testament writers: 1 Pet. 2:23; Heb. 12:3), impartially compassionate, and forgiving of those who hurt him and betray him. Jesus defies classification for he subverts "normal" human expectations.[11] In the Gospels he is presented as one whose methods, words, and actions confound not only his enemies but also his family and friends (Mt. 7:28-29; 13:54-57; 22:15-22, 33; Lk. 2:46-51; 8:25; 9:43-45; Mk. 3:20-21; Jn. 4:27; 7:2-10; 10:19-21). While the claim made by liberation theologians is correct that Jesus identified with the economically poor, economic poverty was not the exclusive criterion in determining his identification and activity (praxis). Not poverty, but human need—whether physical, mental, or spiritual—was the basis of Jesus' action or praxis. He identified not only with the economically poor but also with all those who were considered outcasts: tax-collectors, prostitutes, and lepers—not all necessarily economically poor [Zacchaeus (Lk. 19:2-10), Matthew (Mt. 9:9-12; Lk. 5:27-31)]. Moreover, while Jesus may have had a preference for "the lost sheep of Israel," he certainly did not exclude Pharisees [Nicodemus (Jn. 3:1-15), Joseph of Arimathea (Mt. 27:57-59)], Samaritans (Jn. 4), Romans (Mt. 8:5-13; Lk. 7:2-10), and Greeks (Mk. 7:25-30; Jn. 12:20). Jesus did not draw the lines between the economically oppressed and the oppressors as sharply as the liberation theologians are wont to do. Jesus, then, can be described as single-minded in his sense of mission, but his actions, as related by the Gospels, reveal that he conceived of his mission as much broader in scope than economic or political liberation. This latter form of liberation was precisely what many Jews expected from the Messiah; in that respect Jesus of Nazareth turned out to be a very confusing and frustrating Messianic figure to his people and ultimately a great disappointment to many of them. Yet it is this latter form of liberation which the liberation theologians seek to make Jesus champion.

There is incoherence, therefore, between the Evangelists' characterization of Jesus and the liberation theologians' characterization. The christological discourse of liberation theologians is put forth as a public moral discourse: it commends a way of acting in the world. However, it is a narrative based on another public discourse, the Gospel accounts. Because liberation theologians lead their audience to believe that their portrayal is based on that of the Gospels, the incoherent characterization gives reason to question their reliability as witnesses to Jesus Christ. Instead this characterological incoherence makes it seem as if liberation theologians are seeking to present a Jesus who will give sacred or ultimate legitimation to their penultimate endeavor.

There also seems to be, therefore, incoherence in the character of the narrators themselves. The Evangelists, through their narrative, seek to witness to the enigmatic figure which was Jesus of Nazareth and thus further the integral transformation of the cosmos, while maintaining the bipolarity of Christian faith: faith in God and faith in Christ, the transcendent and the immanent, the eschatological and the historical, the sacred and the profane. The liberation theologians, through their discourse, tend to overemphasize one of the poles of Christian faith (the immanent, the historical) to the neglect of the other and consequently overemphasize only one of the aspects of liberation, the socio-economic, to the relative exclusion of all other aspects of liberation, despite their occasional references to integral salvation.

The Narrative Fidelity of Liberation Christology

Liberation theologians concurrently proclaim three rhetorical narratives. The three discourses are: (1) The social reality of Latin America is one of oppression and so it must be changed (liberated) by revolutionary praxis. (2) Christian theology is functioning as a legitimating ideology and so it must be changed (liberated) by ideological critique. (3) To proclaim "Jesus of Nazareth is the Christ" is not relevant in Latin America and so the proclamation must be changed through hermeneutical criticism to "Jesus of Nazareth is the Liberator." These narratives or rhetorical discourses are interconnected and each should be assessed in terms of their fidelity. In spite of the interconnectedness of the discourses we will have to limit ourselves to evaluating the third rhetorical discourse and discuss the other two only when relevant to christology.

In assessing narrative fidelity, arguments/discourses are evaluated in terms of "those elements that provide warrants for accepting or adhering to the advice fostered . . ." (Fisher 1989, 107). Does the discourse provide good reasons for its acceptance? What statements are offered as a basis for accepting the value judgment implicit or explicit in the discourse? Fisher argues that in assessing narrative fidelity we must first determine if the "truths" or "facts" proclaimed correspond to the truth and facts as we know them. This entails asking the following questions about the rhetorical narrative: (1) Are its statements that purport to be "facts" indeed "facts?" (2) Have relevant facts been omitted or have those offered been distorted in any way or taken out of context? (3) What patterns of reasoning are utilized in making the argument? (4) What is the relevance of the individual arguments (the various christologies) to the decision the message concerns (in our case, to engage in a revolutionary praxis) ? (5) Does the message deal with the questions on which the whole matter turns or should turn? (Fisher 1989, 108-09)

This is not all, however. In determining if there are good reasons for accepting the liberationists' discourse, we must also explore the values that are being espoused by the narrators and promoted to their audience, for "whatever is taken as the basis for adopting a rhetorical message is inextricably bound to a value—to a conception of the good" (Fisher 1989, 107). We need to compare the values communicated in the story with values we know to be true and worthwhile in our own lives. We must ask five questions concerning values: (1) What are the values implicit/explicit in their discourses? (2) Are the values appropriate to the nature of the decision that the messages (discourses) bear upon? (3) What would be the effects of adhering to these values? (4) Are the values confirmed or validated in one's personal experience, in the lives or statements of others whom one admires, and in the conception of the best audience that one can conceive? (5) Do these values constitute the ideal basis for human conduct?

We will first assess the "facts" of the christological discourse and subsequently the values communicated therein.

Assessment of "Facts"

1. Are the statements made about Jesus by liberation theologians "factual," i.e., are the messages confirmed by consensus or reliable witnesses?

The essence of the liberationist message is that Jesus is the Liberator and his mission (or "project") was and continues to be, to a great extent, a political project. There is consensus that Jesus is the Liberator but there is not a clearly established consensus on what he liberates *from* and *how* he liberates. For instance, a key question is whether we can legitimately speak of the *praxis* of Jesus, political activity oriented toward the transformation of society. Are we not reading a concept into the text, imposing a foreign ideology upon it?[12] There is historical consensus that the biblical text presents Jesus as the liberator who effects a cosmic (integral) liberation. The issue is, however, *how* that liberation is to be realized, particularly on the structural level, i.e., in the polis, as opposed to the individual level.

This lack of consensus on the issue of "how" liberation is to be realized is pointed out by Segundo himself when he argues that as soon as Jesus died, the early Church embarked on a *different* approach from that of the historical Jesus; the historical Jesus' project was to effect liberation by raising the consciousness of the oppressed and "dismantling the ideological mechanisms of religio-political oppression" (Segundo 1985, 148); the project of the early Church was to effect liberation by proclaiming Jesus as Messiah. Jesus' approach was political and historical, the Church's approach was religious and spiritual (Segundo 1985, 185-86). Liberation theologians clearly want to shift the consensus of Church leadership in the direction of the historical Jesus rather than the early Church; however, there are many in the Church who convincingly argue that the early Church's project was in continuity with Jesus' own project.[13] (The Evangelists themselves attempt to make this case.)

2. Have relevant facts been omitted or have those offered been distorted in any way?

The most serious distortion is that Jesus sought to subvert the politico-religious structures and that he pursued a revolutionary praxis to accomplish that aim. The distortion lies in the interpretation which the liberation theologians give the Gospel narratives, for although the Gospels clearly present Jesus in conflict with the Jewish religious authorities, Jesus appears almost indifferent to Roman rule and the Herodian puppet government, and he refuses to identify with any of the rebel groups active at that time. Consequently, in order to make Jesus the inspiration for modern political activism, liberation theologians must distort the historical facts and make the Pharisee-Sadducee religious hegemony of great *political* importance in Palestine, while the Gospels reveal them to be very limited in power (for instance, this hegemony could underhandedly manipulate the system to get Jesus executed, but when it challenged Roman power directly, it could not even get the sign posted over Jesus' cross changed! [Jn. 19: 19-22])

3. What patterns of reasoning are utilized in making the argument?

Using the standards of informal logic elaborated by Stephen Toulmin in *The Uses of Argument* we can assess the reasoning of the liberation theologians and the place of christology in their reasoning. Toulmin views argument as "a movement from data, to warrant, backing for the warrant, to reservations, and to conclusion" (Fisher 1989, 44). The liberation theologians' argument can be schematized as illustrated in Figure 1:

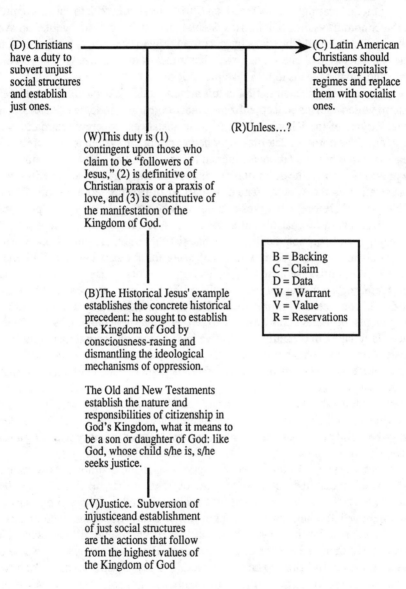

(D) Christians have a duty to subvert unjust social structures and establish just ones.

(C) Latin American Christians should subvert capitalist regimes and replace them with socialist ones.

(R)Unless...?

(W)This duty is (1) contingent upon those who claim to be "followers of Jesus," (2) is definitive of Christian praxis or a praxis of love, and (3) is constitutive of the manifestation of the Kingdom of God.

B = Backing
C = Claim
D = Data
W = Warrant
V = Value
R = Reservations

(B)The Historical Jesus' example establishes the concrete historical precedent: he sought to establish the Kingdom of God by consciousness-rasing and dismantling the ideological mechanisms of oppression.

The Old and New Testaments establish the nature and responsibilities of citizenship in God's Kingdom, what it means to be a son or daughter of God: like God, whose child s/he is, s/he seeks justice.

(V)Justice. Subversion of injusticeand establishment of just social structures are the actions that follow from the highest values of the Kingdom of God

Figure 1: Anatomy of the Argument

The illustration makes clear that christological discourse enters in as backing for the arguments' warrant. Latin American Christians should seek to subvert oppressive socio-economic systems (capitalist systems) and establish more egalitarian systems (socialist) because all Christians have a moral duty to seek social justice since that is what it means to love one's neighbor, what it means to actualize God's Kingdom on earth, and what it means to be a disciple of Jesus.

There is a basic assumption in this argument that is debatable: that the relative systems which humans conceptualize/actualize constitute, in some instances, concrete actualizations of the Kingdom and, in other instances, concrete retardations of the Kingdom. The norm for determining whether or not the system is a concretization of the Kingdom is humanization: are human beings benefitted? But as we pointed out in the previous chapter, the definition of what is humanizing or what benefits humanity is as relative as the systems which purport to fulfill this moral norm. Liberation theologians, therefore, must presumptuously claim that their vantage point affords them the best view of what ails Latin America and how its problems can be solved. For the majority of liberation theologians what ails (or rather, victimizes) Latin America is capitalism, and the system which will bring the greatest humanizing benefits is socialism. But this discourse is rhetorical, in the worst sense of the term, since the labels refer to "a rather undefined socialism [that] becomes the bearer of all the hopes and ideals connected with liberation. Capitalism, without any differentiation of its components, becomes simply the evil to be overcome" (McGovern 1989, 178). Such loaded language can certainly be effective in demarcating or singling out the protagonists and the antagonists (whether they be systems, structures, or individuals) in a tragic situation, but it also smacks of demagoguery and manipulation since, as McGovern points out: "No system produces only positive or only negative effects. Either-or choices between capitalism and socialism ignore the possibility of building structures that take the best from each and reject what is worst in each" (McGovern 1989, 183). But most liberation theologians present their audience with only an either-or choice.

The absence of formally stated reservations in the liberationists' argument led to the criticism that liberation theology advocates a utilitarian ethic that is willing to sacrifice the rights of the individual for the liberation of the whole. For many critics this foreboded totalitarianism. Consequently, many liberation theologians have shifted their position in the last few years, qualifying their calls for socialism by claiming that their quest is for a *democratic* socialism, which preserves some of the human rights felt by critics to be endangered.[14] The problems in this shift, however, are that in calling for democratic socialism, liberation theology ends up advocating a reformism not much different from the reformist ideology of the Social Christian or Christian Democratic Parties. There is, therefore, a problem of identity.

4. What is the relevance of the individual arguments (the various christologies) to the decision the message concerns (in our case, to engage in a revolutionary praxis) ?

The particular argument of liberation theologians invites a decision to enter into a praxis that will achieve social justice. Christology, we said, serves as the backing for the warrant, but also, (by making Jesus into what Segundo calls a "referential witness") it is intended to provide inspiration and guidance concerning the values and virtues which the primary actors in the social drama (the oppressed) are to have. But with the shift in the message of some liberation theologians—no longer calling so much for revolution as for democratic participation[15]—and as democratic mechanisms become fairer and more effective, the uncompromising, subversive Jesus of liberation christology is becoming more and more irrelevant to the sorts of decisions concerning social transformation the oppressed need to make.

There is, therefore, a problem of consistency or coherence in the liberationist discourse, for the gradualist, reformist approach now advocated by some liberation theologians hardly conforms to the uncompromising praxis exemplified by Jesus the Liberator; the character and activity now being called for by some of these theologians hardly conforms to the radical, "willing-to-die-for-justice-sake," character which liberation theologians portray Jesus as having. In all fairness, however, in some places—like Haiti and El Salvador, for instance—political participation and voting can certainly cost one his/her life, and so the story of Jesus the Liberator's radical commitment can still inspire and illumine praxis.

5. Does the message deal with the questions on which the whole matter turns or should turn?

Liberation theologians, in their christologies, give a great deal of attention to the issue of whether the Historical Jesus' activity was political. The key questions, however, which I believe are not sufficiently considered, are the following. Given the fact that we are reflecting from a historical horizon, is the Historical Jesus' activity normative for today—not only his intentions but also his methods? If so, why? If not, then why is it necessary or important to reflect on this Historical Jesus?

Assessment of Values

We said earlier that in order to find out if there are compelling reasons for accepting the liberation theologians' arguments about Latin America, theology, and christology, we will need to assess the values being espoused and proclaimed in the respective discourses. For this assessment, we will ask the following questions of the rhetorical discourses proclaimed by liberation theologians:

1. What are the values implicit/explicit in their discourses?

The values implicitly assumed by liberation theologians in their meta-theological discourse are: (1) relevance: theology and christology in particular must speak to the concrete historical situation, (2) effective change: the best theology, and christology in particular, will be that which best facilitates the transformation of society, and (3) suspicion: theologies or christologies that do not further values #1 and #2 above must be viewed with suspicion.

The value explicitly held in their argument as absolute is justice, social justice (See Figure 1). This value is non-negotiable. The means to the realization of this value, however, *are* negotiable. Since justice is absolute, the existence of unjust social structures necessitate their subversion. The methods of subversion will have to vary in accordance with the context. In some cases violence may be necessary (as a last resort), in other cases democratic mechanisms may be used. The determining criterion (or implicit value) is efficacy: whatever means are most effective in achieving social justice are the ones to be employed.

2. Are the values appropriate to the nature of the decision that the messages (discourses) bear upon?

The decision that this discourse calls one to make is to transform Latin American society by engaging in a concretely historical subversive praxis, and to that end the values which liberation theologians hold are made part of the christological narrative which will further this social transformation. They deconstruct christology so as to free the discourse from those values—communicated by the traditional narrative— which preserve an oppressive status quo by furthering passivity and resignation, values such as contentment (acceptance of one's lot as part of God's will), unconditional love (impartiality), peace at all costs (which implies non-violence, unilateral reconciliation), submission to authority, individual eschatological salvation, and contemplation (inner spirituality). Liberation theologians have sought to animate a liberative praxis by linking their values to their christological discourse. The values which they hold and communicate through their christology are: absolute justice, bilateral reconciliation, partiality, solidarity, autonomy (self-mastery), popular participation, social historical salvation, efficacious action, and perseverance. The values, therefore, are relevant to the decision that needs to be made.

3. What would be the effects of adhering to these values?

Adherence to these values by the majority of Latin Americans would have various effects on society, theology, and the Church. Socially, adherence to these values would lead to social conflict, as the oppressed are mobilized against the oppressors, in order to advance social change. Such was the case in Nicaragua in 1979, and in places like Brazil, Mexico, Chile, and Peru, adherence to these values by the public have spurred the establishment of democratic mechanisms and social reforms.

Theologically, adherence to these values would transform (and already have) the method as well as the content of theology, but perhaps at the expense of the doctrinal unity of the Church achieved through centuries of reflection on Scripture and Tradition. A related effect would be the creation of a plurality of contextual christologies and ecclesiologies, which could result in further fragmentation within Christianity. This has been one of the fears of the Vatican with regard to the liberationist discourse and the Ecclesial Base Communities, namely that the values espoused by liberation theologians may form the basis for another—different— church, hence the various "Instructions" and warnings on liberation theology issued by the Vatican.

A result of espousing these values would be the polarization of the Church— again, as has occurred already in Latin America—into progressives and conservatives, each with their own "Christ" to support their values. Each group in the Church (would be) is faced with tough decisions: in order to maintain true unity, the conservative Church would have to start a process of restructuration (as Boff calls for in *Church: Charism and Power*), while the progressive Church would have to bring its teachings and emphases more in line with official declarations.

4. Are the values confirmed or validated in one's personal experience, in the lives or statements of others whom one admires, and in the conception of the best audience that one can conceive?

Certainly everyone agrees with the value placed upon justice—equality, participation, and social welfare—by liberation theologians through their primary argument (Discourse #1) that the social reality of Latin America is one of oppression and so must be changed (liberated) by revolutionary praxis. Yet recent events in Eastern Europe and in China have brought into question the capacity of socialist systems to fulfill the aims of social justice and validate the aforementioned values. It is true, as liberation theologians might retort, that Latin America is a different situation, but if they have a unique socialism in mind, the best audience that one can conceive would certainly have a basis in history to be a bit cynical about such claims to uniqueness.

Many would not agree with the liberationist argument that Christian theology is functioning as a legitimating ideology (Discourse #2), and particularly with the value these theologians place on change in theology. This valuation seems based on a caricature of traditional theology as socially ineffectual (hence the need for change). Liberation theologians seem to overlook the many instances in which traditional theology has been an agent for positive change. They seem so captivated by the "New- is-Better" ideology that they fail to see how the "old" Story has effected changes in consciousness and in concrete history.

5. Do these values constitute the ideal basis for human conduct?

In my view, it is agape love rather than justice that constitutes the *ideal* basis of human conduct. Justice, understood as "liberation" by the liberation theologians, is the *ultimate* value, one actualized through a relevant, active, and suspicious way of doing and theologizing. The problem, however, with the primary value of justice or "liberation" is that it is a value pursued on the basis of utilitarian calculations (efficacious praxis), and such justice is implicitly equated with Christian love. Segundo, for instance, makes an unconvincing argument that love necessarily involves violence (Segundo 1976, 156-62). Liberation theologians fail to distinguish between the absoluteness of Christian love and the relativity of justice (that justice necessarily involves coercion)—a distinction made by Reinhold Niebuhr. Agape love excludes utilitarian calculations as a basis for action and requires self-denial not just for the sake of one's friends but also for one's enemies. Agape love constitutes a truly radical ethic and provides the Church with a norm unparalleled by the rationalistic ethics of the humanisms to which it often seeks to conform. The ethic of agape is what gives Christianity its uniqueness.

Justice is certainly a worthy value to pursue as a *minimum* standard of human conduct, but the Christian ideal is love. Thus to equate revolutionary praxis (justice) with the ideal of Christian conduct is to fail to grasp the radicality of Jesus Christ.

Concluding Assessment

Using Fisher's questions for assessing the narrative rationality of the liberation theologians' rhetorical discourse, we find many points in it that are commendable and worth considering, but the argument is not wholly coherent, either methodologically or christologically. Methodologically, we saw in Chapters 3 and 4 that the liberationist christological discourse is based on contradictory assumptions and is mediated through an arbitrarily chosen ideology. Christologically, we have found that the discourse is materially and characterologically incoherent. In terms of the liberation theologians' fidelity to the "facts" as these have been communicated by the witnesses closest to the events and to the values inherent in the original story, it is clear that there are crucial points of incongruence. The result is that the liberationist narrative about Jesus Christ (Political) Liberator fails to be persuasive because it does not ring true; it does not conform to the "facts" publicly affirmed nor does the story wholly correspond with the historic vision of what constitutes Christian truth and Christian love. Moreover, when we examine how this christological narrative fits into the overall argument made by liberation theologians, we find the reasoning fallacious.

I have said previously that there are three discourses or arguments being promulgated by liberation theologians: (1) Latin America must be liberated (from dependency or neo-colonialism), (2) Theology must be liberated (from ideological orthodoxies), and (3) Jesus Christ is the Liberator (from all forms of oppression and the concomitant oppressive ideologies). The theological warrant for discourses #1 and #2 is discourse #3, but in order to establish the credibility of discourse #3, one needs to presuppose the validity of discourses #1 and #2. Let me explain this more clearly: Latin America must be liberated from economic oppression since Jesus Christ calls on Christians to pursue an integral liberation, not just the liberation of the soul from sin and death, but also liberation from sinful social structures that dehumanize and destroy life. Theology must also be liberated from static orthodoxies whose transcendent absolutes keep human beings from acting in love since Jesus Christ himself rejected static orthodoxies (of the Pharisees, for example) that kept people from doing good for the sake of some religious value. To affirm discourse #3, that Jesus Christ is the Liberator—not just from individual sin but also from structural sin, and that he is the Liberator from static orthodoxies—and to get to this discourse by first reflecting on praxis in light of the Word, one must assume the validity, *a priori*, of discourses #1 and #2, for one would not be engaged in revolutionary praxis unless one accepted the validity of the assessment that Latin America must be liberated from economic oppression, and one would certainly not begin to theologize from a praxiological starting point unless one had first assumed that orthodoxy (or the deductive theological method) had nothing to offer a liberative praxis (that it could not be deduced from the transcendent absolutes of orthodoxy), in brief, that orthodoxy is useless for this social liberation.

If I could express the liberationists' arguments more clearly:
1. Latin America must be liberated from political/economic oppression since Jesus is the Liberator from all oppression.
2. Theology (Christology) must be liberated from ideological distortion since Jesus is the Liberator from religious ideologies.

But what is the backing for the warrant, discourse #3? How do we know that Jesus is the Liberator from political and economic oppression and religious ideologies? We come to know Jesus as Liberator by first reflecting on the praxis of the oppressed, which of necessity implies presupposing the validity of discourses #1 and #2, that Latin America is politically/economically oppressed and that christology is ideologically distorted. Once these discourses are accepted as valid, then it becomes possible to see Jesus as Liberator from economic oppression and ideologized theologies (cf., the hermeneutic circle).

In brief, the reasoning seems to be: The arguments are valid if the warrant is true, the warrant is true because the arguments are valid. Liberation theologians might claim that there is a dialectical relationship between the first two discourses and the third; clearly, it is rather a logically and rhetorically incoherent form of arguing.

Notes

1. According to Williston Walker, for Socinus "Christ was a man, but one who lived a life of peculiar and exemplary obedience, filled with divine wisdom, and was therefore rewarded with a resurrection and a kind of delegated divinity. . . ." "Christ's death is a great example of the obedience which every Christian should, if necessary, manifest . . ." (Walker 1970, 398).

2. For Abelard,"the work of Christ was conceived psychologically rather than metaphysically. The interest for Abelard was not its effect upon God, but its effect upon us" (Wells 1984, 117).

3. Because liberation theologians are primarily concerned with praxis, with relevance to present suffering, they are averse toward considering speculative theological problems, such as determining how God is affected by the death of Jesus Christ.

4. The liberation theologians' concept of salvation tends to be Semi-Pelagian: the human will is free and can choose to cooperate with God in the process of salvation. Semi-Pelagianism underestimates the extent of the Fall and denies irresistible grace and predestination (as Augustine argued against Pelagius).

5. This lopsided discourse is indicative of a trend evolving within Christianity since the eighteenth century of eliminating one of the poles of Christian faith: faith in a transcendent God (the other pole is faith in Christ). In recent years Christocentricity has been taken to its limit: "to a form . . . so exclusive that it does not seem to contain any reference to a transcendent God" (Milet 1981, 190). So argues Jean Milet in his book *God or Christ: The Excesses of Christocentricity.* He demonstrates how the christocentric emphasis has led to various forms of "atheistic Christianity" such as Bonhoeffer's theology, "Death of God" theologies, and liberation theologies. He specifically mentions the christologies of two liberation theologians, J. I. Gonzalez Faus and Jon Sobrino, as examples of this atheistic Christianity; these are christologies that present Jesus Christ as a "God without God." According to this type of theology "it is fitting for all the disciples of Jesus Christ to have some 'idea' of an 'atheistic Christianity.' It is a matter of lucidity and honesty, so [John] Robinson tells us. That

is his major thesis. . . . We find it [the thesis] again . . . in the Spanish theologian J. I. Gonzalez Faus, who sees in Jesus the 'absolute man' in whom humanity achieves a truly 'divine' level. The God of Jesus Christ is the highest 'idea' that Jesus ever conceived; it is the idea which inspired him; it is the ideal which he dreamed of handing on to men. We also find echoes of these analyses in . . . J. Sobrino and X. Pikaza. In these two different cases there is resolute talk of an atheistic Christianity. In other words, the reference to God has completely disappeared: better still, the idea of God must be rigorously banished. Here theocentricity has completely vanished, and by reaction christocentricity is triumphant" (Milet 1981, 200).

6. David Tracy states that there are five basic models in contemporary theology. Liberation theology can be seen as belonging to the fifth model, "radical theology." Of this model, Tracy notes that "The corresponding weakness of the radical position is . . . [this]: can one really continue the enterprise of Christian theology if there is no meaningful way to affirm the reality of God?" (Tracy 1975, 32). If the reality of God and, relatedly, the saving activity of God, cannot be meaningfully affirmed, then there is no basis for theological discourse and for the sort of evangelistic proclamation to which the New Testament bears witness and which has been the mission of the Church throughout its history: to call human beings to repentance from sins and to trust in the promise of resurrection.

7. A similar viewpoint is echoed by Raúl Vidales, Mexican liberation theologian: "The overcoming of all dualisms is of definitive importance to all theological work. It no longer has to do . . . with seeing concrete situations in light of the Word; it has to do with understanding from the beginning that the only history which exists, human history, is not only the environ, field or circumstance of salvation but that in itself it is inchoate salvation moving towards final fulfillment. . . . From this perspective it will have to be understood that the action of God manifests itself as human efficacy in the creation of a more just society . . . " (Vidales 1978, 27).

8. The history of dogma demonstrates that the most important struggle in Christianity, and an important reason for the formulation of doctrine, was the struggle to maintain the tensions, the antinomies or polarities, related in the christology of witness. Early on there was a tendency to collapse one or the other of the poles: the Ebionites denied Jesus' divinity, the docetic Gnostics his humanity, the Arians denied his *full* divinity while the Apollinarians and the Eutychians denied his *full* humanity. The Councils of the Church attempted to correct these excesses and reaffirm the tensions present in the story.

9. In order to give coherence to the story of Jesus' life and their own experience

with Jesus of Nazareth, the disciples connect not only Messianic prophecies with Jesus of Nazareth but also Suffering Servant prophecies.

10. Segundo writes in a footnote "I am not suggesting that any one key can explain the whole life of a human person. In the case of Jesus, for example, we have religious and moral teachings that cannot be explained solely in a political key; such an explanation would be sheer reductionism" (Segundo 1985, 219). This suggests that many valid christologies can be produced employing a variety of interpretive keys. But in spite of Segundo's qualification, he appears to contradict himself by suggesting that for any explanation of Jesus' words and deeds, "the political key used throughout this volume remains the most adequate. Christologies will have to start from there" (Segundo 1985, 188). In short, reducing Jesus' life to the political is the best way of making sense of it.

11. John Dominic Crossan, for instance calls Jesus "the Parable of God" to express the subversive nature of his person, for like a parable, he subverts our worlds. (Crossan 1988, 102)

12. Jacques Ellul argues that in constructing "a materialist theology one would have the right to refer only to the proletarian praxis of *Christians*. And in no way can one refer to Jesus' praxis, since, . . . (1) no proletariat was involved; (2) the interpretation of Jesus as having had a revolutionary practice in the modern sense depends on a series of wordplays and forcing of the text; (3) no one could begin claiming Jesus had a revolutionary praxis until the time when the ideology of Marxist revolution became part of our thinking. In other words, *this* Jesus is discovered not on the basis of what He is, but on the basis of a presupposition acquired from one's social milieu" (Ellul 1988, 130-31).

13. The lack of consensus on *how* Jesus liberates is very much tied to the question of *who* Jesus is, and on this latter question there is much diversity of opinion as evidenced by the plethora of books on christology, such as: *The Myth of God Incarnate, The Truth of God Incarnate, The Myth/Truth of God Incarnate.*

14. Paul Sigmund traces this shift in his book *Liberation Theology at the Crossroads: Democracy or Revolution?* and puts the turning point in the publication of two documents: the Vatican's "Instruction on Christian Freedom and Liberation" (*Libertatis Conscientia*) on April 5, 1986 and the pope's letter to the Brazilian bishops on April 12, 1986. The documents essentially called on liberation theologians to make clearer the distinction between liberty and liberation, an instruction that was received with mixed feelings by some liberation theologians, such as Ellacuría, Sobrino, and

Boff, who saw it as an attempt by the Vatican to universalize bourgeois notions of liberty and democracy, while others (such as Gutierrez and Assmann) welcomed it and took it as a challenge to deepen their theological reflection. (Sigmund 1990, 167-75)

15. Hugo Assmann, for instance, one of the most radical liberation theologians, now says that members of the Latin American left "must now reestablish the organic relation to the popular majorities which never understood their abstract revolutionism," and that "Democratic values are revolutionary values" (Sigmund 1990, 174-75).

CHAPTER 6

NOTES TOWARDS A POSTMODERN LIBERATION THEOLOGY

Christological discourse is crucial for the legitimation of Christian social ethics, as it has been throughout Christian history. The Jesus event has been a perennial source for the communication of values and ideological agendas[1] and nowhere is this more true than in Latin America where, as liberation theologians have pointed out, for the past five hundred years traditional narratives of Jesus have served to legitimate oppression. Liberation theologians, for their part, seek to inject into cultural awareness a different image of Jesus: Jesus the Liberator, a Jesus who identifies with the oppressed, who struggles for their liberation, is killed because of his struggle, and whom God ultimately vindicates by raising him from the dead. In order to communicate such values as justice, human dignity, effective action, and solidarity to the larger Latin American culture, the theologians have made use of a recognizable cultural symbol, a well-known narrative, and brought to light meanings that had been obscured. Latin American liberation theology, then, depends a great deal on its christological discourse to establish the validity of revolutionary praxis as a Christian endeavor.

In order to accomplish this rhetorical aim of effectively communicating a mode of being human, a framework of values for action, liberation theologians take the predominant narrative concerning Jesus of Nazareth, the Theological Code, and deconstruct it by applying to it the presuppositions of historicism, praxis, and ideological distortion. Then, in order to make christology liberative, the narrative is reconstructed by mediating it through positive ideology, i.e., through categories of social analysis that expose the forms of political and economic oppression that exist as well as suggest the means to undo these forms of oppression.

We have seen, however, that at each step in the construction of their rhetorical narrative, liberation theologians fall into a variety of errors. Firstly, liberation theologians are not wholly consistent in using historicism, praxis, and ideology as hermeneutical categories. These serve to relativize traditional intepretations of Jesus and of Christian ethics by relegating them to particular historical, cultural, and social loci and by showing these interpretations to be politically ineffectual. The main problem with these presumptions is that liberation theologians are inconsistent in their application—other christological discourses are evaluated in light of these presumptions, but not the theologians' own discourses. Liberation theologians fail to be sufficiently self-critical; they do not subject their discourse to the same canons of adequacy by which they judge other discourses.

Secondly, when they begin to reconstruct their christological discourse by mediating through ideology what remains after deconstruction, liberation theologians demonstrate an arbitrariness, an intellectual authoritarianism, unbecoming of those who presumably desire the liberation of all from oppression, for they hardly consider (or encourage the oppressed to consider) the variety of explanatory theories, put forth in the past few years, concerning Latin America's economic problems. For the majority of liberationists, the problem is capitalism and the solution is socialism. There is no room for discussion since all other explanations are, in their eyes, ideological distortions. Such arbitrariness and authoritarianism in the choice of an ideology is produced by impatience and desperation—they need a sociology that, by pointing out identifiable and manageable causes, will justify quick and radical changes. One can hardly blame liberation theologians for the desperation that is the fruit of poverty and repression, but desperation is hardly the handmaiden of prudence.

Finally, when we consider the liberationists' narrative itself, we find that it is rhetorically incoherent. It fails to correspond fully to the highest values historically proclaimed by Christianity: unconditional love, forgiveness, reconciliation. Moreover, although their christological narrative is internally coherent, it fails to cohere with the Gospel sources and fails to present a portrait of Jesus that coheres with the radical values and attitudes that make him unique in history. In short, their discourse is neither materially nor characterologically coherent. Because of these various forms of incoherence, the narrative does not provide good reasons for assent.

For their narrative to be more persuasive, therefore, liberation theologians will have to articulate a discourse that is more faithful to the people's and the New Testament's understanding of Jesus' identity, values, and methods; one that presents Jesus as Liberator not only from economic oppression, but also sexual, racial, cultural, religious, and ecological oppression, and which demonstrates greater self-criticism and openness to alternative economic explanations and proposals.

The Liberationist Contribution to a Postmodern Christology

In spite of the criticisms made throughout this work of the christology of liberation theology, there is no doubt that this theological genre has made a positive contribution to the quest for a christology relevant to a postmodern world. Its contribution can be noted in the following aims pursued by liberationists, aims which theologians everywhere should attend to in their own theologizing.

First, liberation theology seeks to recover the totality of Jesus' life for christology. There is no question that the divorce of the cross and resurrection from Jesus' pre-paschal life has had a deleterious effect on the concrete practice of Christians throughout history. Traditional christology makes Jesus' life irrelevant to Christian ethics, in spite of claims to the contrary. However, liberation theologians do not fare much better, as I have argued.

Secondly, liberation theology consciously seeks to relate christology to Christian social ethics. Traditional christology has treated the description of Jesus Christ as an end in itself. Liberation theologians, however, have sought to make all theological reflection, and christology in particular, relevant to concrete existence. In contrast, much of traditional christology has remained on the level of apologetic and polemical discourse, trying to prove or explain to the unbelieving world that Jesus Christ is God. Liberation theologians, in postmodern disdain for philosophical reason, presuppose throughout their christological reflection that what is truly important is not so much what people *think* or even believe about Jesus Christ but what people *do* because of Jesus Christ, although thinking and acting do influence each other.

Thirdly, liberation theology seeks to develop a concept of God as God presents himself in Jesus Christ's words and actions. Traditional christology seems to impose a concept of God upon Jesus of Nazareth, a Platonic concept that refuses to grant that God can suffer, that God participates in human history. Liberation theology, like political theology before it (e.g., Moltmann), has opened the way for the construal of a Suffering God, a God who is involved in human suffering.

In this regard, however, liberation theologians have not gone far enough. Their respective christologies make allusions to the idea of a "Suffering God," but they do not develop it. If they would develop the idea, they would consequently have to develop an ontology, which they sorely need to provide a philosophical basis for their reflections on oppression-liberation. Having such a philosophical basis would help liberation theology avoid the charge of reductionism by establishing a broader horizon of Christian practice that would include not only political activity to help the economically poor but also activities that challenge all forms of oppression: sexual, cultural, racial, and religious oppression, plus the exploitation of children and the environment. I will say more about this philosophical shortcoming in discussing liberation theology's use of "praxis" as an epistemological and methodological category.

Because christology lies at the core of Christian faith, whatever epistemological assumptions or hermeneutic presuppositions are brought to the construction of christological discourse affect the theology as a whole. The presumptions of the priority of praxis and ideological conditioning that we looked at earlier (in Chapters 3 and 4) with regard to christology affect the whole of liberation theology in negative ways. As we conclude this work, therefore, it will be useful to see how the methodological weaknesses we saw in the construction of the christological discourse impact the theology as a whole. We will first look at how giving praxis absolute priority in the process of theological reflection poses various problems to liberation theology and raises questions to be addressed. Secondly, we will see how the conceptual tool of ideology which is used by liberation theologians for critique and mediation, in deconstructing traditional christologies and in reconstructing their own, can reveal certain dangerous tendencies within liberation theology itself.

Liberation Theology and the Appeal to "Praxis"

In giving the priority to praxis, liberation theologians reflect the shift made in contemporary theology to make theology socially relevant. The need for social relevance is all the more imperative in Latin America because of the strong religious fervor which exists among the people, on the one hand, and the repressive, exploitative regimes which are found all over the continent, on the other. It is tragic that in so religious a continent, religion should have so little impact on the oppressive situation under which the majority of people live. In giving the priority to praxis, therefore, Latin American intellectuals and theologians are giving voice to a sense of frustration and outrage over Christianity's other-worldly, escapist approach to social reality, especially in the face of a reality of economic disparity, exploitation, and repression. The influence of Marx on these intellectuals, and particularly his critique of religion, has moved them to take Marx's challenge seriously and see how they can transform theology from a form of false consciousness into an instrument of liberation.

Marx himself had said in his Eleventh Thesis on Feuerbach: "The philosophers have so far only interpreted the world; the object, however, is to change it." In this statement Marx disparaged the tendency since Aristotle, to divorce theory from praxis in epistemology. "Theory" was seen as "pure" knowledge and so the primary aim of the philosopher was to develop the proper theory from which the correct praxis would ensue. The philosophers spent years refining their theories without ever affecting the world around them. Marx sought to give praxis not simply its legitimate place in the dialectic of theory and praxis but rather to give it epistemological primacy.

The liberation theologians have followed Marx in giving praxis this epistemological priority. They criticize traditional theology for being a type of theoretical or speculative knowledge which, like philosophy before Marx, merely interprets reality, leaving it essentially unchanged. In making praxis the starting point of theological reflection, liberation theologians claim they have begun a "new way of doing theology." In fact, the shift to praxis as a *locus theologicus* began much earlier with political theology in Europe. Traditionally, praxis was seen as "the continuation, implementation, or concrete application of a previously defined theory" (Lane 1984,

13). Political theology and, subsequently, liberation theology, viewed the relationship between theory and praxis as a dialectical one, with primacy given to praxis; the Aristotelean epistemological assumptions (of first, theory, then praxis) which had ruled theology for centuries gave way to the Marxist epistemological dialectic of praxis-theory. Consequently, praxis is able to transform theology (theory), and theology, in turn, is able to give transcendent meaning and impetus to praxis. With this epistemological inversion praxis becomes "the matrix of all authentic knowledge and the source of a new kind of discourse about the faith . . . and Christian community" (Lane 1984, 22).

This new emphasis upon praxis is a welcome change for the Church and has much to commend it as an ingredient of theological reflection. It has put the theological enterprise (the "doing of theology") on a course away from a useless scholasticism onto a path of pastoral and social relevance. Specifically, the emphasis on praxis has served to point out that "faith" can and must make use of reason in whatever ways it will enable faith to work itself out concretely, or achieve its moral ends. As the Epistle of James makes clear, faith works, and Christian faith, which has revelation as its fountainhead, makes itself concrete through action, which has reason as its conduit. Faith, as Segundo argues in *Faith and Ideologies*, must be mediated through a system of means, an ideology, or as the Boffs prefer to call it, a "Socio-analytic mediation." It is through these rational mediations that faith becomes praxis, that love is made concrete on a social level.

Moreover, by placing the priority on praxis, theology (or "speech about God"), as a reflective endeavor, is made to demonstrate in its method the character of the God about which it "speaks," a God of action, an Acting God. Liberation theology clearly demonstrates that speech of (about) God is only proper after one has acted as God acts, namely, on behalf of the oppressed. For it is not proper to speak as if one knows what God is about if one has not experienced what God is about, just as it is not proper to say to a mother grieving over the death of a child "I know how you feel," if one has not experienced the death of one's child. Only undergoing the experience enables one to speak meaningfully about that experience.

The inclusion of praxis as part of the method of theological construction, then, is an important and needed change. However, liberation theologians need to address the tendency to view "praxis" as the only valid *locus theologicus*. While Clodovis Boff (Boff 1987) has gone a long way toward clarifying the place of praxis in theology (for him, praxis is the starting point for a theology of the political without denying that there may be other starting points for many other types of theologies), others leave the impression in their writings that any other starting point, any other sort of theologizing, is sheer ideology. Some liberation theologians, in effect, turn "praxis" into a rhetorical weapon for counter-discourse. The following statements by Lamberto Schuurman, approvingly discussing Sobrino's christology, give evidence of this:

> Unless one takes into consideration the particularity of the histor-
> ical Jesus . . . any ontological notions offer an excellent method of
> separating the lion of Juda from his claws. This, according to
> Sobrino, is what is happening in three current christologies:
> doctrinal christology, resurrection christology, and existential
> christology. In all three cases, Jesus is not permitted to define what
> is said about him from the viewpoint of his historical functionality,
> his functional history [Read: his praxis]. . . . The absence of an
> adequate christological epistemology [i.e., one that has Jesus'
> praxis as its starting point] . . . tenders a most welcome succor to
> certain ideological interests. (Miguez-Bonino 1985, 167)

While Schuurman is correct that in doing ontology, the historical Jesus must be considered, the disdain for ontology generally shown by liberation theologians keeps their theology from having the philosophical basis that would make the discourse truly universal and fully liberating. Furthermore, although social relevance *is* a very important consideration in a christological discourse, a functionalist christological epistemology is certainly not the only way of obtaining that relevance or functionality.

It is, moreover, *theologically* and *anthropologically* problematic to make praxis the only *locus theologicus* as some liberationists argue. "Praxis" cannot be conceived as *the locus theologicus* in a strict sense, for that would be to reduce the nature of God and the nature of human being to a narrow aspect of experience. According to Karl Lehmann, reflection on praxis cannot exhaust the meaning of the Gospel or the depth of theology, for theology is "Speech about God," *theo-logos*. To make praxis the only locus of reflection would be to make praxis representative of the totality of God, and thus would shrink reflection to a very narrow conception of God's being and of the experience of God (Lehmann 1978).

Anthropologically, praxis is only one aspect of human experience. Therefore, to theologize *only* from a praxis locus is to fail to address other areas of human experience where theology might have a liberating word to speak. Moreover, human beings are not a complex of mere thinking and action; human beings also feel and intuit. Reflection on the affective aspect of human experience, "pathos," could contribute to Christian theology and ethics.[2] Liberation theologians need to look back at the theological contribution made by Schleiermacher in the nineteenth century, for instance, and they might very well find much that is usable in the construction of a more coherent discourse—one truer to the biblical sources *and* the totality of human experience.

In making praxis the starting point of theological reflection, liberation theologians virtually ignore the affective dimension of human experience, which, if given due consideration, could provide a more coherent discourse about God, Jesus Christ, theological method, and Christian ethics. The entire focus is upon the theory-praxis dialectic, the relationship between action and rational contemplation. There is a further dimension, however—a moment prior to praxis that is mentioned only in passing by liberation theologians—the affective dimension of human experience, the moment of indignation over oppression, the moment of pathos or empathy at the sight of suffering. Rather than there being a dialectical relation between *theoria* and *praxis*, there is actually a dialectical relation between three poles: *theoria*, *praxis*, and *pathos*. "Pathos" has been presupposed, but not explored theologically, christologically, or ethically by liberation theologians. In fact, in some instances, such a focus has been discounted. Leonardo Boff, for example, seems to think that the focus on pathos is that taken by those who advocate the sacramental articulation of liberation theology, an approach which moves change forward by the fuel of emotion but which is not very effective. He favors an analytic approach since it gets to the root mechanisms and suggests efficacious ways of dismantling these mechanisms (Boff 1989; Boff and Boff 1982, 15). But such an approach to Latin America's problems is empiricist and technocratic, which is not much different from the approach taken by the developmentalists Boff and other liberation theologians reject.

The consideration of this affective aspect of human nature would provide a better liberation epistemology than the present one, which is certainly problematic. For although liberation theologians claim that theology starts with reflection on the praxis of the oppressed, in actuality, there must be a prior moment of reflection that recognizes opting for the poor, or struggle for liberation, as the Christian thing to do. For the one who calls himself or herself Christian, there has to have been a prior moment of reflection on the Word of God as announced and taught by the Church, that now leads him/her to understand his/her faith from the standpoint of liberative praxis. In the words of theologian Karl Lehmann: "The historic world is unquestionably the place where the Gospel ought to be reflected upon, but this Gospel does not disconnect itself from it nor exhaust its dynamism within it" (Lehmann 1978). In other words, there has already been at work in society a dynamic which liberation theologians are not recognizing in their methodology.

The praxis on which they are reflecting has not appeared *ex nihilo*. The traditional christological discourses may have served to legitimate oppression, but somehow they have also served to initiate the praxis on which liberation theologians are subsequently reflecting. For instance, it was the Theological Code that legitimated slavery in North America, Latin America, and England. But strangely enough it was that same Theological Code that created the conviction of William Wilberforce, Theodore Dwight Weld, and other Christians to challenge slavery and seek its abolition, and moved Bartolomé de las Casas to defend the Amerindians. Clearly even the traditional Gospel message, the Theological Code, somehow works as a leaven to bring about greater justice in society.

Liberation Theology and the Appeal to "Ideology"

We saw in Chapters 3 and 4 that liberation theologians deconstruct traditional christologies by appealing to a negative view of ideology, i.e., by subjecting traditional discourses to ideology critique, and then reconstruct their christological discourse by appealing to a positive view of ideology, i.e., an allegedly scientific interpretation of Latin American reality, a neo-Marxist sociology.

A few remarks, however, are in order concerning liberation theologians' use of the notion of ideology in their theological construction. These remarks should be taken as caveats since I do not dispute the basic truth of the ideological presumption, namely, that our ideas (theologies) are *conditioned* by the social locus which we inhabit. I say conditioned, not determined, because I cannot fully agree with the notion that consciousness is determined, in the last instance, by material conditions. Traditional Christianity believes in the power of the Holy Spirit to lead into all truth and to convict of sin. And although ideologies might distort the perception of that truth by, say, a European or North American theologian or a Christian in a feudal or capitalist society, there is nevertheless, *some truth* in their discourse. It would be the highest form of conceit if Latin American liberation theologians thought that only oppressed Latin Americans were privy to the truth into which the Holy Spirit wanted to lead the Church, so that they have no need of the reflections of other Christians elsewhere.

But many liberation theologians do not evince a great deal of humility about their own theologizing. Many of them often verge on claiming ideological purity and total truth for their discourses, which are signs of false consciousness. Firstly, liberation theologians write as if their discourse is *pure*; that because it takes its point of departure in the experience of the oppressed, it is thereby free from distortions and presents reality as it really is. Their discourse, therefore, is often not sufficiently self-critical. A truly critical approach would recognize that the social locus of the liberation theologian could be as bourgeois as that of a North American or a European theologian, hence their discourse could be as ideological (false consciousness) as the rejected christological discourses. Most of those writing on liberation theology are well-educated professionals, university professors who travel around the world and enjoy the renown of being theologians on the cutting edge of a theological movement. While I do not want to minimize the dangers to which many of them expose themselves by their writings, they also enjoy privileges that almost none of the oppressed have. Is it possible that this social locus affects their theological reflection in ways they themselves are not conscious of?

Secondly, many liberation theologians imply that their discourse is *total* truth. They often write as if the only valid christological discourse in/for Latin America is one that is relevant to economic oppression, and, relatedly, that political praxis is the totality of Christian activity. Other christological discourses that appeal to other kinds of Christian activity or that reflect on other aspects of human experience are seen as ideological in the pejorative sense. The truth of the matter is that many other forms of oppression besides political or economic oppression must be addressed by Christian reflection and action (which cannot properly be called "praxis"). While liberation theologians provide a much needed discourse in Latin America that speaks to socio-political realities, and while this discourse provides a much needed corrective to the absolutist, allegedly non-political, claims of traditional discourse, liberation theologians must be careful not to claim more for their discourse than what it merits: it speaks to one facet of oppression and one facet only. There are many other forms of oppression which exist in Latin America and elsewhere and many other forms of suffering that cross political, economic, and cultural boundaries, which require other forms of Christian activity and other forms of reflection.

These aforementioned characteristics alone would be enough to raise suspicion about the liberation theologians' discourses as being ideological in the pejorative sense. But other traits show themselves that would confirm the judgment. Lewis S. Feuer elaborates seven traits of ideological thinking, several of which are evident in the discourses of liberation theologians. The first characteristic, according to Feuer, is the empirical ingredient; that is, that an ideology must "avail itself of a minimum perception of social reality, some empirical facts which will lend at least partial credence to its assertions" (Feuer 1975, 96). Liberation theologians attempt to avail themselves of the empirical facts that will give credence to their assertions, particularly the facts concerning the "signs of the times" and "the poor and oppressed." Such empirical data are not lacking but are by-and-large presupposed by liberation theologians in their works. One does not find much statistical data cited by the theologians; rather, they presuppose the validity of the analyses done by neo-Marxist economists and sociologists.[3] Such empirical "facts," liberation theologians assume, are obtainable through the application of the "scientific" method of social analysis: neo-Marxism[4] in the forms of dependency theory and world-systems theory.

But the liberation theologians are not doing economic analyses *per se*; they are doing *theology*, which is a different sort of discourse with its own sort of validation. Consequently, liberationists also need theological "facts" that will give credence to their theological affirmations. These theological "facts" are obtained through the application of exegetical methods that will enable them to validate their affirmations. As we saw in chapter 3, most liberation theologians employ hermeneutical approaches—such as the historical-critical method or the materialist method—the presuppositions of which will make possible the conjoining of the exegetical "facts" thus discovered with the socio-analytic facts previously obtained. Thus empirical economic analysis is fused to theological "proof" to validate the affirmations of liberation christology, affirmations such as "Christ is incarnate in the economically poor."

The second characteristic of ideology is isomorphic projection upon the universe, i.e., world-mythologization. Structural traits which characterize the social myth are projected on the world as a whole as a total myth. "Then after this projection has been accomplished, the ideologist claims to 'derive' his social myth as a special case of the world myth" (Feuer 1975, 99). In the "first stage" of liberation theology—in its early years—such isomorphic projection was much more clearly displayed: the division of the world into conflictive dichotomies such as exploiters and exploited, central and peripheral nations, alienated Christians and consciencitized Christians, reactionary versus revolutionary ideologies. The theory of dependency was the universal narrative of which Latin America was the special case.

In the "second stage" of liberation theology such isomorphic projection still continues but far more subtly than during the 1970s. Although socialism is no longer univocally called for as the socio-economic system to be erected, and although a greater realism has now sobered liberationists' expectations,[5] the international capitalist system is still seen as the primary cause of the woes of the Third World, and of Latin America in particular. Paul Sigmund notes that for the majority of liberation theologians "it is enough to know that capitalism is the root of all evil" (Sigmund 1990, 186). Although such a causal relationship between international capitalism and Latin American underdevelopment has been challenged by many scholars (Sigmund 1990; Berger 1986; Novak 1982), it continues to be the myth which liberation theologians project upon reality, after which they "opt" for the social "science" or method of analysis which demonstrates it to be "true."

The third trait of ideological thinking is a two-fold theory of truth: a theory of "anti-truth," an organon higher than scientific truth and verification. "In other words the higher 'truth' of Marxism transcends all commonplace scientific verifications. . . . The ideologist invokes a higher 'dialectical' conception of 'truth,' a higher 'dialectical reason.' The latter may be defined as: the superimposition on observational facts of unverifiable auxiliary components, or their deliberate misreporting, in order to render them consistent with or irrelevant to the ideological system" (Feuer 1975, 105). "An ideology cannot allow itself to be tested in the manner of a scientific hypothesis. Contravening evidence is either barred, or so mixed with 'truth' that it is repressed, obliterated, distorted, or permeated with obligatory auxiliary hypotheses" (Feuer 1975, 108). "The new wave of ideology . . . challenges the notion that an objective, value free social science is possible" (Feuer 1975, 113).

Liberation theologians demonstrate this trait, firstly, in challenging the notion that an objective, value free social science is possible; instead, they begin with the assumption that all social science, as well as all theology, is committed, wittingly or unwittingly, to political ideologies. Thus it is required that the theologian own up to his/her partisanship and opt for that ideology, those values, which he or she wagers will be the most liberating. Secondly, the liberation theologian as ideologist invokes a higher conception of dialectical truth which he or she locates in "the epistemological privilege of the oppressed" and "the praxis of the oppressed." Such an affirmation of the locus of truth is beyond philosophical and/or empirical verification. Finally, this two-fold theory of truth is evident, on the one hand, in the liberation theologians' granting of scientific status to Marxist social analysis (specifically, historical materi-alism)[6] and historical-critical and materialist hermeneutics, and, on the other hand, in the liberation theologians' refusal to grant any truth value to the charismatic experi-ences of many Latin American poor who convert to Pentecostalism,[7] or scientific status to the functionalist sociologies of Talcott Parsons and Max Weber, or the socio-economic analyses of W. Arthur Lewis, Claudio Velíz, and Carlos Rangel,[8] for in-stance, or validity to other methods of biblical interpretation such as christocentric or symbolic interpretation.[9] Clearly liberation theologians are engaging in an arbitrary process of selection, where they alone are the ones who determine for all Latin Americans which of the options is true and which is false.

Related to ideological thinking is a fourth trait, alluded to earlier: totalism. More specifically, the ideologist argues that his/her analysis is superior to other analyses by virtue of its 'totalist' conception of reality. The ideologist (in our case, the liberation theologian) not only sees the totality of society as corrupt but also sees the totality of his/her ideology as unassailable, pure, and true. "He who thinks that partial reforms are possible is regarded as naive because he does not perceive that the 'total' system is corrupt. Whatever problem is raised . . . its evils will be attributed to the capitalist system as a whole" (Feuer 1975, 131-32). "The ideologist . . . is averse to the comparative weighing of alternatives. . . . The essence of rationality is the comparative evaluation of alternatives. An ideologist, however, in examining any evil in the workings of some social institution, is constrained by his emotional a priori, apart from any consideration of alternatives, to demand 'total' abolition of the existing society. In fact the so called 'dialectical' method forbids asking comparative questions" (p. 132). "Ideologists thus tend to irrationalize all political life. This pattern of 'irrationalization' is perhaps their most important effect on social existence" (p. 134).

The irrationalization of political life is evident in the liberationists' (the ideologists') rhetorical appeal to the affective wellsprings of action and behavior.[10] Since the superiority of the ideology cannot be rationally argued, then the appeal is made to the emotions through the use of images and narratives that clearly delineate characters and plot. The narratives, through their self-involving quality, "captivate" the reader/listener within a universe of meaning and beckon him/her to participate in the narrative, to join with a community united in feeling (a *Gemeinshaft*) (Feuer 1975, 104). We can see, therefore, how and why christological discourse enters in: through it liberation theologians can tap into the images, symbols, and metaphors that have had (and will continue to have) the profoundest influence on the conduct of Christians. Through these narratives the liberationist can avoid the distracting consideration of rational aspects within capitalism or political reformism or theological dogma[11] and thus maintain or elicit from Christians the depth of commitment and the singularity of purpose necessary for effective revolutionary praxis.

The warrant for this totalism that will admit no alternatives, no "third ways" (*tercerismo*) between capitalism and socialism, is not only the Marxist analysis of society (especially, the relation of the superstructure to the base) but also the liberationist christological narrative itself. Totalism is evident in the totalists' interpretation of Jesus' own uncompromising stance towards the politico-religious structures and in his willingness to suffer and die for the cause of liberation, for siding with the oppressed, the cause of God; for Jesus, there was no third way between the Kingdom of God and the kingdom of the world.[12]

According to Walter R. Fisher, a good narrative rhetoric will include such important elements of rationality as "the ability and willingness to support one's claims with evidence [reasons] and regard for the other [reasonableness]," and it is also made evident by a rhetoric that is "self-perpetuating, nonmanipulative, bilateral, deliberative, reflexive, and attentive to data" (Fisher 1989, 117). Most liberation theologians do not seem very interested in furthering dialogue or in encouraging bilateral exchange, or in deliberating interpretations of or approaches to Latin America's problems, or in inviting criticism. Since the liberationist narrative does not foster the individual's rational assessment of the whole spectrum of ideological alternatives, we can say that it is a rhetorically defective narrative. Liberation theologians, therefore, lack rhetorical competence, and their audience should be skeptical of their narratives about Jesus Christ and Latin America.

Prospectus for a Postmodernist Liberation Christology

Liberation theologians are attempting to fashion a new paradigm for doing theology while at the same time providing the oppressed of Latin America with a postmodern christology, a narrative that will mobilize them to act for the creation of a more human society.

There are problems in their attempt, as we have seen, and hence changes will be needed. The most notable weakness is that, in constructing the new paradigm, liberation theologians cling to the very same modernist assumptions that have brought about the crisis of modernity: subjectivity of truth, relativity of values, autonomy, and technologism, to name a few. Because of their inability (or unwillingness) to move beyond these assumptions, their narrative has failed to be convincing and enter the mainstream of Latin American culture. Instead we find that many Latin Americans are turning to a premodern discourse—the Theological Code, as articulated by evangelicals and pentecostals[13] —which for the most part is not a discourse that promotes political transformation, but which resonates with the personalism and enthusiasm (i.e., pietism) characteristic of the piety of the oppressed.

Both narratives, the liberationist and the fundamentalist-charismatic, are inadequate to deal with the problems of Latin America, so a different narrative will need to be proclaimed, one that articulates what is best from each of them and will also address the needs of a postmodern world. What shape might that narrative take?

The disenchantment with modernity which the world is experiencing has given rise to a variety of postmodern narratives, each suggesting ways of living in the world. The deconstructionist narrative (like Mark C. Taylor's, for instance [Taylor 1984]) calls for abandoning closure, for telling stories without endings. Lives must be lived without illusions since closures are "untenable fictions." From such a perspective, Walt Disney's Bambi, the Young Prince, is just as likely to end up as venison stew as he is to end up King of the Forest. Similarly, the christological narrative that follows from this narrative would be one that eliminates hope, that projects nothing, that anticipates nothing. In this view, Jesus' resurrection is wishful thinking. The stories he told and his own life story are subversive stories, they subvert our world, shatter expectations, but there are no ultimate vindications, no moralizing about the structure of reality.

Some might suggest this as a way of being human in Latin America, but such a narrative springs from existential anomie, which others judge as the despair of the bourgeois. In Latin America, the despair is real material despair—the despair of the dehumanized—hence the nihilistic mode of living advocated by this deconstructionist narrative can only lead to resignation and ultimately to real objective misery and death, objective annihilation. The deconstructionist postmodernist story, therefore, may not suit Latin America, not only because of its possible consequences, but also because deconstruction has not yet demonstrated any resonance with pre-modern culture, such as that which is predominant in Latin America.

The liberation narrative, on the other hand, has closure; the story seeks to inspire hope and illusions. Their narrative is postmodern in that it seeks to deprivatize faith and turn it into a valuable factor of social transformation. Yet liberation theologians cling to modernist assumptions and values that clearly make their narrative, first of all, incomprehensible to the vast majorities of oppressed Latin Americans who themselves hold a premodern worldview and, secondly, inadequate to confront the postmodern condition into which the world at large has entered. Some of these modernist assumptions are the subjectivity of truth, the relativity of values, pragmatism, and autonomy. The implicit acceptance of these philosophical presuppositions lead liberation theologians to apply historical-critical assumptions and ideological criticism to biblical narratives and theological reflections (past and present). Moreover, their acceptance results in calls for a contextualized and autochthonous theology: "We must have our own christology, our own truth, relevant to our needs." In some liberationist circles, however, this has resulted in an ironic solipsism where the truth originating from the oppressed is the only truth, their interpretations of Jesus and of society are the only valid interpretations; and these are valid merely because they are suited to the needs of the oppressed, i.e., because of their functionality. Such a particularistic viewpoint, such a regionalistic narrative, might inspire a Guatemalan or Salvadoran Christian suffering oppression to subversive action, but it does not provide him/her, or any other Christian from any other culture or nation, with a narrative in which to live as a human being, as a member of the world-community. Liberation christological discourse, therefore, does not contribute very much to the construction of a postmodern theology which would, in turn, contribute to the construction of a postmodern world.

Another modernist assumption held by liberation theologians is that science—social science and particularly Marxist social science—is capable of giving the one true account of the Latin American reality (=scientism). Postmodernity has belied such an assumption. Rather, we are confronted by a plurality of views and interpretations—whether in religion or sociology—each with their claims to validity. Liberation theologians, however, while not blind to this pluralism, for the most part refuse to come to terms with it and articulate a synthetic discourse, whether in their christological narrative or their social analysis. Instead, they proclaim an anti-thetic discourse, or what Segundo himself calls an anti-christology. It could be said, then, that *a fortiori* and like the deconstructionists, liberationists proclaim an anti-theology; they consciously opt for one discourse among the many, one that shocks and challenges the audience to act for their own material well-being in the here-and-now; one that presents humanity as the Ultimate Reality.

By employing these modernist assumptions and values in the construction of their christological narrative, liberation theologians continue the modern preoccupation with bureaucratic rationalization. Jesus is made the legitimator of a technocratic way of being human, one concerned with the most effective way of loving, i.e., achieving liberation. Technocrats are concerned with means and results. The emphasis which liberation theologians put on praxis puts a premium on efficacy. Consequently, liberation theologians have problems in constructing a convincing story of Jesus, for the story derived from the Gospels and articulated in popular piety (or even the story of the historical Jesus), does not cohere with the story they articulate and want the oppressed to believe, that of a technocratic Jesus, a Jesus concerned with means and efficacy, i.e., praxis.

What would be a better christological narrative? James Breech makes the argument that Jesus' own stories, as well as his own life as narrated by the Synoptic Gospels, aim to show a distinctive way of living: the "personal mode."

> The earliest Christians used their own culturally received concept
> of the resurrection appearances to reflect their conviction that
> Jesus' mode of being human could not be judged by its results, that
> death did not hold the key to the meaning of his mode of being
> human. (Breech 1989, 78)

A more coherent story would affirm this personal mode of living, one that puts a premium on unconditional love and faithfulness rather than efficacy. Determining efficacy implies calculating (claiming to foreknow) results or consequences. The personal mode of living, however, implies a commitment to the other without taking account of results or consequences, without attempting to predict how the other will respond. Such is love (e.g., the ten lepers in Lk. 17:11-19); it is an uncalculated risk. Love does not always conquer all—Judas Iscariot being a case in point. In fact, if "love" is bent on the "conquest" of the other, it is not true Love at all.

Does the acceptance of this narrative, this proposed mode of being human, by the oppressed mean that they must accept oppression? Not at all. It means that one is to act without consideration of results; one does what is right and just for the other, not because of some ultimate goal in view (such as the Kingdom of God, or ultimate vindication in history or beyond history) but because it is the right thing to do. Hence this narrative suggests a deontological Christian ethic, whereas the liberationist narrative argues a teleological ethic that verges on utilitarianism (cf., Segundo 1976, 170). A deontological ethic appears to be more coherent and faithful to the sources.

A postmodern christological narrative, therefore, would provide the basis for a deontological ethic—one that presents the individual in relationship to the cosmos and as responsible for the various spheres within that cosmos. A postmodern christological narrative will be one that maintains the distinctiveness of Jesus Christ's life and work while bringing his particularity to bear on every sphere of human experience. Such a christology will seek to address, not only the historical, political, and economic, but also the personal, cultural, and ecological dimensions of human life.

Liberation theologians have given the world a vision of what theology should be—practical and liberating—and for that vision, we are grateful. The vision, however, needs to be sharpened, and for that a christological discourse will have to be articulated that will enable "reasonable men [*sic*] of different interests, experiences, and vocabulary . . . [to] disagree about some questions . . ." and yet move them to "search for meeting places where they can stand together and explore their differences about the choices life presents" (Booth 1974, 111). Such a discourse is still awaited.

Notes

1. See, for instance, Jaroslav Pelikan, *Jesus Through the Centuries: His Place in the History of Culture* (New York: Harper & Row, 1985) and H. R. Niebuhr, *Christ and Culture* (New York: Harper Torchbooks, 1956).

2. Besides Schleiermacher, some contemporary theologians have made some initial attempts at such reflection on this aspect of human experience. See, for instance, Monika K. Hellwig, *Jesus: The Compassion of God* (Washington: Michael Glazier, Inc., 1985); William M. Thompson, *The Jesus Debate: A Survey and Synthesis* (New York: Paulist Press, 1985), 283-88; Rebecca Chopp, *The Praxis of Suffering* (Maryknoll: Orbis Books, 1986).

3. Arthur F. McGovern states that "Liberation theologians rarely use, or even cite references to specific and detailed accounts of the factors most associated with 'scientific' Marxist analysis: falling rates of profits, cycles of stagnation and expansion, studies of changing modes of production, analysis of class structures, and so forth," but that rather Marxist categories are used heuristically or as moral norms to point out or unmask structural injustices (McGovern 1989, 161-62). My argument throughout this work, however, is that liberation theologians, in referring to Marxism as "analysis" and as "scientific," in extolling its virtues of concreteness, flexibility, practicality, and efficacy, and in claiming its superiority as a mediating ideology, use Marxism as a rhetorical device within their overall argument; it provides a discourse, a vocabulary, for creating a believable narrative about Latin American society.

4. As far as empirical evidence is concerned, liberation theologians can cite specific "sins" committed by some multi-national corporations in particular countries (ITT in Chile, United Fruit Company in Guatemala), but these incidents alone would not be enough to warrant a subversion of the socio-economic system or a call for a new international economic order, nor would such isolated facts explain the poverty that prevails all over Latin America (Berger 1986, 123-25). Neo-Marxism provides causal explanations for this poverty; it provides the narrative structure by which these incidents and other empirical facts (such as the *encomienda* system, and the repressive governments) can be correlated within a universe of meaning.

5. For instance, we saw above that J. L. Segundo calls for historical flexibility in the establishment of political systems, and J. B. Libaînio notes that liberation theology "now speaks of an 'alternative system' to capitalism rather than social-

ism" [Libaînio cited by (McGovern 1989, 181) and (Sigmund 1990, 178)].
Gustavo Gutiérrez writes that "Recent historical events . . . have dispelled illusions
regarding concrete historical systems that claim to eliminate all evils. As a result
we have launched out upon new and more realistic quests" (Gutiérrez 1990).

6. We saw earlier that Leonardo Boff certainly does make such a claim, Sobrino
presupposes it, and Segundo qualifies it and we also noted the weaknesses of such
implicit or explicit claims. Fernando Belo, a liberationist exegete, also affirms the
scientific status of historical materialism, concerning which Jacques Ellul has this to
say: "Belo's entire argument depends on a certain number of ideological *presuppositions* he holds firmly but never demonstrates. . . . Everything related to 'heaven,' 'the
Spirit,' etc., he calls 'mythology.' Only materialism is scientific, and the only science
of history is historical materialism. . . . Belo takes for scientific truths those things he
finds evident, but which I would feel obliged to call mythical, since they are neither
based on reason nor critically examined" (Ellul 1 988, 93).

7. In spite of this well-documented sociological and religious phenomenon
which is occurring among the Latin American poor, liberation theologians have either
ignored the phenomenon altogether or have given it the standard Marxist evaluation
of religion, seeing the conversions as a form of escape, an opiate of the masses or a form
of alienation. In short, liberation theologians have not taken the experience of the poor
seriously at all. (Lernoux 1988), (Martin 1988), (Martin 1990), (Rodriguez 1989),
(Stoll 1990).

8. These three political economists (Lewis is from Trinidad, Veliz is from Chile,
and Rangel is from Venezuela) have provided alternative explanations for the economic disparity between Latin America and First World nations, but these explanations have been virtually ignored by liberation theologians. One likely reason for the
oversight may be that, as "narratives," they lack clear cut protagonists and antagonists
which the people can identify. Consequently, these explanations are, rhetorically, not
very effective. In fact, if anything, some of these explanations tend to put the blame
on Latin Americans themselves—the values and attitudes which are transmitted by the
culture create an ethos that generates economic stagnation and dependence. The
respective works of these political economists are: W. Arthur Lewis, *The Evolution of
the International Economic Order* (Princeton: Princeton University Press, 1978), *The
Theory of Economic Growth* (Homewood: Richard D. Irwin, 1955); Claudio Véliz,
The Centralist Tradition of Latin America (Princeton: Princeton University Press,
1980); and Carlos Rangel, *The Latin Americans: Their Love-Hate Relationship with
the United States* (New York and London: Hartcourt Brace Jovanovich, 1977).

9. Jacques Ellul points out that "In the area of scriptural interpretation we are clearly faced with ideological choices. According to contemporary hermeneutical specialists, there are only three exegetical methods: (1) historical-critical (the venerable method); (2) structuralist, and now (3) Marxist. . . . Specialists eliminate, without even mentioning, for example, christocentric interpretation . . . or symbolic interpretation. These are brushed aside, because they are not 'scientific,' as if the others were, in some basic fashion!" (Ellul 1988, 86)

10. Although liberation theologians make a rhetorical appeal to the emotions, the affective aspect of human experience is excluded from their theological method, as we have discussed above.

11. Segundo might very well argue that such rational consideration, such careful weighing of alternatives, especially by the populace at large, increases entropy, i.e., the loss of energy in the social ecology, and decreases efficiency.

12. Feuer presents several other traits of ideological thinking that could be argued are evident to a greater or lesser degree in some of the liberation theologians' discourses but the argument would be forced. The other traits of ideological thinking according to Feuer are: the authoritarianism of master ideologists, in other words, certain individuals have status as an elite reinforced against criticism. It is not altogether clear how much authority liberation theologians carry over the Base Communities (CEB's) and clearly they themselves are not averse to criticism, but it is unclear how much of this criticism is considered by them in their theologizing.

Another trait is regression to primitivism; the ideologist develops a primitivist tenet, a hostility to ethics, to the requirements and demands of civilization, and a return to primitive modes of feeling, aggression, and thinking (Feuer 1975, 105). The primitive, the original, the root of the self is best. Leonardo Boff makes some comments that might be construed as such a return to primitivism, for instance: "Original does not refer to someone who says entirely pure and new things . . . Original comes from 'origin.' Those who are near the origin and root of things and by their lives, words, and works bring others to the origin and root of their own selves can be properly called original, not because they discover new things but because they speak of things with absolute immediacy and superiority. . . . All those in contact with Jesus encountered themselves and that which is best in them. . . . Confrontation with this source generates a crisis: One is constrained to make a decision and either convert or install oneself in that which is derived, secondary, and part of the current situation" (Boff 1978, 96). Hence everything in the current situation must be oppressive, enslaving, simply because it is not "original," primitive, proceeding from the genius which lies at the root of human nature. Boff goes on to say what this means for today's

Christian: "Therefore, what emerged in Jesus ought to emerge and be expressed also in his followers: . . . a critical spirit in confronting the current social and religious situation . . ." (Boff 1978, 97).

The hostility towards ethics and the demands of civilization which are part of the regression to primitivism can be seen in Boff's view of the Christian's relationship to the law. Disregarding the context and the meaning of "law" and "freedom from the law" in the epistles of Paul, Boff flippantly applies such passages as Rom. 6:15; 1 Cor. 9:21-22; and Gal. 5:1 to the Christian's relation to civil law. "The law [i.e., civil law] is relativized and put in the service of love." The hostility towards institutional religion is seen specifically in his predilection for religious secularity (religion that celebrates the secular; secular reality is seen as the proper realm of God's presence/activity and hence of the believer's discipleship). Boff, of course, views this religious secularity as warranted by Jesus' own comportment.

Other than these comments by Boff, there is little evidence in the liberation theologians' works for these other traits, hence I do not include them in my argument that their christological discourses become pejoratively ideological.

13. I would hypothesize that this turn to Protestantism by Latin Americans is actually a transition not from modernity to postmodernity, but from a premodern worldview to a modern one, for evangelicalism fosters such modern values as individualism, freedom of conscience, anti-authoritarianism (priesthood of all believers), and the separation of religion and politics. What this cultural situation means for liberation theology is that its christological discourse is "ahead of its time" or addressed to those artistic and intellectual elites who are in tune with the modern worldview but who are estranged from the popular religiosity of their compatriots. While being "ahead of its time" may commend a discourse to the larger culture on pragmatic grounds, oftentimes the discourse is, in fact, impracticable or incomprehensible, for the society has not gone through the necessary changes to make sense of it or put it within a larger context of meaning (one need only recall such fiascos as the League of Nations, Esperanto, and the French decimal calendar [1792]). The liberation theologians seem oblivious to the psycho-social dynamics operating within Latin American culture: they articulate a postmodern narrative based on modernist assumptions to a people who live within a premodern narrative or who are barely making the transition to a modern narrative. Can they hope their discourse to be heard?

BIBLIOGRAPHY

Alves, R. A. *A Theology of Human Hope*. Washington, DC: Corpus Books, 1969.

Assmann, Hugo. *Theology for a Nomad Church*. Translated by Paul Burns. Maryknoll: Orbis Books, 1976.

_____. "Power of Christ in History: Conflicting Christologies and Discernment." In *Frontiers of Theology in Latin America*, ed. R. Gibellini. 133-50. Maryknoll: Orbis Books, 1979.

_____. "The Actuation of the Power of Christ in History: Notes on the Discernment of Christological Contradictions." In *Faces of Jesus*, ed. J. Míguez-Bonino, 125-36. Maryknoll: Orbis Books, 1984.

Aulén, Gustaf. *Christus Victor*. Translated by A. G. Herbert. New York: Macmillan Publishing Co., 1969.

Bammel, Ernst and Moule, C. F. D., ed. *Jesus and the Politics of His Day*. Cambridge: Cambridge University Press, 1984.

Batstone, David. *From Conquest to Struggle: Jesus of Nazareth in Latin America*. Albany: State University of New York Press, 1991.

Baum, Gregory. *Religion and Alienation: A Theological Reading of Sociology*. New York: Paulist Press, 1975.

Bercovitch, Sacvan. *The American Jeremiad*. Madison: University of Wisconsin Press, 1978.

Berger, Peter. *A Rumor of Angels: Modern Society and the Discovery of the Supernatural*. Garden City: Doubleday, 1969.

_____. *Pyramids of Sacrifice: Political Ethics and Social Change*. Garden City: Anchor Press, 1974.

_____. *The Capitalist Revolution: Fifty Propositions about Prosperity, Equality, and Liberty*. New York: Basic Books, Inc., 1986.

Berryman, Phillip. *The Religious Roots of Rebellion: Christians in Central American Revolutions.* Maryknoll: Orbis Books, 1984.

Boff, Clodovis. *Theology and Praxis: Epistemological Foundations.* Translated by R. R . Barr. Maryknoll: Orbis Books, 1987.

Boff, Leonardo. *Jesucristo y Nuestro Futuro de Liberación.* Bogotá: Indo-American Press Service, 1978.

_____. *Jesus Christ Liberator: A Critical Christology for Our Time.* Translated by Patrick Hughes. Maryknoll: Orbis Books, 1978.

_____. "Christ's Liberation via Oppression: An Attempt at Theological Construction from the Standpoint of Latin America." In *Frontiers of Theology in Latin America,* ed. Rosino Gibellini, 100-32. Maryknoll: Orbis Books, 1979.

_____. *Pasión de Cristo, Pasión del Mundo: Hechos, Interpretaciones y Significado, Ayer y Hoy.* Translated by Juan Carlos Rodríguez Herranz. Santander: Sal Terrae, 1980.

_____. *Way of the Cross-Way of Justice.* Translated by John Drury. Maryknoll: Orbis Books, 1980.

_____. *La Vida Más Allá de la Muerte.* Translated by José Guillermo Ramírez. Bogotá: Confederación Latinoamericana de Religiosos - CLAR, 1981.

_____. *Liberating Grace.* Translated by John Drury. Maryknoll: Orbis Books, 1981.

_____. "Images of Jesus in Brazilian Liberal Christianity." In *Faces of Jesus: Latin American Christologies,* ed. José Miguez-Bonino. Maryknoll: Orbis Books, 1984.

_____. *Church: Charism & Power.* Translated by John W. Diercksmeier. New York: Crossroad, 1985.

_____. *El Destino del Hombre y del Mundo: Ensayo sobre la Vocación Humana.* 4a ed., Vol. 2. Coleccion Alcance, Santander: Sal Terrae, 1985.

_____. *Jesucristo el Liberador: Ensayo de Cristología Crítica Para Nuestro Tiempo.* 4a ed., Colección Presencia Teológica, Santander: Editorial Sal Terrae, 1987.

_____. *Trinity and Society*. Translated by Paul Burns. Theology and Liberation Series, ed. Leonardo Boff, Sergio Torres, and et al. Maryknoll: Orbis Books, 1988.

_____. *When Theology Listens to the Poor*. Translated by Robert R. Barr. San Francisco: Harper & Row, Publishers, 1988.

_____. "The Contribution of Liberation Theology to a New Paradigm." In *Paradigm Change in Theology: A Symposium for the Future*, ed. Hans Küng and David Tracy, 408-23. New York: Crossroad Publishing, 1989.

_____. *Faith On the Edge: Religion and Marginalized Existence*. Translated by Robert R. Barr. San Francisco: Harper & Row, Publishers, 1989.

_____. "The New Evangelization: New Life Bursts In." In *1492-1992 The Voice of the Victims*, ed. Leonardo Boff and Virgil Elizondo, 130-40. London: SCM Press, 1990.

Boff, Leonardo and Clodovis Boff. *Libertad y Liberación*. 2nd ed., Salamanca: Ediciones Sigueme, 1982.

_____. *Salvation and Liberation*. Translated by Robert R. Barr. Maryknoll: Orbis Books, 1984.

_____. *Introducing Liberation Theology*. Translated by Paul Burns. Maryknoll: Orbis Books, 1988.

Boff, Leonardo and Virgil Elizondo, eds. *1492-1992 The Voice of the Victims*. London: SCM Press, 1990.

Booth, Wayne. *Modern Dogma and the Rhetoric of Assent*. Chicago: University of Chicago Press, 1974.

Bowden, John. *Jesus: The Unanswered Questions*. Nashville: Abingdon Press, 1989.

Branson, Mark Lau and Padilla, C. René, ed. *Conflict and Context: Hermeneutics in the Americas*. Grand Rapids: William B. Eerdmans Publishing Company, 1986.

Bravo, Carlos, S. J. *Jesus Hombre en Conflicto*. Serie Teología Actual, Mexico: Centro de Reflexión Teológica, 1986.

Breech, James. *Jesus and Postmodernism*. Minneapolis: Fortress Press, 1989.

Bruce, F. F. "The History of New Testament Study." In *New Testament Interpretation: Essays on Priniciples and Methods*, ed. I. Howard Marshall, 21-59. Grand Rapids: William B. Eerdmans, 1977.

Burtchaell, James T. "How Authentically Christian is Liberation Theology?" 50 (2 1988): 264-81.

Bussmann, Claus. *Who Do You Say?: Jesus Christ in Latin American Theology*. Maryknoll: Orbis Books, 1985.

Calvert, David G.A. *From Christ to God*. London: Epworth Press, 1983.

Castillo, Alfonso. "Confesar a Cristo el Señor y Seguir a Jesús." In *Fe en Jesús y Seguir a Jesús*, 47-82. 3. Mexico, D. F.: Centro de Reflexión Teológica, 1978.

Clarke, Thomas E., S. J., ed. *Above Every Name: The Lordship of Christ and Social Systems*. Vol. 5. Woodstock Studies. Ramsey: Paulist Press, 1980.

Clévenot, Michel. *Materialist Approaches to the Bible*. Translated by William J. Nottingham. Maryknoll: Orbis Books, 1985.

Coste, René. *Marxist Analysis and Christian Faith*. Maryknoll: Orbis Books, 1985.

Cox, Harvey. *Religion in the Secular City: Toward a Postmodern Theology*. New York: Simon & Schuster, Inc., 1984.

Crites, Stephen. "The Narrative Quality of Experience." *JAAR* 39 (3 1971): 291-311.

Croatto, J. Severino. *Exodus: A Hermeneutics of Freedom*. Translated by Salvator Attanasio. Maryknoll: Orbis Books, 1981.

Crossan, John Dominic. *The Dark Interval: Towards a Theology of Story*. Sonoma: Polebridge Press, 1988.

Curran, Charles E. and McCormick, Richard A., S. J., ed. *The Use of Scripture in Moral Theology*. Vol. 4. Readings in Moral Theology. New York: Paulist Press, 1984.

Dias de Araújo, João. "Images of Jesus in the Culture of the Brazilian People." In *Faces of Jesus: Latin American Christologies*, ed. J. Míguez-Bonino, 30-38. Maryknoll: Orbis Books, 1984.

Dussel, Enrique. *A History of the Church in Latin America*. Translated by Alan Neely. Grand Rapids: William B. Eerdmans Publishing Company, 1981.

Eagleton, Terry. *Literary Theory: An Introduction*. Minneapolis: University of Minnesota Press, 1983.

Ebeling, Gerhard. *The Problem of Historicity*. Translated by Grover Foley. Philadelphia: Fortress Press, 1967.

Echegaray, Hugo. *The Practice of Jesus*. Translated by Matthew J. O'Connell. Maryknoll: Orbis Books, 1984.

Ellacuría, Ignacio. *Freedom Made Flesh*. Maryknoll: Orbis Books, 1976.

Eller, Vernard. *Christian Anarchy: Jesus' Primacy Over the Powers*. Grand Rapids: William B. Eerdmans Publishing Co., 1987.

Ellis, Marc H. and Otto Maduro, ed. *The Future of Liberation Theology: Essays in Honor of Gustavo Gutierrez*. Maryknoll: Orbis Books, 1989.

Ellul, Jacques. *The Ethics of Freedom*. Translated by Geoffrey W. Bromiley. Grand Rapids: William B. Eerdmans Publishing Co., 1976.

_____. *The Subversion of Christianity*. Translated by Geoffrey W. Bromiley. Grand Rapids: William B. Eerdmans Publishing, 1986.

_____. *Jesus and Marx: From Gospel to Ideology*. Translated by Joyce Main Hanks. Grand Rapids: William B. Eerdmans Publishing, 1988.

_____. *The Presence of the Kingdom*. Second ed., Translated by Olive Wyon. Colorado Springs: Helmers & Howard, 1989.

_____. *What I Believe*. Translated by Geoffrey W. Bromiley. Grand Rapids: William B. Eerdmans Publishing, 1989.

Elster, Jon. *Making Sense of Marx*. Cambridge: Cambridge University Press, 1985.

Feuer, Lewis S. *Ideology and the Ideologists*. New York: Harper & Row, 1975.

Fierro, Alfredo. *The Militant Gospel*. Translated by John Drury. Maryknoll: Orbis Books, 1977.

Fisher, Walter R. *Human Communication As Narration: Toward a Philosophy of Reason, Value, and Action*. Columbia: University of South Carolina Press, 1989.

Flannery, Austin P., ed. *Documents of Vatican II*. Grand Rapids: William B. Eerdmans Publishing Co., 1975.

Gardner, E. Clinton. *Christocentrism in Christian Social Ethics*. Lanham, MD: University Press of America, 1983.

Geuss, Raymond. *The Idea of a Critical Theory: Habermas and the Frankfurt School*. Modern European Philosophy, ed. Alan Montefiore. Cambridge: Cambridge University Press, 1981.

Gibellini, Rosino, ed. *Frontiers of Theology in Latin America*. Maryknoll: Orbis Books, 1979.

_____. *The Liberation Theology Debate*. Translated by John Bowden. Maryknoll: Orbis Books, 1988.

Glebe-Möller, Jens. *Jesus and Theology: Critique of a Tradition*. Translated by Thor Hall. Minneapolis: Fortress Press, 1989.

González, P. Carlos Ignacio, S. I. *El Es Nuestra Salvación: Cristología y Soteriología*. Vol. III. Teología Para la Evangelización Liberadora en América Latina, Mexico: Consejo Episcopal Latinoamericano, 1987.

Gonzalez-Faus, José Ignacio. "La Fe en Jesucristo: Raíz, Plenitud, y Compañera de la Liberación Humana." In *Fe en Jesús y Seguir a Jesús*, 7-45. 3. Mexico, D. F.: Centro de Reflexión Teológica, 1978.

Grillmeier, Aloys. "The Figure of Christ in Catholic Theology Today." In *Theology Today*, ed. Johannes Feiner, Josef Trütsch, and Franz Böckle, 66-108. 1. Milwaukee: The Bruce Publishing Company, 1965.

Gustafson, James M. *Christ and the Moral Life.* Chicago: The University of Chicago Press, 1968.

Gutiérrez, Gustavo. *A Theology of Liberation: History, Politics and Salvation.* Translated by Sister Caridad Inda and John Eagleson. Maryknoll: Orbis Books, 1973.

_____. *The Power of the Poor in History.* Translated by Robert R. Barr. Maryknoll: Orbis Books, 1983.

_____. *Dios o el Oro en las Indias.* Salamanca: Ediciones Sígueme, 1989.

_____. *The Truth Shall Make You Free: Confrontations.* Translated by Matthew McConnell. Maryknoll: Orbis Books, 1990.

Haight, Roger, S.J. *An Alternative Vision.* New York: Paulist Press, 1985.

Harvey, Van Austin. *The Historian and The Believer: The Morality of Historical Knowledge and Christian Belief.* New York: The Macmillan Company, 1966.

Hauerwas, Stanley. *A Community of Character.* Notre Dame: University of Notre Dame Press, 1981.

_____. *The Peacable Kingdom: A Primer in Christian Ethics.* Third ed., Notre Dame: University of Notre Dame Press, 1983.

Hauerwas, Stanley and L. Gregory Jones, ed. *Why Narrative?: Readings in Narrative Theology.* Grand Rapids: William B. Eerdmans Publishing Co., 1989.

Hauerwas, Stanley, Richard Bondi, and David Burrell. *Truthfulness and Tragedy: Further Investigations into Christian Ethics.* Notre Dame: University of Notre Dame Press, 1977.

Hawkin, David J. *Christ and Modernity: Christian Self-Understanding in a Techno-logical Age.* Waterloo: Wilfried Laurier University Press, 1985.

Hellwig, Monika K. *Jesus: The Compassion of God.* Second ed., Vol. 9. Theology and Life Series, ed. Monika K. Hellwig. Washington: Michael Glazier, Inc., 1985.

Hennelly, Alfred T. *Theologies in Conflict: The Challenge of Juan Luis Segundo.* Maryknoll: Orbis Books, 1979.

Hennelly, Alfred T. "Steps to a Theology of Mind." In *American Academy of Religion Annual Meeting in Chicago, Illinois*, The Currents in Contemporary Christology Group 1988.

_____. "The Search for A Liberating Christology." *RSR* 15 (1 1989): 45-47.

_____. *Theology for a Liberating Church: The New Praxis of Freedom*. Washington, D.C.: Georgetown University Press, 1989.

Hewitt, Marsha A. "Review: Jesus of Nazareth Yesterday and Today." *RSR* 15 (1 1989): 47-51.

Krieg, Robert A. *Story-Shaped Christology: The Role of Narratives in Identifying Jesus Christ*. Theological Inquiries: Studies in Contemporary Biblical and Theological Problems, ed. C. S. P. Lawrence Boadt. New York: Paulist Press, 1988.

Lane, Dermot A. *Foundations for a Social Theology: Praxis, Process and Salvation*. New York: Paulist Press, 1984.

Larrain, Jorge. *The Concept of Ideology*. Athens: The University of Georgia Press, 1979.

Lehmann, Karl. *Problemas de la Teología de la Liberación*. Mexico, D. F.: Secretariado de Pastoral Social de la Arquidiocesis de Mexico, 1978.

Lernoux, Penny. "The Fundamentalist Surge in Latin America." *CC* 105 (January 20 1988): 51-53.

Lohfink, Gerhard. *Jesus and Community: The Social Dimension of Christian Faith*. Translated by John P. Galvin. Philadelphia: Fortress Press, 1982.

Lyotard, Jean-Francois. *The Postmodern Condition: A Report on Knowledge*. 6th ed., Vol. 10. Translated by Geoff Bennington and Brian Massumi. Theory and History of Literature, ed. Wlad Godzich and Jochen Schulte-Sasse. Minneapolis: University of Minnesota Press, 1988.

MacIntyre, Alasdair. *After Virtue*. Notre Dame: University of Notre Dame Press, 1981.

_____. "Epistemological Crises, Dramatic Narrative, and the Philosophy of Science." In *Why Narrative? Readings in Narrative Theology*, ed. Stanley Hauerwas and Gregory L. Jones, 138-57. Grand Rapids: William B. Eerdmans Publishing Co., 1989.

Magaña, José, S. J. *Jesús Liberador: Hacia una Espiritualidad desde los empobrecidos*. Mexico: Librería Parroquial, 1985.

Maier, Gerhard. *The End of the Historical-Critical Method*. Translated by Edwin W. Leverentz. St. Louis: Concordia, 1977.

Martin, David. *Tongues of Fire: The Explosion of Prostestantism in Latin America*. Cambridge: Basil Blackwell, 1990.

Martin, David and David Lee. "Speaking in Latin Tongues." *National Review*, September 29 1988, 30-35.

Macquarrie, John. *Jesus Christ in Modern Thought*. London: SCM Press Ltd., 1990.

McCann, Dennis P. *Christian Realism and Liberation Theology: Practical Theologies in Creative Conflict*. Maryknoll: Orbis Books, 1981.

McCann, Dennis P. and Charles R. Strain. *Polity and Praxis: A Program for American Practical Theology*. Minneapolis: Winston Press, 1985.

McClendon, James W. *Ethics: Systematic Theology*. Vol. 1. Nashville: Abingdon Press, 1986.

McGovern, Arthur F. *Liberation Theology and Its Critics: Toward an Assessment*. Maryknoll: Orbis Books, 1989.

McKnight, Edgar V. *Post-Modern Use of the Bible: The Emergence of Reader-Response Criticism*. Nashville: Abingdon Press, 1988.

Mesters, Carlos. "How the Bible is Interpreted in some Basic Christian Communities." *Concilium* 138 (October 1980): 41-46.

Metz, Johann Baptist. "A Short Apology of Narrative." In *Why Narrative?*, ed. Stanley Hauerwas and L. Gregory Jones. 251-262. Grand Rapids: William B. Eerdmans Publishing Co., 1989.

Miguez-Bonino, José. *Doing Theology in a Revolutionary Situation*. Philadelphia:

Fortress Press, 1975.

_____. *Toward a Christian Political Ethics*. Philadelphia: Fortress Press, 1983.

_____, ed. *Faces of Jesus: Latin American Christologies*. Maryknoll: Orbis Books, 1985.

Milet, Jean. *God or Christ: The Excesses of Christocentricity*. Translated by John Bowden. New York: Crossroad, 1981.

Min, Anselm Kyongsuk. *Dialectic of Salvation: Issues in Theology of Liberation*. Albany: State University of New York Press, 1989.

_____. "How Not to Do a Theology of Liberation: A Critique of Schubert Ogden." *JAAR* LVII (1 1989): 83-102.

Miranda, José. *Marx and the Bible: A Critique of the Philosophy of Oppression*. Translated by John Eagleson. Maryknoll: Orbis Books, 1974.

Mulholland-Wozniak, Anne. "Dangerous Stories in the Theology of Liberation: The Subversive Ethic of Latin American Liberation Theology." Ph.D. Dissertation, University of Southern California, 1987.

Nealen, Mary Kaye. "The Poor in J. L. Segundo's Christology: The Synoptics and Paul." In *American Academy of Religion Annual Meeting in Chicago, Illinois*, The Currents in Contemporary Christology Group, 1988.

Nelson, Paul. *Narrative and Morality: A Theological Inquiry*. University Park: The Pennsylvania State University Press, 1987.

Novak, Michael. *The Spirit of Democratic Capitalism*. New York: Simon & Schuster, Inc., 1982.

Nuñez, Emilio A. *Teología de Liberación: Una Perspectiva Evangélica*. 3rd ed., Miami: Editorial Caribe, 1988.

Oden, Thomas C. *After Modernity...What? : Agenda for Theology*. Grand Rapids: Zondervan Publishing House, 1990.

Pelikan, Jaroslav. *Jesus Through the Centuries: His Place in the History of Culture*.

New York: Harper & Row, 1985.

Popper, Karl R. *The Open Society and Its Enemies*. Vol. II. The High Tide of Prophecy: Hegel, Marx, and the Aftermath. Princeton: Princeton University Press, 1966.

Pottenger, John R. *The Political Theory of Liberation Theology: Toward a Reconvergence of Social Values and Social Science*. Albany: State University of New York Press, 1989.

Rangel, Carlos. *The Latin Americans: Their Love-Hate Relationship with the United States*. New Brunswick: Transaction Books, 1987.

Rejón, Francisco Moreno. "Seeking the Kingdom and its Justice: The Development of the Ethic of Liberation." *Concilium* 172 (2 1984): 35-41.

Richardson, Alan. *The Political Christ*. Philadelphia: Westminster Press, 1973.

Ricoeur, Paul. *Lectures on Ideology and Utopia*. ed. Gorge H. Taylor. New York: Columbia University Press, 1986.

Rodriguez, Richard. "A Continental Shift: Latin Americans Convert from Catholicism to a More Private Protestant Belief." *Los Angeles Times*, August 13 1989,

Root, Michael. "The Narrative Structure of Soteriology." In *Why Narrative? Readings in Narrative Theology*, ed. Stanley Hauerwas and Gregory L. Jones, 263-78. Grand Rapids: William B. Eerdmans Publishing Co., 1989.

Roth, Robert Paul. *The Theater of God: Story in Christian Doctrines*. Philadelphia: Fortress Press, 1985.

Rottenberg, Isaac C. *Redemption and Historical Reality*. Philadelphia: Westminster Press, 1964.

Rubenstein, Richard L. and Roth, David K., ed. *The Politics of Latin American Liberation Theology: The Challenge to U.S. Policy*. First ed., Washington, D.C.: The Washington Institute for Values in Public Policy, 1988.

Ruether, Rosemary Radford. *To Change the World: Christology and Cultural Criticism*. New York: Crossroad Publishing Company, 1988.

Runia, Klaas. *The Present-day Christological Debate*. Issues in Contemporary Theology, ed. I. Howard Marshall. Downers Grove: Inter-Varsity Press, 1984.

Rupp, George. *Christologies and Cultures: Toward a Typology of Religious Worldviews*. Paris: Mouton & Co., 1974.

Sanders, Jack T. "The Question of the Relevance of Jesus for Ethics Today." In *The Use of Scripture in Moral Theology*, ed. Charles E. and McCormick Curran Richard A., S. J., 45-65. 4. New York: Paulist Press, 1984.

Scannone, Juan Carlos. *Teología de la Liberación y Doctrina Social de la Iglesia*. Vol. 1. Trilogía sobre Fe, Religión, y Cultura en Iberoamérica, Madrid: Ediciones Cristiandad, 1987.

Schillebeeckx, Edward. *Jesus: An Experiment in Christology*. Translated by Hubert Hoskins. New York: The Crossroad Publishing Company, 1987.

Schweiker, William. "The Liberation of Theology and The Revolution of Love: An Engagement with Juan Luis Segundo's *Faith and Ideologies*." In *American Academy of Religion Annual Meeting in Chicago, Illinois*, The Currents in Contemporary Christology Group, 1988.

Schweitzer, Albert. *The Quest of the Historical Jesus*. London: Black, 1910.

Scriven, Charles. *The Transformation of Culture: Christian Social Ethics After H. Richard Niebuhr*. Scottdale: Herald Press, 1988.

Segundo, Juan Luis, S. J. *The Liberation of Theology*. Translated by John Drury. Maryknoll: Orbis Books, 1976.

_____. "Capitalism vs. Socialism: Crux Theologica." In *Frontiers of Theology in Latin America*, ed. Rosino Gibellini, 240-59. Maryknoll: Orbis Books, 1979.

_____. *Faith and Ideologies*. Vol. I. Translated by John Drury. Jesus of Nazareth Yesterday and Today, Maryknoll: Orbis Books, 1984.

_____. *The Historical Jesus of the Synoptics*. Vol. II. Translated by John Drury. Jesus of Nazareth Yesterday and Today, Maryknoll: Orbis Books, 1985.

_____. *The Humanist Christology of Paul*. Vol. III. Translated by John Drury. Jesus of Nazareth Yesterday and Today, Maryknoll: Orbis Books, 1986.

_____. *The Christ of the Ignatian Exercises*. Vol. IV. Translated by John Drury. Jesus of Nazareth Yesterday and Today, Maryknoll: Orbis Books, 1987.

_____. *An Evolutionary Approach to Jesus of Nazareth*. Vol. V. Translated by John Drury. Jesus of Nazareth Yesterday and Today, Maryknoll: Orbis Books, 1988.

Shea, John. *The Challenge of Jesus*. Chicago: The Thomas More Press, 1975.

Sigmund, Paul E. *Liberation Theology at the Crossroads: Democracy or Revolution?* New York: Oxford University Press, 1990.

Slater, Peter. *The Dynamics of Religion: Meaning and Change in Religious Traditions*. San Francisco: Harper & Row, 1978.

Snook, Lee E. *The Anonymous Christ: Jesus as Savior in Modern Theology*. Minneapolis: Augsburg Publishing House, 1986.

Sobrino, Jon. *Christology at the Crossroads*. Translated by John Drury. Maryknoll: Orbis Books, 1978.

_____. "The Following of Jesus and Faith in Christ." In *The Myth/Truth of God Incarnate: The Tenth National Conference of Trinity Institute*, ed. Durstan R. McDonald, 122. Wilton: Morehouse-Barlow Co., Inc., 1979.

_____. "The Epiphany of the God of Life in Jesus of Nazareth." In *The Idols of Death and the God of Life: A Theology*, ed. Pablo Richard et al., 66-102. Maryknoll: Orbis Books, 1983.

_____. *Jesus in Latin America*. Maryknoll: Orbis Books, 1987.

_____. "The Crucified Peoples: Yahweh's Suffering Servant Today." In *1492-1992 The Voice of the Victims*, eds. Leonardo Boff and Virgil Elizondo, 120-29. London: SCM Press, 1990.

Stoll, David. *Is Latin America Becoming Protestant? The Politics of Evangelical Growth*. Berkeley: University of California Press, 1990.

Strain, Charles R. "Ideology and Alienation: Theses on the Interpretation and Evaluation of Theologies of Liberation." *JAAR* XLV (4 1977): 473-490.

Taylor, Mark C. *Erring: A Postmodern A/theology.* Chicago: University of Chicago Press, 1984.

Taylor, Mark Lloyd. "The Boundless Love of God and the Bounds of Critical Reflection: Shubert Ogden's Contribution to a Theology of Liberation." *JAAR* LVII (1 1989): 103-47.

Thiselton, Anthony C. *The Two Horizons: New Testament Hermeneutics and Philosophical Description.* Grand Rapids: William B. Eerdmans Publishing Co., 1980.

Thompson, John B. *Studies in the Theory of Ideology.* Berkeley: University of California Press, 1984.

Thompson, Kenneth. *Beliefs and Ideology.* Key Ideas, ed. Peter Hamilton. Chichester: Ellis Horwood Limited, 1986.

Thompson, William M. *The Jesus Debate: A Survey and Synthesis.* New York: Paulist Press, 1985.

Tilley, Terrence W. *Story Theology.* Vol. 12. Theology and Life Series, ed. Monika K. Hellwig. Washington: Michael Glazier, Inc., 1985.

Toulmin, Stephen E. *The Uses of Argument.* Cambridge: Cambridge University Press, 1964.

Tracy, David. *Blessed Rage for Order: The New Pluralism in Theology.* Minneapolis: The Winston • Seabury Press, 1975.

Tucker, Robert C. *Philosophy and Myth in Karl Marx.* Second ed., Cambridge: Cambridge University Press, 1972.

Vidales, Raúl. *Desde la Tradición de los Pobres.* Mexico, D.F.: Centro de Reflexión Teológica, 1978.

Walker, Williston. *A History of the Christian Church.* 3rd ed., New York: Charles Scribner's Sons, 1970.

Wells, David F. *The Person of Christ: A Biblical and Historical Analysis of the*

Incarnation. Foundations for Faith, ed. Peter Toon. Westchester: Crossway Books, 1984.

Witvliet, Theo. "In Search of a Black Christology: The Dialectic of Cross and Resurrection." *CC* 37 (Spring 1987): 17-32.

Yoder, John Howard. *The Politics of Jesus*. Grand Rapids: William B. Eerdmans Publishing Company, 1972.

_____. *The Priestly Kingdom: Social Ethics as Gospel*. Notre Dame: University of Notre Dame Press, 1984.

Zeitlin, Irving. *Ideology and the Development of Sociological Theory*. Prentice-Hall Sociology Series, ed. Neil J. Smelser. Englewood Cliffs: Prentice-Hall, Inc., 1968.

Zimbelman, Joel. "Christology and Political Theology in the Thought of Juan Luis Segundo, S. J." In *American Academy of Religion Annual Meeting in Chicago, Illinois*, The Currents in Contemporary Christology Group, 1988.

INDEX

Abelard, P., 116, 134n
adoptionism, 19
Alfaro, J., 103
Althusser, L., 80, 89n
Alves, R., 71, 83
American Jeremiad, 107
anarchy, 6, 15n
Anselm, 71
anthropological faith, 58, 97-102
Apollinarians, 135n
Aquinas, T., 71
Arians, 135n
ascending christology, 116
Assmann, H., 64, 68, 72, 82, 137
Atonement, 21, 27, 116
Austin, J. L., 15n

Barth, K., 25
Bateson, G., 89n
Baum, G., 106
Belo, F., 59, 76, 96, 155n
Bercovitch, S., 107
Berger, P., 15n
Bloch, E., 96
Boff, C., 60, 64, 89n, 143
Boff, L.,
    on Jesus, 21, 22, 25, 28-29, 31-46, 48;
    on hermeneutics, 49, 51-52, 54, 66, 68,
        70, 83, 84, 88n, 89n;
    on ideology, 92-97, 100;
    and rhetorical intent, 121;
    and the Church, 131, 137n;
    and pathos, 145;
    and historical materialism, 155n;
    as pejoratively ideological, 156-57n
Bornkamm, G., 51
Breech, J., 153
Bultmann, R., 9, 21, 34, 51, 56-59
Bussmann, C., 74

Calvin, J., 71
Cardoso, H. F., 80

Carthage, Council of, 71
Casalis, G., 4, 86-87, 108, 120
CELAM, 35, 67, 68
Chalcedon, Council of, 19, 71, 115, 119
Chalcedonian, 72, 76
characterological coherence, 120-22
Chopp, R., 154
Christ of faith, 51, 73
Christians for Socialism, 66
Clévenot, M., 59
Constantinople, 71
Councils, 27
Cox, H., 15n, 82
Crites, S., 11
Croatto, S., 59
Crossan, J. D., 136n

de las Casas, B., 80, 117
deconstruction, 49
demythologization, 51, 84-85
descending christologies, 116
developmentalism, 80, 81, 102
dialectic, dialectical, 94, 100, 107, 134,
    148-49
dialectical sociologies, 96
Dias de Araújo, J., 85
divinity, 99
docetism, 19

Ebionites, 135n
Ecclesial Base Communities, 131
Ellacuría, I., 2, 21, 117, 136n
Ellul, J., 6, 15n, 75-76, 96, 136n, 155-56n
Engels, F., 39
Ephesus, Council of, 71
ethics, 117, 119, 132
Eutychians, 135n

Fierro, A., 9
Fisher, W. K., 113, 125, 132
Frankfurt School, 80
Frei, H. 48n